"It takes a special kind of American to perceive and interpret the contemporary European. Stuart Miller is one of the very few who does it with flair. He could rightly say, 'Tocqueville, here I come!' "
— JEAN-LOUIS SERVAN-SCHREIBER
Philosopher and journalist
CEO, The Expansion Group of Companies

"Through [*Understanding Europeans*], business executives interested in today's global economy are provided a practical guide to the European market psyche.... And by better understanding the place that is, to most of us, our 'other home,' we can better understand ourselves."
— THOMAS R. HORTON
President and CEO,
American Management Association
Author of What Works for Me

"I read Stuart Miller's [*Understanding Europeans*] with great interest and pleasure. His statements ring true. What he says is penetrating, often fresh, free of the usual American illusions about Europe, and throughout seems based on real depth of feeling and knowledge."
— PROFESSOR HENRY MAY
Department of History
University of California, Berkeley

"Stuart Miller's latest book is not only a fun read but has insights of real value to those who work with the Europeans."
— CHARLES THOMAS
Principal Deputy
Secretary of State for
European and Canadian Affairs

"[*Understanding Europeans*] gets down to the springs of motivation instead of symptoms and will achieve three things: Americans certainly will see Europeans in a different light, Europeans will understand the citizens of the world better, and those of us who straddle both worlds will find a sufficient number of rationalizations to make us feel better about our prejudices."
— GEORGE LANG

"A terrific book. There's no question that, better than anything else I've read recently, [*Understanding Europeans*] crosses bridges and eliminates the potential for misunderstanding and suspicion."
— DAVID PUTTNAM

"It's fascinating, interesting, and fun. A shrewd appraisal of Europeans that works. The discussion of terrorism, one of my areas of particular expertise, is original and illuminating."

—DAVID APTER
Professor of Political Science,
Yale University
Author of Against the State

"Stuart Miller, along with a handful of Americans such as Henry James, understands Europe. His book is as useful for the tourist as it is for the expatriate U.S. multinational. It's also a great read and can make a difference in Euro-American relations."

—WARREN G. BENIS
Distinguished Professor of
Business Administration,
University of Southern California
Coauthor of Leaders

"Through his sage rumination on the intellectual chasm separating Americans and Europeans, Stuart Miller helps to bridge that divide with insight and understanding."

—SENATOR CLAIBORNE PELL
Chairman, Senate Foreign
Relations Committee

"An exceedingly well-argued and well-written book that should be read by everyone who is interested in Europe, including all who are going, have gone, or plan to go there."

—IRVING HALPERIN
Professor of English and Creative
Writing, San Francisco State University

"The most necessary understanding for our survival is our understanding of the other nations of the world. Stuart Miller has given us a picture of Europe, the nations over which hostile armies have marched for centuries. This is an excellent book not only to help us understand Europe but also to understand ourselves."

—ROLLO MAY

"Shocking. Destroys the usual clichés about Europe and its people. For a European, it even hurts, but in a good way. It lays bare the European subconscious on which our ways of thinking and behaving depend."

—DR. PIERO FERRUCCI
Director, Center of
Psychosynthesis Studies,
Florence, Italy

UNDERSTANDING EUROPEANS

Understanding Europeans

Stuart Miller

John Muir Publications
Santa Fe, New Mexico

This edition is dedicated to my father, Irving, to my son, Antony, to my friend, David Forrest, to Jacqueline, and to the loving memory of my mother, Annette. Pauca pro multis.

Originally published as Painted in Blood: Understanding Europeans
© *1987 by Stuart Miller*

John Muir Publications, P.O. Box 613, Santa Fe, NM 87504
© *1990 by Stuart Miller*
Cover © *1990 by John Muir Publications*
All rights reserved. Published 1990
Printed in the United States of America

FIRST EDITION. FIRST PRINTING

Library of Congress Cataloging-in-Publication Data

Miller, Stuart.
  [Painted in blood]
  Understanding Europeans / Stuart Miller. — 1st ed.
    p. cm.
  Originally published under title: Painted in blood.
  ISBN 0-945465-77-7
  1. Europe—Civilization—1945- 2. National characteristics,
European. 3. Ethnopsychology—Europe. I. Title
D1055.M55 1990
940.55—dc20   *90-6370*
                                                      CIP

Distributed to the book trade by:
W.W. Norton & Company, Inc.
New York, New York
Cover art by Sally Blakemore
Printed by Banta Company

Contents

Preface

to this edition

It's a complex fate, being an American, and one of the responsibilities it entails is fighting against a superstitious valuation of Europe.

—Henry James

This is an unusual traveller's guide, for it is psychological. I am after the human essence of those alluring, fascinating and often infuriating Europeans, who they are and what makes them tick. As Malcolm Forbes pungently described it after reading my manuscript, "where they are coming from, which isn't where we are."

More precisely, as Hamlet might say today, this is a "psycho-socio-econo-politico-cultural-historical" guidebook. For to deeply understand such a broad group, one must put together insights from many perspectives. In the beginning and in the end, however, I am not after ponderous intellectuality but something very warm and concrete —the inner workings of our cousins "over there."

Why bother? Why must we try and understand Europeans? After all, we never tried much before.

True enough. We didn't have to. Then, we could be casual travellers when we visited, even blank tourists. Now, however, as the Italians say, *tutto il mondo è paese*, the whole world is our hometown. We and they are *neighbors* now: economically, politically, and in every other way. The warm critical reception the earlier edition of this book enjoyed from readers of every sort— from business people to tourists, foreign relations leaders to social scientists, historians and psychologists to literary writers—indicates how deeply and widely felt is the need to understand not just those whose culture is new to us (like the Japanese) but, perhaps even more urgently, those who seem very much like us in many ways yet, at the same time, are so bafflingly different.

Europe particularly cries to America for comprehension now. Our interdependence, always great, is climaxing. In the beginning, centuries ago, Europe was the cultural mother of the

United States. Then, for decades since the Second World War, Western Europe has been our largest overseas trading partner and tourist destination, our closest and most powerful military and political ally, and the most important foreign influence on our fashion, industrial design, literature, art, food and technology. Now, the unification of the Western European countries into the tariff-free European Community, expected in 1992 and continuing thereafter in every field including economics, politics and culture, creates the world's largest market at a time when we Americans are troubled by serious trade deficits. Furthermore, with the Iron Curtain suddenly lifted, Western Europe is our bridge to the newly opened and volatile East. To be successful in business, to keep up with rapidly changing military and strategic realities as East joins West (and as the European part of the West becomes more independent of the United States), we must finally get with these people. Quite simply, our peace and prosperity depend on our understanding Europeans.

Speaking more personally, I also had more subjective reasons to research and write this work. As the reader will discover, the book includes the human record of one man's complex, lived encounter with a foreign people. Though I had visited Europe many times and stayed for as much as a year—as writer, editor, psychologist, and research administrator—and though I had studied and taught its literature, languages and culture, it was only when I found myself living there for what turned out to be fully six years that I felt compelled to get to the bottom of many European ways that had troubled and intrigued me even from my first visit. Being involved with my Belgian former wife's family made understanding a personal imperative.

I found myself puzzling as all travellers do over everyday incidents and observations that seemed, well, so *foreign*. Why didn't the Brusselois or Parisians or Florentines give me a cheery "hello" in the street, the way people would at home, especially after passing them day after day? Why did so many Europeans look so much more interesting than we bland Americans? Why did Europeans seem so private, so reluctant to talk about their incomes, their fears, their problems, when we Americans would tell our whole life story to almost any stranger sitting next to us on an airplane? Why were they so ritualistic, so formal in business, especially when it came to matters of hierarchy and authority? Why did

Europeans seem at one moment so rude and aggressive and another so exquisitely polite and courteous? What does it mean that their locks and keys are more elaborate than ours? That their store windows are covered with iron shutters? That they drive faster? That they seem more cautious and even pessimistic but also more sure of themselves and of what they think?*

These and many related questions began to fascinate me, as they briefly do even the most casual tourist. I found myself sitting late at night in hotel lounges puzzling with American compatriots over these questions. When these short-term travellers left, I continued to ask long-term American residents and to ask Europeans themselves, to listen and to read between the lines of what I was being told.

The result is this guidebook, which is grounded in a personal quest and the real experiences of everyday life. The reader will find many intimate anecdotes here, the outcome of all these meetings with the European people.* I found much to be critical of in Europeans. Like any American visitor, I found a lot of their behavior off-putting, even aggravating. At first I tried to make excuses for them; later, after studying the situation, I saw there were times I had a right to be critical. Many American readers will feel relieved in the early chapters to see I am not, as James put it, under the spell of any "superstitious valuation" of Europeans. We Americans have our virtues, I believe, and we have ways— many of them — in which we are even superior to Europeans. But then, as we shall see later, they have their wonderful superiorities, too. And, in both cases, the merit is not so much in the individuals of today as in the historical conditions which shaped the two peoples. Out of comprehending *why* each of us is the way

---

*Since I first wrote this book, Americans have become somewhat less hopeful, themselves, and Europeans somewhat more. Europeans also seem a little more flexible and dynamic. These are reactions to changing economic, political and social conditions. But the basic character differences I discovered remain in these regards as in others. The historically shaped characters of whole peoples change slowly even when outer conditions are moving with fair rapidity.

*To protect the confidentiality of my informants, from experts in various fields to friends and family, I have in many instances changed names and other revealing details of identity.

we are can come the compassion which should lead to mutual forgiveness and the deep knowing we so desperately need.

As is clear, already, despite the concreteness of this book, I shall be leading the reader to entertain ideas of considerable generality. Such a general understanding is the first step to knowing others in depth. Of course, generalizations are always partial in their accuracy and completeness, and they certainly must be so when hundreds of millions of individuals are being so briefly comprehended as here. Moreover, at a time when Americans and Europeans are growing rapidly alike and when massive political and economic changes are accelerating, all generalizations must be carefully weighed.

My specific scope here is Western Europe. But I am not writing about the Germans or the Portuguese or any other specific nationality. What interests me is the impression all Americans have that every one of these people is different from us and more like one another than like us. The collectivity I examine when I talk about ''Europeans'' here comprises the inhabitants of that ancient civilization existing between the Mohammedan, Byzantine, and Slavic which historian Marc Bloch calls the ''Romano-Germanic'': the group bounded by the Elbe and the Atlantic, the Tyrrhenian and the Adriatic, including Scandinavia and the British Isles. Even examining this large area, I shall leave out big groups, like peasants, who are no longer representative, and other subgroups outside the typical mainstream of today. I am after the mass of urban and suburban TV-watching people, plugged into the modern world by the market system, political parties and a hundred other means. The Eastern European people are only just coming back into the fold, and I have not, for that reason, treated them as modern Europeans. But *much* of what I say about Western Europeans applies also to today's Yugoslavs, Czechs, Hungarians, Poles, Romanians, Lithuanians, and even Russians, among others. For the deepest historical reasons, as we shall see, Americans are nearly unique among civilized people. Understanding Western Europeans, then, is a way of knowing much about the other peoples of the whole world.

Equipped with the concepts in this book, travellers will find themselves more at ease, less irritated and confused by daily encounters with the wonderful but at times aggravating Europeans. Furthermore, if we are doing business, sight-seeing, vacationing, studying or pursuing any kind of negotiation, our way will be smoothed. We Americans can overcome our confusion, reticence and tentativeness, not through gimmicks but through knowledge. Just because the two people are becoming more alike and more in touch with each other, the possibility exists, at last, for true understanding.

—S.M.

PART ONE

PRELUDE: PAINTED IN BLOOD

Homo homini lupus ("Man is a wolf to Man")
—**Latin proverb**

Like many American visitors to Europe, I have always felt that it is more peaceful than the United States. One feels that there is less street violence than we are used to. In the nighttime subways and the lonesome streets of old, dark cities, one is unafraid. The statistics confirm our impressions: urban, criminal violence is much less likely. Depending on the country, Europe suffers six to eight times fewer murders and violent assaults than America.

But the person who stays in Europe long enough begins to sense other stirrings behind the aura of European civility. Even when Europeans joke with condescension about our own violent tendencies, calling Americans "cowboys"—by which they mean we are irresponsible and undisciplined people, often unable to master ourselves—one feels that they are not completely free of those same tendencies.

For me, this suspicion is repeatedly renewed by European highway manners. There is, for example, the violent blinking of lights on the *Autobahn* in Germany. A Mercedes pulls up behind you and rides the tail of your car. You glance down to learn you are already going 140 kilometers an hour—10 kilometers higher than the posted speed limit and a respectable clip of 85 mph. But it is not sufficient for the car behind you. You feel the quick flame of his wrath, you see in your mirror the eyes beginning to bulge, you hear the hand now banging on the horn. He would toss you off the road if he had a gadget that could do it: not a mine sweeper, a car sweeper is what he yearns for. You yield the fast lane, and he passes you by as if you were standing still, not even pausing as he makes violent gestures with his right arm, his mouth seen through the glass open in what must be shouts, outraged that you have not ceded him his place sooner. Even in city traffic,

3

there is a continuous and thorough aggressiveness, no chance missed to get ahead, to slice past you and reach that red light first. Over and over, irritating horns are used to punish the slightest hesitation or delay. If you both happen to meet at the next stoplight, he looks at you furiously. He may even roll down a window and lean over to express his contempt for your abilities as a driver, with a ready and automatic venom.

True, you soon learn that all this carrying on is not going to propel your European out of his car, baseball bat in hand, as happens in America when, much more occasionally, feelings run so high. That realization makes you feel, again, safer than at home, though still you wonder why their nerve endings are so raw. You read that in Western Europe auto accidents kill ten to thirty times as many people each year as do homicides. During his lifetime, one European in two can count on being hurt in an automobile accident. And yet, in most countries, attempts to regulate dangerous driving fail every year.

But, driving aside, there is something in the air, some kind of vague thing that bothers. One begins to wonder, for example, at all the shutters—white in Belgium, gray in France, green in Italy, red in Germany—the old-fashioned sort that swing shut like double gates over farmhouse windows or city apartments. My mother-in-law in Brussels tells me that her late husband used to lower their wooden shutters, the kind that roll down from boxes above the windows in the house, all nineteen of them, every night. She herself would do it now, she says, but it requires more physical energy than she has at eighty years.

One of the sounds at daybreak and sunset that I get used to is the raising and lowering clatter or the opening and closing bang of those European shutters. What we call "riot gates," the steel accordion shutters that American merchants installed over ghetto shop-windows at the end of the sixties, European shops have had for generations. You find them all over southern and central Europe. And where we install paltry double locks on our better-guarded front doors, to keep out urban intruders, many Europeans inherit ancient wooden beams of bolts and strong locks that throw another metal bolt when you turn the key fifteen times. The typical modern apartment I now occupy in Florence embodies the latest technical advances on such old systems. The front door has a double-edged key so complex that a duplicate can be made only by hand and will take a master locksmith the better part of an hour. The lock not only thrusts a metal bolt into the wall near itself—by means of various connecting gears and rods that occupy the interior of the door—it also slides eight other three-inch bolts, hardened alloy, into sockets in the four walls surrounding the door. It is like the door of a safe, a strong room, a bank vault. In my complex of modern buildings, three hundred apartments come with doors like this, standard equipment. They cost two thousand dollars each, are faced with sheets of heavy steel, and cannot be broken down by shoulders or even axes. Shooting away the lock would still leave those nine three-inch bolts in place. To break into my apartment, you need to smash down the whole front wall.

The very landscape of Europe, that man-cultured countryside, and even the old cityscape, so eagerly sought by Americans for relief from our own more monotonous spaces, are full of monuments to violence. Not just, I notice, those machine-gun pockmarks, still unrepaired, on scattered farmhouse walls from Norway to Greece. What seems a charming old castle is really an engine of self-defense; so too the girdling town walls; so too the huge, metal-studded, heavy doors of ten thousand cathedrals and parish churches. The ubiquitous equestrian statues of men on horseback, stern figures on bulging steeds—Godfrey de Bouillon in Brussels near the Musée de l'Art Ancien or Marcus Aurelius in Rome on the Capitolium—celebrate a tradition of conquest and domination. I come to see that we should not look upon these objects as if they were mere symbols of the human mind, sculptures of the hero archetype. They are, instead, celebrations of fighters.

At first, we apprehend castles and town walls, medieval gates and watchtowers, as picturesque—tourist attractions. We mythologize them, we lend them the colors of romance and forget they were conceived in fear. We psychologize them and enjoy them as poetic images of safety, imaginatively appropriating them and unconsciously placing ourselves in their symbolic protection. Their height, solidity, and artfulness seem guarantors of our peace and safety. We locate them and ourselves in a literary world, a world of charming fairy tales.

But European history tells the tale of a world painful and unsafe, a world not yet safe, and the European dwells in that history. It marks the experience of his parents and grandparents and lives in their vivid recollections, their unconscious memories. It is transmitted directly by them to him. It marks, as we have seen, his physical environment, the windows and front door of his dwelling, the fortresses and walls of the cities where he grows up. These ancient fortresses, refurbished, are often local head-quarters of the army or the militarized police. When the European child goes to school, the endless succession of military rulers is explained in history class. Imagine being ten years old and learning that for two thousand years, the city you live in has been under attack, ten, fifty, a hundred times. Attacks come to seem like air and sunshine, not incidental occurrences in an otherwise peaceful world but essential elements of life.

Only by plunging ourselves into a sense of the enormous weight of historic violence can we begin to understand the European soul. We must think of a vast South Bronx of a continent, repeatedly devasted not for ten or twenty years but, as men experience time, forever. The Roman Empire itself, the beginning of what we think of as Europe, was an organization for domination and defense. Everywhere still are the remains of Roman fortifications; from one extreme of Europe to another, they abide, stone piled on stone, as far north of Rome itself as the wall the emperor Hadrian built across England, to protect his Romanized citizens from the barbarians still farther north.

One might say that the Roman Empire fell a long time ago and that European life and personality are based on more recent experiences, but the line of violence is heavy and persistent. The sociologist Talcott Parsons writes that after the fall of the empire, during the slow Middle Ages, "physical security was . . . the most pressing problem. . . . Beside the original barbarian invasions of the Empire, disorder throve on long-continuing incursions . . . Muslims . . . Huns . . . Scandinavians . . . and internecine strife induced by political fragmentation. A premium was thus placed on military safeguards against violence. With support from the traditions of antiquity, a predominantly military class became as-cendant in secular society and secured its position."

In contrast, America has seldom been invaded and what in-vasions there were have been small (the War of 1812 being the largest) and brief. "Internecine strife induced by political frag-mentation," with the single big exception of the Civil War, has not been the American way. Never has the American military been the dominant class, the "military-industrial complex" notwithstanding.

The pattern of European violence has also been typified by collective action—organized, traditional, political; armies, invasions, crusades; sects, neighborhoods, regions, political parties, and classes against one another. Violence in the United States has tended not to have this institutionalized character, this heavy organization, this sense of permanence. Our violence has been mostly anarchic, individualistic, spontaneous. But in European medieval life, violence was written into the structure of society itself. As the historian Norbert Elias points out, with the ruling class being warriors, existence revolved around rapine, the hunt for men and animals, and combat: "The documents suggest unimaginable emotional binges where each man, when he could—with some rare exceptions—abandoned himself to the extreme joys of ferocity, murder, torture, destruction, and sadism." In Oxford alone, there were four to seven times more murders in the thirteenth century than in the average big American city today. In European medieval society generally, few men reached adulthood without being mixed up, more or less intimately, with a murder.

The prestige of the soldier is one with the prestige, not entirely vanished, of the aristocracy in Europe. The European nobility was first a group of tough guys and their molls; it was as if Billy the Kid and his kind took over and spawned dynasties. There is no such ancestral link in American history between institutionalized violence, defense, and the rewards of prestige and high status among the ruling elite. It is not that we are an exceptionally peaceable nation: we now have the highest rate of violent crime in the developed world by far, we virtually destroyed the Indian, and we held blacks in more or less brutal subjection for nearly four hundred years. But until recently, except in time of war, our armed forces were small, miserable affairs.

The European military tradition did not cease with the end of the Middle Ages and the foreign invasions. With the coming of the Renaissance, there occurred a commercial revolution that opened up worldwide trade on a scale which permitted the accumulation of surplus capital and, for many, a prosperity hitherto undreamed of. Had this new wealth been applied to peaceful purposes, hunger and plague might have been severely curtailed, even done away with. But the rulers of Europe—secular and ecclesiastical alike—chose otherwise: "When pestilence and famine were ceasing to be necessities imposed by nature," writes R. H. Tawney, "they reestablished them by political art. . . . For approximately three-quarters both of the sixteenth and . . . seventeenth centuries, Europe tore itself to pieces. The spiritual fires of Renaissance and Reformation alike were trampled out beneath the feet of bravos. . . . By the middle of the sixteenth century the English government . . . was in a state of financial collapse, and by the end of it Spain, the southern Netherlands . . . and a great part of France . . . were ruined. By the middle of the seventeenth century wide tracts of Germany were a desert."

In the eighteenth century, the story is not essentially different. England, France, and Spain lost nearly 500,000 men in colonial wars while wars in Prussia and Austria decimated thousands. The nineteenth century, after the terrible losses of the Napoleonic wars fought all over Europe, was relatively quiet. Wars were small among the so-called great powers. But European imperialism gave birth to war on a world scale. Innumerable invasions and colonial police actions were the rule. In our century, the First World War killed nearly ten million Europeans. In the Second World War, nearly fifty million people died worldwide, of whom only sixteen million were soldiers.

Casting his eye over eleven nations and empires of Europe and over twenty-five hundred years, sociologist Pitirim Sorokin notices that from one century to another, war was about equally frequent: in European history, one year in five is a year of armed conflict. War is a normal condition.

This tradition of systematic group violence marks the European, but a parallel tradition of personal violence also marks him. Personal violence has steadily declined with industrialism, education, and increased prosperity, but this is a comparatively recent development. In the closed world of the traditional village, distractions were rare, and every quarrel either exploded immediately and was conducted openly, or ripened with time, often dangerously within the family. Combat did the duty of the courts. One didn't go to judges, mysterious and too far away. One fought. Village life was more violent than that of the cities, hates more intense. In schools, the violence of masters on pupils, with canes and even whips, was normal. The life in the cities is easily evoked by a trip to what we normally see as simply picturesque San Gimignano near Siena. There, medieval families built high towers as homes. The remnants of those many fortified domestic skyscrapers can serve to recall all of Europe's history of urban family against family. It was as if today's apartment dwellers were to pile brick on brick and make a fortress against the attacks of neighbors.

It takes a European to plumb the depths of this hatred of others that, in less obviously violent fashion, still exists. The Polish poet Czeslaw Milosz, who has lived as a refugee in France and now in America, writes: "The violence of nineteenth century human clashes in America took place on the surface, in the open. The violence in Europe became formalized, coalesced with class divisions hallowed by centuries; it was interiorized, ingrained, or baked in." Milocsz's Europe consists of societies more or less permanently divided, drenched in resentment. I realize that, partly as a result of this past, the inner life of Europeans must be different from ours, that their present is every day influenced by the past. Even when they watch the world's latest faraway little war on news-time television, they watch with different eyes from ours because it has happened to them. That memory too is "baked in" in a hundred subtle and unspoken ways, and it is important that we grasp the deep imprint of organized horror on the European soul. We should look around us in their sunny plazas or on rainy-day museum afternoons, and beside all the uplifting beauty, or perhaps beneath it, see a continent painted in blood. We must become visitors with imaginative vision, who can do better than to transform history into mere pageantry and heroics. Everywhere, on the fronts of buildings, in the eyes of a waiter, beneath the desks of travel agents, abide the reminders of institutionalized horror.

Like the military historian John Keegan, we must become "time-travellers" as well as space travelers and see the killer everywhere in Europe: "The image of the warrior, the outline of his form, the print of his foot, the press of his palm, the trace of his tools on the stones of his strong places, the touch, sight, almost sound, smell and taste of him, await rediscovery by the time-traveller at every level and turning-point of the journey into Europe's past." We must catalogue the myriad guises of the European killer:

> Who is he, this universal man of Europe as widespread in his wandering and settlement as the tiller of the soil and, from age to age, almost as commonplace? As warrior, he is Everyman, builder and destroyer, trader and pirate, citizen and slave. He is hoplite, legionary, Frank, Visigoth, Viking, knight, crusader, condottiere, Landsknecht, streltsi, pandour, estradiot, grenadier, hussar, guerrillero, zouave, marsouin, Frontkämpfer, poilu, Tommy, para. He is the ever present man of war, war of city-state, civil war and war of empire, war of religion and war of ideas, feudal war and war of nations, war of kings and war of peoples.

Aiming one's imagination at the monstrosity of history upon which Europeans live brings gradual illumination about their condition. Most Americans are afraid of war because we know abstractly that it means potential death. The European is afraid in a more intimate and concrete way. Europeans know that war *hurts*. You go cold and hungry. You are wounded. They can peel the skin off you. You are impressed and tortured and ordered over the top in a gas attack. War is not a story, not a simple end to living. War is not death, but torture.

In Milan one night, I watch a TV documentary about the Second World War. Italian troops retreat over snow from bloody Russian counterattacks. I realize that from where I sit, nobody in Europe can be said to have won that war. The Russians, yes, technically, if you call sixty million casualties a victory. The French, yes, technically, if you call foreign occupation, Gestapo seizures and deportations, collaboration, shame, disgrace, hangings, and firing squads "winning." The British, if you call vast numbers of wounded and dead, and loss of empire, national will, and prosperity, "winning." Bitter defeat for the Axis, bitter but grateful survival for the Allies.

It was different for most of us in the United States. True, many families suffered casualties, but for most of us at home the last big war, our favorite, was the stuff of John Wayne propaganda films. America had a good time during the war. We were a little worried, even frightened, at times, about possibly being on the losing side, about losing the Philippines, about losing England. About maybe a small air raid.

Phantom fears. We won it big. The dollar was king and prosperity soared. Despite the sufferings of some, most of us won an abstract and distant moral battle of good against evil. And if Vietnam and Korea and some of our other adventures have not done us so well, we can take it, we weren't really that involved— faraway stuff. For the Europeans, it was just yesterday, and just the other side of the hill or valley or tenement. They remember war and they remember that it wounds the body, the feelings, the mind and the spirit. In all dimensions, it makes you suffer.

Like many of us, I am no Gibbon, one who might easily intuit the past in the present. He could be stirred by the sound of monks singing in the Temple of Jupiter to write of the decline and fall of the Roman Empire and to penetrate its meaning in some pungent phrase: "the triumph of barbarism and religion." To keep before my present consciousness the shaping past of European collective violence, I must talk to people rather than just read books and exercise my historical imagination. But many Europeans—most, in fact—are reluctant to talk in detail even about a war that ended forty years ago. It is painful to face it again, it is inconvenient to face it, and it is dangerous. For many Europeans, I learn, war, as is natural where conflicts are fought on one's home ground, has the character of civil war. One doesn't have to go back to fratricidal Florentines in the Middle Ages, Guelphs against Ghibellines or Whites against Blacks, those hoary conflicts kept forever alive in Dante's *Commedia*. An American psychiatrist who works with Europeans, most of them practicing psychotherapists themselves, tells me: "People in my training groups are just beginning to come to terms with the Second World War. So many, all over Europe, from Norway to France, were Nazis or worked with Nazis, or just turned their backs." Nor was that grand treason easily forgotten. In 1944, the murder rate in Europe was twenty-three times that of 1936. Summary executions, vengeance, and evening the score created still more painful memories.

Another American psychologist who works in Europe says with sorrow and pity: "The generation of Germans now in their late thirties are troubled by father problems—his being around or not being around when they were children, and which side he was on. You ask one about his father and he looks very sad, even dead: 'He left when I was a year and a half old. Never came back. Just a photo on the wall with big staring eyes.'" A Massachusetts woman athlete who gives occasional aikido workshops abroad (black belt, 105 pounds), and who is known to her students at home for her gentleness in this mildest of martial arts, reports: "The Germans nowadays are supersoft. Those big guys, they found me too violent, like I was a bone-crusher or something!"

All over Europe, the postwar generations carry the war in their blood. A Dutch nurse remembers 1944: "We still call it the 'Winter of Starvation.' I recall people in a freight train were stopped near our village; for a whole day, they screamed for water. I was six. My mother said, 'Hush, we don't talk about that, come away.'" And a thin Dutch reporter whose father was a Nazi tells me his story: "My mother was German. When the Allies invaded, she had the wrong idea and took us three children back to Germany. She thought we would be safe there!" He snorts at the irony, then continues: "I remember trains, an endless succession of trains; day and night, getting on and off, people pushing, planes strafing, my mother screaming a lot. I put it behind me, I thought. I became an aggressive, very left-wing journalist, until one day, driving home, I heard a hand grenade explode inside the car." I look at him in wonder, for he seems in one piece. "It wasn't real," he explains, "a memory, a hallucination; I guess I cracked up. I'm better now."

The European civil war, which scars such memories deep into the collective psyche, continues today. Group still wars with group; Protestant and Catholic Irish still mount their bloody reprisals; so too Basques against Spaniards, Corsicans against French, Flemish against Walloons, Greeks against Turks, right-wing and left-wing terrorists against all Italians, against Germans. The list seems endless and the pot continues to simmer, though it has not boiled over in a big way in more than forty years.

Nevertheless, as recently as 1962, during the Algerian conflict, civil war was widely feared in France (as it has been feared since in Spain, Portugal, and Greece, among other countries). In the late seventies, it was thought by many that sheer anarchy would follow the paralyzing attacks of the Italian Red Brigades. Their gunmen seemed able to destroy at will judges, police chiefs, and even the prime minister (who was trying to reconcile Christian Democrats and Communists). Many were similarly worried about the stability of Germany, with its own terrorists. As recently as 1980, it was feared that the election of a socialist government in France would lead to hardening of political positions on both sides and then to another civil war. Every day, headlines all over the continent report the continuing toll of organized violence. A bomb blows the legs off a police sergeant, a blast kills seventy in the Bologna railroad station, another destroys scores more in a tunnel on the same line, unknown persons machine-gun Jewish children getting on an Antwerp bus to go to summer camp, police in every country move their armored cars around to cover a shifting list of endangered foreign embassies, consulates, airline companies. American visitors from tourists to residents prefer not to look too close. We skip from springtime castle to quaint city wall, to sculptured man on horseback, glad to be away from our little routine lives.

I do the same. One July, I go to vacation in peaceful Switzerland. My wife and I spend a few days at the house of a friend's mother. During a long summer's evening, we talk with her, a pleasant, elderly, thoughtful German woman. We talk after dinner in her chalet, an expensive house in the old wooden style, above one of the country's many prosperous mountain valleys. The living room is full of good Oriental rugs and antiques. When we can't find a word in English, we go to German, which I am feeble in, or to French. The fire slumbers in the cool August night, the wine in green glass beakers is sweet and light.

She tells me that though she lives in Switzerland and California now, she grew up in Hamburg and spent her years as a young woman in Munich, including the years of the Second World War. She says she is Jewish.

I am startled. I hadn't known that Jews could survive in Nazi Germany. She explains that if one was married to an "Aryan," one was "privileged." "Of course," she adds, "if the war had lasted longer, we would have been taken to the camps, me and my daughter and my son. In fact, an order did come for us, but it was very late in the war, everything was in chaos, and we just didn't show up. Before that, being married to an Aryan helped, and I was not a practicing Jew, and he was the eldest son of a very old, rich brewing family, so even the local Nazis in the village where we finally took refuge from the bombing were cautious with us.

"Naturally, it wasn't easy," she says with calm. "Especially toward the end. Everybody was starving and there was always a threat of deportation, extermination, one didn't exactly know what."

As if she had anticipated my inner thoughts, she adds: "People all over still hate the Germans for that. They consider them all Nazis. They wonder how, otherwise, it could have happened at all. But I understand how all those people, virtually a whole nation, could have done it."

It is a lot to understand, I think. "How?" I ask.

"They were scared. That's all. Of losing their jobs. Of losing their social position. Of being physically hurt. Of ending up in jail or concentration camps. And when people are scared, they do what they are told."

We sit and look at the fire for a long minute. A loud crack from the logs sends up a scattering of sparks. "Courage is rare," she resumes. "Most people don't have courage. This is true not only in Germany. People do what they are told everywhere—in the Communist countries, in wars, everywhere. Perhaps the Germans are more this way; they are great practitioners of obedience. If you told a German soldier to shoot these two hundred Jewish men, women, and children, he did it."

It is a heavy, pregnant moment, as if having survived out of her turn, she will reveal something of great importance. But her tone, as she resumes, is matter-of-fact. "I am by nature optimistic. I used to believe in the forward progress of man. But I have learned that there is too much evil, too little courage. Now, at the end of my life—I am seventy-two—I have to say that all those youthful ideas, those ideals I still hold, are, in fact, illusions. It is an illusion. My second husband was a paleontologist. He worked in China with Teilhard de Chardin. I love still to read Teilhard. He never talks about evil, the devil, the dark things. You never read about wars. It is all going, he says, toward an inevitable happy ending. I would like to believe that. But it is an illusion."

I am chilled. Too big to want to look at for long, too grand and dark. Ridiculous, in a way, ensconced here on the slope of this dark valley, the lights of the village cheerful below, the rich furnishings, the carpets and the decanter and the carefully joined wooden walls. And we are in Switzerland, protected by neutrality since 1515. One doesn't shrug off what she has said, one lets it go by. She herself has taken pains not to be dramatic, not to give much detail, a mere summary of horror from which one can turn away. Except my wife and I are not let off quite so easily by the circumstances.

"Tomorrow night I can't invite you again to dinner," my hostess says apologetically. "I'm going to a concert with some people and there are no extra seats, sold out. So you'll have to make your own supper." We are staying in her little guesthouse, a charming cottage, all very cute and quiet and ordered and Swiss. "I've left you stuff in your refrigerator there," she says with solicitude, "but you'll need some noodles."

Noodles. A good peaceful concept after Hitler. Noodles.

I follow her into the roomy kitchen, where she opens the hand-carved cupboards in vain. "We'll have to go downstairs," she says, leading the way to the cellar. There she opens row upon row of metal cupboards. They are full of neat boxes with Magic Marker writing on them. Five large cases declare: "Noodles. Spaghetti. Spaetzle." Next to them are six ten-kilogram sacks of sugar, and twenty boxes of lump sugar, each weighing half a kilo. I see stacks of canned vegetables and large bags marked "Coffee Beans." She takes down one of the boxes marked "Spaetzle" and before I can wonder if this hoarding is a product of her wartime experience, she explains: "It's a Swiss law that you have to have a certain quantity of food stored in the house." And before I can imagine why (the wine has made me a little less than keen at this late hour), she explains again: "Sixty days' worth; in case of war."

The peaceful, neutral Swiss. But like all Europeans, they remember. Boxes of starches, sugar, canned goods in every home as reminders. The next day I inquire and they tell me every Swiss man up to the age of sixty is in the active army reserve; he must keep his rifle and ammunition at home, in case. I hear about the atomic bomb shelter program, fortified holes no more than fifteen minutes away from 90 percent of the population. I hear the scraping sound of supersonic aircraft through the valleys, the Swiss air force endlessly crisscrossing the tiny country, on guard. They run only a few flights in the tourist-ridden summer, but in winter the practice maneuvers are so constant and noisy that many citizens protest.

At the end of the week's stay, driving north, my wife and I stop for coffee at a restaurant on the superhighway. It is a sunny day, but the peace of the outdoor café is disturbed by incessant noises which seem to come from just beyond a man-made grassy mound that cuts off the view beyond the parking lot. When I ask, the waitress explains that it is army target practice and that some army installations are located on the highway for quick maneuvering. When we stop at another such restaurant for a last coffee before the frontier, the sounds are the same: Bam! Bam! Bam! Once over the border, the scraping noises of military jets, with German markings this time, echo those in Switzerland. I remember seeing the same planes, with Italian air force identification, dip in practice into the Casentino Valley near Poppi in Tuscany, and how my car was stopped on the road near Fiesole by army patrols with red batons, so that Italian troops could complete their maneuvers in the woods beyond.

They go about their business, the Europeans. My Swiss hostess goes to her concert; the Swiss summer tourists in the restaurant parking lots calmly check the ropes that hold windsurfers to the tops of their cars and carefully place rubbish in neat garbage cans, keeping their cars immaculate; the Germans and Italians don't even look up at the planes anymore. And yet what is it but a whole continent on alert? *Force de frappe* in France on my left as I drive north. Enough atom bomb shelters for the whole population ahead of me in Sweden. The road signs I pass on the German *Autobahn* give two speed limits: one for cars and one for tanks.

Like the Europeans, one must turn away, go about one's business. But the mind is still set in restless motion. It seems doubtful, but I ask myself whether it will be a European who presses the button first. Could the weight of historical habits prevail? I remember how at the beginning of the Falklands tension, I listened fascinated to the BBC coverage. Almost everyone they talked to laughed at the whole affair: "It's just rocks and penguins and a few hundred company employees, isn't it?" Eighty-five percent of the public polled thought England should do nothing about the Argentine invasion. Within a few weeks, however, there were patriotic speeches, high-sounding denunciations of "the Argentine dictator," a growing go-get-'em climate. The coverage was constant and I found myself listening with increasing horror at the speed with which public opinion swerved and became bloodthirsty: kick the Argies out, go get those spics, defend our people's freedom, send in the fleet! Within six weeks, the peaceful, civilized British public, the most orderly country in Europe, had reversed position: 85 percent supported war.

Like me, the European retreats from such awarenesses, but his life is, nonetheless, conditioned by what he has always known, and his character is shaped by it. The background of collective violence, combined with other historical forces like memories of massive poverty, makes the European closed and defended in ways that are typically un-American.

PART TWO

PRINCE IN THE CASTLE

It takes seven years, seven weeks, and seven days to know with whom you're dealing.

—Breton proverb

Since I am too poor to buy any other horse, at least the Horse of Pride will always have a stall in my stable.

—French peasant

The bulk of mankind on their part are not excessively curious concerning any theories whilst they are really happy; and one sure symptom of an ill-conducted state is the propensity of the people to resort to them.

—Edmund Burke

Rye was not a restful place. It had the atmosphere of a china shop. It urged you to remark on the pretty houses and the well-kept gardens and the self-conscious sign-painting, and then it demanded you move on. But it was not just the quaint places in England that looked both pretty and inhospitable. Most villages and towns wore a pout of rejection—the shades drawn in what seemed an averted gaze—and there were few places I went in England that did not seem, as I stared, to be whispering at me all the while, *Move on! Go home!*

—Paul Theroux

CHAPTER ONE

Defensiveness

Remember Jean Gabin? Anna Magnani? Charles Laughton? Faces. Those wonderful European faces which make Americans think that behind them is a profundity, a density of personality, to which most of us cannot even aspire. Those strongly etched foreign countenances, the wrinkles of European experience, the eyes full of depth, the irregularities that speak of true individuality, are in direct contrast to the cultivated insipidness which is the American heartland preferred look.

Encounter a typical European, of almost any class, and you will find not only a "real face," as one upper-class Boston housewife put it to me, but behind it a whole worldview. One of my own first memories of Europe, over twenty-five years ago, was a conversation with a German furniture salesman on a train who made sophisticated remarks about the latest political events; he seemed not only to understand them but also to have an understanding of *everything*. Behind his tight, tough countenance, his long, bony chin, dark skin and hard, black eyes, a cheek engraved by a crease, were a philosophy, a politic, an ethic, even a psychology—all rather well worked-out and seemingly unique to him alone.

For many historical reasons, we Americans tend to be different. Indeed, because of our national experience, we become increasingly more plastic. So often wrenched by that major tendency in modern life which sociologists call "alternation"—the continual shift of social norms and expectations—we are more open and therefore more bland.

We have lived a long time now with constant change. What was yesterday's truth became shattered when we went to college; the philosophy professor took apart the views our parents had handed on and demonstrated their logical flimsiness. Technological innovation relentlessly undermined any stable belief. So did the multiple images of acceptable conduct presented by mass communications. So did moving, as we have tended to do from community to community.

It is no wonder that as a people we are fascinated by tales of total personality conversion. Incredible as it may seem, more Americans knew who Patty Hearst was during her period of active celebrity than knew who was president. Ditto for the Reverend Jim Jones and Jonestown. And some of us still remember the shock we felt when it was announced that the Chinese Communists had "brainwashed" (a new term then) a number of our soldiers in Korea. We feared that with our modern suppleness, we could become anything. We believe, after all, in positive brainwashing: American self-improvement. But we are, consequently, sometimes afraid we don't have souls. And so, we think, we even hope, that those Europeans with their decisively individual countenances and definite views on everything (whether the views be Communist or right-wing, aesthetic or ethical, religious or atheist) are truly whole personalities.

Unfortunately, the integrity of the European character is at best a mixed business.

The European's intellectual style is one personality trait that typically contributes to this impression of apparently finished integrity. Any American who has ever come up against a European in discussion has probably found himself in quick trouble. One is immediately impressed by what seems to be considerable thought about the topic at hand—whether it be films, child-rearing, politics, science, art, or whatever. Moreover, the European tends to be tenacious and inventive in such encounters. He objects easily to what you say, disagrees forcefully, points out inconsistencies with determination and seems an expert at shifting the subject to grounds on which he is a master of the material.

For me, the words *eristic* and *irenic* describe the essential difference in their way of discussion and ours. *Eristic,* from the Greek *eristikos,* "fond of wrangling," means "warlike, given to disputation." It is the standard European style. *Irenic,* on the other hand, also of Greek origin, means "peaceful, seeking to combine thoughts into a working consensus." One can say that this is the natural American intellectual style of our day: cooperative, democratic, and practical.

In the eristic style, the European advances ideas like battalions of tanks, holds the ground he wins, blasts you as you come toward him, brings in other battalions to reinforce a position. Intellectually, he justifies this procedure by claiming he is "refining truth through dialectic." But the antagonistic and competitive social atmosphere this approach engenders is almost never productive of higher synthesis.

By turns baffled, impressed, frustrated, and annoyed, I have inquired how it is that Europeans seem so intellectually formidable and why so many of them feel they have to look as if they've figured everything out.

A lot of what they say is, indeed, merely for show. One Spanish physicist confides to me: "In Europe, you seldom admit a new thought from someone else into your mind in public. You defend your ideas as you would defend yourself. Later, when you're alone at home at night, you might incorporate your opponent's ideas into your arsenal, for the next go-around. You Americans are much more open—you don't seem to understand that when we Europeans argue, we are doing it, above everything, to try and impress each other and you."

But it is no mere pastime or Johnsonian "talking for victory." The sense of self is at stake. I talk about it, for example, to a French girl, Georgette Lambert, barely twenty years old. She spent a year as a high school senior in Glendale, California—mainstream suburban America—living with an American middle-class Catholic family that had ten children. Bony and petite in the French way, with a pleasantly angular face and the figure of a boyish girl rather than a woman, she describes her struggle to understand how the two minds—the French and the American—differ.

"In Europe, you're *judged* by what you think. If you have a lot of friends in France, you are considered superficial, while in America, it is important to be popular. In America, people want to be loved, so they must learn to agree with others. But here, we want to fulfill a certain image: we want to appear adult, reasonable, mature, wise, even wised-up. After only a month's touring around, all my French friends, for example, had very clear opinions about the U.S. They were, as I knew they would be, very critical, America is *débile,* they said, crazy. But if you ask a typical American about his European visit, he'll say, 'It was great!' If he really doesn't like it, he'll say, at worst, 'It's okay.'" She goes on to tell me that she got to like America, very much. But she had to learn "to become like them: not critical, at least at first. You mustn't offend."

The intellectual or ideological variety of Europeans is as varied as their particular mugs. They feel a need to differentiate themselves by their ideas, while we like to blend with one another. Europeans have always remarked on the "intellectual conformity" of Americans. A recent Swiss visitor, a graduate student nearly thirty years old, echoes that observation. She reports that except for her stays in New York City, she had to learn that one was not really supposed to air definite likes and dislikes, along with a well-thought-through rationale. "People at cocktail parties would just shy away if I said that such and such a film was thin, insubstantial, naïve; or if I criticized a book or a political party. In America, I found a padded world where personal attitudes can't be strongly affirmed." One German political scientist remembers emptying a small dining room at the Harvard Faculty Club during the McCarthy era by strongly condemning Franco's Spain: "People grew silent; then, gradually, just drifted away. The next day one of them asked me, if you can believe it, whether I was a Communist!" On the other hand, the same professor loves what he calls the "openness" of college students in America. "In Europe, by the time they get to the university, students have already constructed their political position and they don't let in anything."

Curious about how this style is created in each new generation of Europeans, I go back to Georgette. "How did you learn to have so many opinions about everything?" I ask her. "Was it in school that you learned you had to do that?"

"In school, certainly. But more fundamentally, it was expected by my parents. Dinner in our family was a running discussion of political, social, and religious issues. My father and mother frequently disagreed, but above all it was my brother who sharpened me up. He was older and he would have crushed me if I hadn't learned to stand up for myself in argument."

The social roots of this European tendency toward theorizing and argument go far back in time. A former White Russian prince who now lives in Sweden on welfare recalls to me "the famous lesson of Talleyrand: how to drink brandy. First you pour it in a round snifter. Then you hold the snifter in the palm of your hand to warm it. Then, you bring the snifter close to you and you smell the fumes of the brandy. Then, you put the glass down and you argue."

But other roots are darker and harder to uncover.

A European intellectual like Milocsz, even though he loves living in America and reveres its many virtues, confesses that he finds himself uncomfortable, deviant: "In an attempt to find a name for what set me apart, I came to the conclusion that it was by a tendency to argue from some basis—that is, an inclination to abstraction—which deprived many of my judgments of their usefulness, and even more, perhaps, my shame at making concessions, though no one around was ashamed to, if the disposition of forces required that concessions be made."

What causes someone as sophisticated as Milosz to be so emotional about intellectual consistency? Why is a world famous poet *ashamed* to yield, to make concessions? Was European thought always so passionate?

With the exception of the Eristics, the ancient Greek philosophers were not angry men nor passionate defenders of tight intellectual positions. Plato, the greatest by universal consent, wrote ironic dialogues, even symposia, often embodying several views of an issue. Frequently, he raised more questions than he answered, and Aristotle, his greatest pupil, can hardly be thought of as a fervently *engagé* spirit. What made the eristic style, once so despised by most ancients, into the European way was above all the passionate tradition of Christian theologizing. It broke the pagan tolerance and made argument into an ardent enterprise, one upon whose outcome your very salvation might depend.

Until recently, we must recall, Europeans had little sympathy with religious differences. In their various localities, they burned deviant people, broke them on the rack, went on Crusades. Though violent and massive persecutions of those with different religious beliefs continued in many European countries through the end of the Second World War, in general, religious passion was gradually replaced by toleration beginning in the eighteenth and nineteenth centuries. But then the fierceness of intellectual contest, the eristic habit, was transferred to politics.

There, a combination of clashing class interests and a human need to seem to know what was right found and still finds an outlet for passion. Moreover, Marxism, the most broadly held political philosophy of our time, has been called, with justice, a religion, meaning it not only serves to answer social and political questions but also provides methods for realizing personal and collective redemption. Other European political beliefs have been charged over the same fires of human need: monarchism, fascism, individualistic anarchism, even social democracy.

The American experience with theology, ideology, and theory was rather different. America was settled in part by Europeans who fled the continent's religious intolerance. Although the Puritan settlers of Massachusetts were as intolerant as those they fled, the same cannot be said of the Virginia colonists and, even in New England, few years passed before Roger Williams established the principle of religious toleration. Then, America broke with the eristic tradition.

It was perhaps inevitable that we do so. America was a land of open uncertainty. For two centuries and more after the Puritans came to New England, for example, there were no reliable maps of the continent. When the Louisiana Purchase was bought from Napoleon, no one even knew whether it extended just to the Mississippi or farther to the Pacific, if it included Canada or not. In such an atmosphere, intellectual precision, abstract theory, and passionate commitment to particular ideas all seemed laughable. Similarly, the American language stayed vulgar, democratic, and unbounded. Whitman praised this openness and imprecision: "Slang, profoundly consider'd, is the lawless germinal element, below all words and sentences, and behind all poetry, and provides a certain perennial rankness and protestantism in speech." Even the march to the frontier, the great expansive adventure of the nineteenth century, had a seeking quality that tended to destroy any interest in linear systems of thought. As Daniel Boorstin writes, it was not always a march or movement west, rather it was movement in the West: "The churning, casual, vagrant circular motion around and around was as characteristic of the American experience as the movement in a single direction. Other people had followed expeditions toward a definite place or a vivid ideal, in crusades, invasion, or migrations. But the Americans were a new kind of Bedouin. More than almost anything else, they valued the freedom to move, hoping in their very movement to discover what they were looking for. Americans thus valued opportunity, or the chance to seek it, more than purpose."

Just so, in their thinking, Americans do not feel the need to specify broad purposes or destinations, or even general points of departure. As much as anything else when we talk, Americans are searching for something that might turn up. Ours is often heuristic conversation. We are inclined to think out loud, trying on ideas for size and rejecting them without shame if they don't fit. Since so many of us do this, we are tolerant. We don't have to hold the other guy to one position because we know he doesn't expect it of us. We believe that life is rich, or it should be; there's still a continent to be taken; there's something doing up there, I heard there's jobs down that-a-way, you can find oil there, gold another place. Many times, the orderly progression of ideas, the patient, symmetrical construction of the sort of intellectual basis that Europeans cling to in discussion, and even the rules of formal logic, all seem irrelevant and purposeless to us.

Politics itself, the field of combat where European children like Georgette learn to prove themselves around the family dinner table, also had a different character from that of the European nation-state. Our politics were decentralized, with each community, county, state, and region having its own large tasks and authority to perform them. Political ideology was replaced by practical expediency—the need to get together to solve problems.

This pragmatic view and lack of real interest in theory touched even our most intellectual politicians, the Founding Fathers. It is little remembered that they actually declared our independence from England on July 2, 1776, and not on the fourth, telling a subcommittee, including Jefferson, Franklin, and John Adams, to draw up a "statement of reasons." The eventual "Declaration" was put together between the second and the fourth of July. Why this putting theory after fact? Because, in typical American fashion, one wanted to forestall excessive discussion and get the job done.

A product of vastly different historical circumstances, the European avails himself of eristic intellectualism to serve the deep psychological function of protecting his ego from assault. The eristic style also protects the person more generally from the object of all thought: the confusing universe itself, which he and his ancestors have been trying to figure out and pin down for thousands of years. By erecting his own theoretical system early in life, the European feels that he has Reality well in hand. Such a belief is, on the face of it, absurd, for talk to a hundred Europeans and they will give you a hundred different, contradictory, but personalized versions of that reality. Obviously, many of these must be wrong, but in practice no one is willing to be the first to admit that his is.

The drive toward system-building also fosters a certain kind of inner self-fashioning, and intellectual signature. There must indeed be a certain personal deepening that comes with undertaking such a task, but inevitably the individuality, because it is built, so to speak, in the teeth of others' criticism and opposition, is flawed by its narrowness and bad temper.

Such European habits have long tended to corrupt their intellectual life and also our own. Because the American university has looked to the Old World for intellectual leadership, the snarling contentiousness of our professoriat is nearly proverbial, the subject of a hundred novels by writers in temporary academic residence, who choke on the aridity, the competitiveness, and the ill will that characterize our official intellectual discourse. But all of these are essentially un-American qualities. A maverick professor of American Studies at a western university summed it up. He is a stout man in his late fifties, a person with the gruff manner and practical wisdom of one who was a foot soldier in the Second World War, European Theatre—GI Joe grown up, a Lou Grant among scholars. He has also conducted hundreds of seminars and lecture programs in Western Europe during the last twenty years. He says he is glad the eristic style is passing out of fashion in our universities:

> This worship of European intellectuality, typified by our enormous respect for their recognition—the Nobel Prize, for example—is coming to an end. I have known many visiting European professors and graduate students and a large number are not really serious. They tend, for example, to be terrified of making a mistake. But as most Americans intuitively know, mistakes are useful. Their European habit of carping, insisting on what they call "rigor," is frequently

nothing more than a power game. They load minor intellectual issues with affect for the sake of maintaining an illusion of superiority. That stuff is no more than veiled hostility. And it's not particularly academic: hostility is not
helpful to clear thinking. We need more American values in
our universities: forsaking punishing habits that put people
down and keep them isolated, giving minorities a chance,
open enrollments, caring about teaching, and helping people improve.

Certainly, Americans are more inclined to cooperate, to
merge their ideas with those of others. Paradoxically, however,
this easy willingness to yield and to be seen to have erred may
itself be a psychologically defensive maneuver. Looking for common ground prevents conflict, but it may also save one from the
discomfort of considering radical or revolutionary alternatives.
Moreover, since we define ourselves as a people willing to dare
greatly, we are inevitably vulnerable to great errors, and our un-
ashamed public confession of such errors can be, in part, a defense against feeling overwhelmed by guilt. In the European case,
errors cannot be admitted because there is no cultural excuse for
guilt, no tradition of getting another chance. One is mercilessly
punished for not seeming "wised-up"—to quote Georgette—and
mistakes must be hidden in oneself and uncovered only in others.
But we, by being unabashed at admitting our own mistakes in
public, give our confessions of error the quality of public ritual,
a purgation of our guilt before it gets too deep.

Our own defensiveness aside, however, it doesn't surprise
me that the eristic habit is starting to go, even in Europe. It is
too naïve for modern life. I talk to the chairman of a university
history department in Rome. Socialist, but partly trained in the
United States, he tells me that he doesn't teach his students his
"truth" anymore. "I try to show them how that truth is for the
liceo, the high school. Now, at the university, they need to put
together their own understanding of the past and, more important, to realize that it, too, will change as they get more information: it is only a *temporary* truth." A professor of law in
Bologna tells me that his students are beginning to be less ideological now: "Ideology is passé, the world is multipolar, and
pragmatism rules."

In typical European fashion, this statement dogmatically exaggerates the truth: In fact, the speed of change is slow. Nonetheless, change is under way. The habits of modern science, where our understanding of reality is constantly subject to evolution, if not to what historians have called "scientific revolution," are corroding the intellectual foundations of European personal dogmatism. Some Europeans are not at all sad about it. As a thirty-five-year-old book editor, mild-mannered, soft-spoken, and wispily blond-bearded in the Dutch way, puts it: "In Europe, even in relatively efficient northern countries, there is a tendency not to act. One has many meetings and people give their usual speeches. The American may be spongy and plastic in not carrying around an intellectual structure, but he tends to be more adventurous in action." One senses in many quarters, despite the wavering of attitudes caused by momentary political developments, an enthusiasm for American practicality and turning away from European theorizing. Indeed, more and more Europeans seem to admire the quality Tocqueville so well described: "For an American the whole of life is treated like a game of chance, a time of revolution, or the day of a battle."

It is more than getting lost in personal theories about the universe and defending them with rigor that keeps Europeans from action. Arising from their felt knowledge of history's terrible chances, a diffuse pessimism also serves to protect the European personality from the shocks of further defeats. Part of the European intellectual manner, pessimism is a collective basic assumption. As the French are given to say: *Le pire est toujours certain*—"The worst is always certain." (By undermining any belief in positive progress, pessimism also reinforces the tendency to speculate and otherwise enjoy contentious talking in the eristic style.)

Even the British are becoming masters of pessimism. They disguise it as self-criticism, and, rushing to be the first to admit everything's going to the dogs, they say: "We're awful. This country is hopeless. We're never prepared for anything. Nothing works properly." Luigi Barzini has described Europe as "pessimistic, prudent . . . and parsimonious, like an old-fashioned banker. It has learned not to rush into anything, even if it is the obviously necessary or advantageous thing to do. It always prefers to wait and see. . . . It is sagacious . . . and its frequent miscalculations are often the product of its excessive sagacity."

The true desperate depths of European pessimism reveal themselves in infinite little examples of everyday life, each one incarnating and making manifest the typical attitudes of a continent's people. A forty-year-old blond Austrian editor I interviewed said she had gained sudden insight one day about the difference between Europe and America. Returning home from her tour of the United States, her plane arrived at Kennedy Airport a full hour later than expected. Having to transfer at another airline terminal, she fretted about missing her next plane. She was hot, nervous from the journey, and her baggage, she realized, would be so late coming off the first plane that she wouldn't be able to get it on the second. Increasingly agitated and worried, waiting at the carrousel, watching everyone's bag but hers slide off the belt, she was moved to blurt out her dilemma to a tall American man, about fifty years old, standing next to her. "He told me, quite simply, to 'have faith.' And that advice, remarkably, calmed me for the moment. That mundane remark focused all the force of the America I had seen. Like many Europeans, I had felt overwhelmed by the vastness of the American West, and of America in general. In Europe, you are seldom more than a few kilometers from water, shelter, a village, people. So I had wondered what could have given men and women the strength to settle and subdue this land, so harsh and immense, so different from the small forests and rivers of Europe. It was that faith! In fact"—she laughed—"my bag did arrive in time!"

Listening to her, I am impressed at how an American commonplace about "having faith" reveals her own lack of it, a lack that is deep and typical in everyday European pessimism. By and large, faith in all senses is now lacking there: in God, in life, in the future. She speaks of faith the way we might speak of ancient chivalry: as something exotic, barely remembered, almost unknown.

Pessimism exists in subtle layers, wrapped onionlike around the European personality. This Austrian editor went on to tell me that she had been particularly nervous about losing her bag that day because she is one of those people who is afraid of flying. "It gets worse and worse," she said, "not a real phobia but still unpleasant." "In that case," I replied, eager to be helpful, "why don't you just take a couple of sleeping pills or a tranquilizer, or drink a couple of glasses of wine and then wake up on the other end?" I teased her about what I thought must be the likely obstacles to her adopting such simple solutions: "Are you worried about addiction or something? Or about seeming 'weak'?"

"Oh, no," she said, "I'm afraid that my mind wouldn't work quickly enough then." She saw my blank look and rushed to explain what seemed an obvious enough concern to her: "In case of an emergency on the plane!" I could only laugh and laugh, out loud, at the well-rehearsed darkness of her outlook. Fortunately, she took my laughing with good grace and, for the moment, laughed at herself too.

It is not that most Europeans are worried about flying or afraid their bags won't arrive on time, but the incident reveals how Europeans protect themselves by being habitually prepared for the worst. There are national variations, as usual—the Scandinavians being generally more optimistic (not cheerful, but optimistic, an intellectual attitude in which the future is expected to be good) than the Latins; and there are variations among the national populations even from year to year, which pollsters now diligently report. But, in general, the European exists in an inner world where things won't get better and life is not very good to begin with. Psychologically, this view shelters him from some of the shocks and disappointments of existence. Practically, such an attitude leads to the caution necessary for confronting what experience has shown to be a dangerous and intractable universe.

American optimism is a contrast and Europeans don't always like or understand it. With some severity, a tweedy young British expert criticizes our optimism in his field of international development: "There is an American approach to foreign aid: every problem can be solved, high technology solutions, and an easy brotherhood of man. When the European hears such ideas, he wonders what somebody is trying to put over on him."

Europeans are often surprised when they finally figure out that Americans are generally not trying to put anything over on anybody in such discussions. At the most, they may be trying to prove a general point and for largely disinterested purposes. Americans are acting out of their national character as formed by their national experience. Though we are not a country of theoreticians or intellectuals in the European sense, everyone who knows us understands that we are the last of the eighteenth-century *philosophes*. We believe in the Enlightenment vision of the power of mind; above all, we believe in the power of mind to solve practical problems.

We are also the inheritors of a special tradition that is ultimately spiritual in origin—a national faith in which even the helpful fifty-year-old man at the luggage carrousel participates. This is why the more we encounter European pessimism, the more annoying it seems to us. For our national assertion in the earliest days was that America was literally the promised land. The Puritans, Cotton Mather among them, saw the work of their contemporaries and Massachusetts ancestors as preparing nothing less than that glorious end to history described in the New Testament Book of Revelation. Prototypes of what we now scorn as American "cults," the Puritans claimed that not only their Massachusetts Bay Colony but the whole land of America was blest by God Himself, that its divine mission included no less than the redemption of a continent, nay, the entire world, under God. Like ancient Israel they—America, itself—would be blessed not merely with this great spiritual opportunity but with its outward signs of worldly success. They must not be stopped; indeed, they, America, could not be stopped.

Such soaring optimism, at once apocalyptic and practical, was reinforced by the founding of the Republic. To the suprarational prophetic context were added the more soberly exuberant discoveries of the Enlightenment. What God had decreed Man now could clearly do. *Novus Ordo Seclorum,* as it says on the dollar bill: "a new order of the centuries."

The next great movement was the settling of the vast continent—an apparently endless success story. After that, what other great wonders: building the world's foremost industrial and agricultural power, saving Europe in 1916–18, and the whole world in 1941–45, teaching the Old World imperialists how to behave (Wilson's Fourteen Points, for example), going to the moon, and so on.

Against such centuries of faith realized, from Puritan prophecy to the perennial triumph of American know-how and practical success, what are our defeats but momentary setbacks? Even the disgrace of slavery yielded to the grandeur of a moral crusade unlike any ever taken. The 600,000 martyrs of the Civil War seal America's greatness; the reform movement begins the redemption of the cities and helps control the trusts; the New Deal makes the Great Depression another forward step. What if Vietnam and other foreign involvements have temporarily showed us our weakness or the Bomb reduced our swagger? America's long history pushes us toward ever renewed faith in undreamed-of solutions.

Despite the perhaps excessive tough-mindedness of recent years, and the forgoing of religious language and piety by many in today's America, especially intellectuals, our American breasts still swell to hear tell of our purity of heart and our spiritual, democratic, even economic mission toward all men. If such high phrases and ideas do not always describe the way we actually are now, they do capture the way we feel we must, we will, be again. Tocqueville rightly bases much of his understanding of our national character on the spiritual difference between the original Massachusetts settlers and European colonists in other parts of the New World. Unlike many other colonizers, the Puritans were educated, prosperous, talented, and accomplished, and they came with their wives and children. "But what most distinguished them from all others was the very aim of their enterprise. No necessity forced them to leave their country; they gave up a desirable social position and assured means of livelihood; nor was their object in going to the New World to better their position or accumulate wealth; they tore themselves away from home comforts in obedience to a purely intellectual craving; in facing the inevitable sufferings of exile they hoped for the triumph of an idea." And that idea was the twin notion of worshipping God in their own way and, with his help and to thank Him for their election, to build a godly society that would redeem the world.

There were other Europeans besides the Puritans who didn't emigrate after the Reformation but who had similar beliefs in the mission of their own groups. But these beliefs dwindled and then were irrevocably tarnished by centuries of fratricidal wars, loss of empires so recently acquired, harsh class struggles during the last two centuries, and all the weight of bitter history as symbolized in many of the old monuments of Europe. Only Americans were able to keep the optimistic faith.

*   *   *

Europeans have gone further in their disillusionment than a mere loss of faith and optimism. They routinely drink the bitter cup of cynicism itself. Like pessimism, cynicism is pervasive, and it comes up in regular ways in the most everyday situations. My wife and I are in our car in Andalusia; she's driving. Though she is Belgian by nationality, by ancestry and constitution she's even more French. Sometimes, she acts like one of those women in French movies who get very emotional, explosive, full of fireworks. Very often, I find this Latin volatility captivating; at certain times, however, what she rightly calls my "Anglo-Saxon conditioning" makes me wish for more calm, a greater distance between herself and what's happening. At this particular moment, because of unusually bad information from two Spaniards whom we had stopped for directions, she finds herself staring at a wall which abruptly ends a road they claimed, wrongly, would lead to our destination. We are already an hour late for our appointment. In the hot irritation of the July sun, she begins her frustrated French number. Full of fury, her mouth turns into a sneer, and she even stamps her foot as she complains. Sitting beside her, I imagine the next step will be for her to send smoke out of her ears because the temperature in the car suddenly seems to rise. I try to quiet her, for my sake as well as hers: "Look, it's not that important, you can calm down." "I can't and I won't," she says and bangs the unoffending steering wheel, obviously overwrought and as mad at herself for being so upset as she is at the two men: "Look how upset I am!" It is time, think I, for praise: "Well, if you're not calm, you are good!" for she is a most high-principled creature and the nub of her fury now is the fury itself; she wants always to be temperate, indulgent, kind. She is angry at her anger. Suddenly cold now, looking straight ahead at the wall, she remarks, to my astonishment: "Some of my European friends would take that as an insult."

Amazed, my eyes widen yet again. She explains: "In French, they say, '*bonne et bête.*' Good and stupid! Be good and somebody will always take advantage of you. To be good in a world like theirs simply means you're dumb."

My wife is no cynic, but she can easily recite part of the European cynical credo. It is proverbial, she meets it in her friends, and I have found it to one degree or another in nearly all Europeans. Cynicism is another defense. It is an intellectual position which pretends that everything and everyone tends toward the debased and corrupt. Only naïve people, like Americans, would believe the contrary. As the scornful Italian phrase for the innocent goes, *tre volte buono*—"He's a person who is good three times over." If Americans believe that hard work and good faith can solve every problem—an aggressive, progressive idea—Europeans believe that behind every action is a conscious, self-interested thrust toward self-advancement.

In *Portrait of a Lady*, Henry James captures the defensive function of European cynicism. The Countess Gemini, an American by birth but thoroughly Europeanized by an unhappy marriage to an Italian, is impressed that Henrietta Stackpole has come all the way from America to help the similarly unhappily married heroine of the book, Isabel Archer.

> "Yes, I wanted to look after her," Henrietta said serenely.
> Her hostess stood there smiling at her with small bright eyes and eager-looking nose; with cheeks into each of which a blush had come. "Ah, that's very pretty—*c'est bien gentil!* Isn't it what they call friendship?"

This is the normal European cool, though it isn't always so blatant. The countess's pretense is that friendship is so rare that when an example of it manifests before your own eyes, you have to reach back into what you have heard about, even to what you have read in books, to identify this aspect of normal human concourse. "Isn't it what they call friendship?"

Henrietta, 100 percent American, sails on through the sarcasm: "'I don't know what they call it. I thought I had better come.'"

"'She's very happy—she's very fortunate,'" the countess goes on about Isabel, her tone visibly changing. "'She has others besides.'" James adds: "And then she broke out passionately. 'She's more fortunate than I! I'm as unhappy as she. I've a very bad husband; he's a great deal worse. And I've no friends. I thought I had, but they're gone. No one, man or woman, would do for me what you've done for her.'"

James remarks that "Henrietta was touched; there was nature in this bitter effusion. 'Look here, Countess, I'll do anything for you that you like.'"

But the countess reverts to her European cynicism—she *knows* there is no hope, that friendship is false and worthless, she's been foiled too many times before by life. With a quick change of tone, she simply dismisses the offer of the generous, naïve American: "Never mind."

Not all Europeans are like the countess, but her attitude touches them all, as "*bonne et bête*" touches my wife. To be different, as Jacqueline is, a European must resist the cynical attitude with every bit of strength, with a conscious idealism; even then it reasserts itself. It is held in reserve to cover over effusions of nature, as James calls them, or more openly mustered to refuse hope. Cynicism is the bitter eye that discerns the bitter reality. It is the epistemological tool that justifies pessimism.

It is an attitude that allows one to accept corruption, in oneself and in others. A German woman acquaintance, just thirty-five years old, a clinical psychologist but a most vulnerable and sensitive person, confided to me once that she had been having crying spells all week. Then, pulling herself together, she seemed to brighten and harden at once. Her blue eyes twinkled with malice and, with an air of vaunting her cold-bloodedness, she described how she had taken her "open marriage one step further. I'm having a secret affair," she says. "With my husband's younger girl friend." After pausing to monitor my discomfort at such complex power plays, she added with a matter-of-fact triumph: "The girl is more in love with me than she is with him!" When I confessed to shock at her cool removal and manipulativeness and selfishness, she laughed lightly: "I knew you would be—sometimes you're *so* American!"

Such cynicism, masquerading as worldliness, is perfectly European but largely strange to the American sensibility. Too easily, it seems to ignore the vulnerability of the young girl, of the husband, and even of the wife herself. As if such vulnerabilities didn't exist. The assumption is that everyone will be as tough as needed, and that all in life can be managed well if one has enough cool.

One Canadian journalist who was educated in Europe and now lives there tried to explain the horrible outbreaks of fratricidal wars by saying that the European character was nearly geologic in structure. "It's as if in one of those outbreaks, suddenly, everybody has had enough of *savoir vivre*, of cynical acceptance

of everyone else. They give up their toleration of the Germans or
the French, the English or the Russians, and they go for them."
Not only in politics does cool European cynicism yield to fanat-
ical loathing. When the cynical defense crumbles, as it does momentarily with the countess, it can let out a repressed higher
nature and sensitivity which may take ugly forms. Paradoxically,
his worldly efforts to give up on hope and foolish crusades can
lead the European to unchain sudden rushes of hate often accompanied by idealistic theorizing.

The coexistence in the same skin of cynicism and enraged
idealism surprises, but it should not. Even Machiavelli, that great
early codifier of modern European cynicism in politics, was himself an ardent idealist, hankering after Italian unity, democracy,
and all sorts of other high causes. A landowner, he liked at the
end of the day to strip off his crude farm clothes soiled by super-
vising work in the fields, to turn from the common talk of stable
hands, dress himself afresh, and, as he puts it in a famous letter,
"go and dwell in the air for which" he was "made." He would
give himself to the company of the ancient Greek and Roman
classics, with all their brave perceptions and high thoughts. But
the same man gave political science its amorality. He showed men
to be at their most cynical when it came to power and for centuries was considered in the northern countries of Europe an
apostle of the devil for his cynicism. Later, those very northern
countries would adopt cynicism as an essential part of their collective and personal character armor.

CHAPTER TWO

Concealment

Intellectual integrity, eristic argumentativeness, pessimism, and cynicism are primarily mental or philosophic protections. For much of their day-to-day dealings, the European must add another ring of defenses which directly affects how he views others, what he expects of himself and them in a relationship, the speed with which he gets close to people, how he acts around them, and even how he dresses for them.

On the airplane taking us to settle in Europe, Jacqueline, a sophisticated and well-educated woman, surprises me when she leans over and says: "When we are living there, don't tell anybody anything personal. It's not like America here. Why, for example, does everyone have to hear what you earn? It's best if people don't know about you. You can never be sure when something you say will be used against you later on."

As an American, thinking about her statement, I am first surprised, then amused, finally even a little shocked at this exhortation to caginess. Then I recall my very first trip to Europe, twenty-five years before, when one still came by ship. Ten days of steaming from New York to Naples. I was twenty and so excited the night before we docked that I could not sleep. I asked the three old men with whom I shared the crowded third-class cabin (they were Italo-Americans returning one last time to the home village for a nostalgic look and a final in-gathering by the clan): "If you could give me one piece of advice, what would it be?" I imagined they would speak of women to be courted, of wines to be tasted, or old ruins and spectacular landscapes to be seen. Instead, like some comic chorus from Aristophanes, as one they replied: *"Non si fida di nessuno!"* "Don't trust anybody!"

Later, I learned the old Italian saying *Fidarsi è bene, non fidarsi è meglio.* "To trust is good, not to trust is better." As a student back then, relatively sheltered from everyday life, with a mysteriously large fellowship that provided me an excess of valuable greenbacks, I found such talk amusing, even quaint: benighted Europeans with their benighted attitudes. I encountered little to make me distrust.

But now, as I go deeper into European attitudes, I discover the reflex of secrecy and mystification everywhere. The elegantly balanced French saying goes: *On n'est jamais aussi content d'avoir bien su parler qu'avoir bien su se taire.* "One is never as happy at having known how to speak well as one is at having known how to keep silent." An Italian sociologist asks me if I know the verb *imboscarsi.* Literally, it means to "in-wood oneself," to lose oneself in the forest. He calls it "a very Italian attitude," but I discover it is also more generally European. The idea is to find a place where no one—not your political party, your confessor, the tax authorities, your wife, or your boss—will be likely to be able to bother you. "Blend in with the woodwork," as we sometimes recommend, is a daily strategy for European living. A gray-haired American publisher who works in Spain has a Swedish woman as his chief assistant. He recalls to me how she screens the letters he writes and regularly censors them: "'No! Take that out,' she says. 'You don't have to tell him that. He doesn't expect you to. It's not like America here.'" A go-getting American management consultant in Frankfurt complains that Europeans can be taught American styles of modern management but, "they don't pass the knowledge on to subordinates coming up the promotion ladder. They hoard what they know, protecting their territory. It's instinctive for them and it means more work for me. Every couple of years, once the old guys get promoted, I'm brought in again to train the new ones."

One longtime observer of the French, an American who has managed a small advertising company in Paris, notes in a bitter mood: "They don't trust their own mothers over here. Why, when they make a turn in traffic, they put on their blinker at the last moment. That way, if they are hit, they are in the legal right; and if they're not hit, they haven't given away any information!"

Toward the end of an interview with a well-known Spanish journalist I will call "Jorge Delgado," I ask how Europeans de-

fend themselves. Early in our conversation, he has gone out of
his way to boast that his father was a colonel in the police before
retiring and that he himself, as a young boy, was trained by his
father's men in the use of pistols, rifles, even automatic weapons.
He wants me to fear him. "There are many ways to defend ourselves, but you have not been aware of the most obvious," he
says. "We avoid letting people know anything about us. Even
when Europeans seem very warm and expansive and open—
Greeks and Italians, for example—we are still inwardly distant.
We reveal nothing of our depths, only our best sides. We calcu-
late.

"Look, you've been questioning me for an hour, and you've
tried various methods to get me to talk about myself in regard to
all these ideas. What do I do?" he asks rhetorically. "I waltz you
around intellectual speculations, stuff I'm making up as we go.
To your direct questions, I reply indirectly or I say 'Perhaps' or I
argue with the general conception behind the question. You have
even tried what the group dynamics people call 'modeling,'
haven't you? Telling me about *your* childhood hurts, *your* arguments with your best friends, *your* personal worries. And still I
avoid telling you anything about myself. We have lots of ways of
mystifying. Don't you see?" He allows just a trace of insult to
creep onto his face.

Indeed, I had seen all along. I had been shocked that after
agreeing to an off-the-record interview, he had used the time to
avoid contact, to size me up and to reply with nothing of himself.
I have gotten used to such ways, however, and have discovered
that the European habit of mystification, often excused as an innocent desire for privacy, is actually full of fear and of an institutionalized, defensive contempt for others.

European wariness extends, naturally, to all of their dealings
with money. George Snyder, an American marketing analyst married to a Belgian, tells me that when he and his wife vacationed
at her family home, his prosperous mother-in-law gave him a bill
for all the long-distance calls he'd made, calculated to the last
Belgian franc. When he handed her a thousand-franc note for
expenses of 989 BF, she insisted, because she didn't have the right
change at the moment, that she would give him the eleven francs
(about twenty-two cents) the next day. When he waved aside her
promise and, the next day, also waved aside the proffered coins,

she insisted he take them, saying: "It's good to keep precise accounts."

Even when one allows for the former poverty of all Europeans during and after the world wars, or when one allows for such people not having been rich in their youth, something doesn't make sense. It is easier for the American to understand such an incident if he keeps in mind the atmosphere of distrust and rancor in which Europeans have always lived. The violent, contentious, impoverished past has created an unconscious reflex in them. They avoid any occasion which might conceivably cause unnecessary resentment. Even a debt of twenty-two cents might give rise to such an occasion. It's not that George's mother-in-law doesn't trust him. It has nothing to do with him personally. Rather, she knows from ancestral experience that money is one among many dangerous topics. Therefore, one must follow the rules of the game most carefully so as not to invite trouble. Most Europeans don't assume it innocent that you wave away extra money—maybe you wish to seem generous for a reason, or maybe you really want that last centime but are pretending not to. No. Better make it right to the last little coin, to be on the safe side. Let us note that personal hospitality, as opposed to niggling formal debt repayment, is generous in Europe. But it too is measured by strict standards of expected reciprocity.

Such an atmosphere of secretive self-protection would never permit the American custom of allowing and forgetting to thrive. In the old American West, a man would arrive from nowhere and make up a new name. No inquiries were made about him. He was taking his American second chance. Even without assuming a new identity, the American has a tradition of entitlement to multiple lives, to forgiveness and new starts.

Not in Europe. There, instead, everyone keeps comprehensive files on everyone else. One chance is all you get. Oh, to be sure, in a moment of natural, sentimental, human weakness or through a fault of memory, people may forget details of a specific offense, but the general recollection remains that there was once something wrong, whether a daughter too sick to marry, or a fur coat appropriated when the owner died in war, or a job given to a brother which you should have rightfully had yourself. Personal weaknesses and wrongs are mixed, everything is carried on the books. True, it is not as bad as it once was, when the peccadilloes or sins of a single member could for generations cast doubt on the worth of a whole family. Nevertheless, the European is further driven to conceal himself from others because everything he does reveal will be taken down and for many years may be used in evidence against him; and he is further pushed to be distrustful because he knows others are engaging in the same maneuvers of concealment as he.

This defensive mistrust and concealment paradoxically help the European develop and sustain relationships. Because he refuses to reveal anything about himself easily, those to whom he does show himself even a little, or who know him by long association, are apprehended as true familiars. A hundred times, as little slivers of fear and desire have been gradually revealed, risk has been taken. The progress of a stranger from the outer rings toward the center is charged with meaning for the European.

When an American casually reveals everything about himself—how much money he makes, what and where he comes from, and what deeply troubles him, the European—Delgado, the Spanish journalist, is an example—not only regards such openness as obscene, he also wonders how he will go about establishing a real relationship to such a person. For the European, withholding creates tension that charges the rapport. Some Europeans occasionally become used to our frank ways, telling themselves these are "charmingly American, charmingly naïve," but most come to think that the American has no substance. For the European's substance is, in large part, his defenses, and they are full of meaning to him. Letting someone in, however little, is heroic. When a European too quickly knows someone's personal details, as with Americans, he paradoxically feels himself to have arrived nowhere.

This is why so many Europeans derogate Americans for "being friendly." They will use the English words and wiggle the fingers of both hands to signify quotation marks. "Sure they tell you how much they make when they first meet you, they tell you to 'help yourself to anything in the refrigerator.' But it's not real friendship." And Europeans are correct in saying so. Such gestures of familiarity mean almost nothing personal to an American. He would do the same with nearly anyone.

Such is the case also with the American's habit of revealing aspects of the self, like personal preferences, hopes, and weaknesses. What, to the European, is a baffling American custom of self-disclosure ultimately derives from our Puritan tradition of public confession of sins, the desire to appear absolutely innocent to the community of men or to ask public forgiveness. It also derives from a more generally Christian sense that all men are brothers and so are to be trusted, and beyond that, if they hurt you, you are to turn the other cheek. Most Europeans don't behave that way, even if otherwise they are good Christians and churchgoers. They think they know that honesty is not the best policy and, unlike the idealistic American, they are not trying to prove anything.

Once having gradually and carefully established their relationships, Europeans defensively cling to them. The European feels it vital to maintain a personal group of people one has known for a long time, even if one doesn't always like them anymore. Here is a reason it is hard for Americans living abroad to integrate into European society. A newspaper editor from Turin, thirty-three years old, talks about how his father is a judge, living and working in the north, but born in southern Italy. "He gets long vacations. One month he always spends down there in the Abruzzi—every year. The other month he goes with my mother, who is Swiss, to Basel—every year. Eight years ago, my own best friends moved from Turin to Rome, but nearly once a month they come back for a visit. I see them almost as much as I could if they lived here."

Europeans try not to need new people. In many countries, and especially in many cities, as the anthropologist Edward Hall says, "propinquity means nothing. The fact that you live next door to a family does not entitle you to visit, borrow from or socialize with them or your children to play with theirs. . . . To the best of my knowledge those [Americans] who have tried to relate . . . purely on the basis of propinquity seldom, if ever, succeed."

The family is, of course, the first line of defense. For many reasons, Europeans do not stray far from their birthplace, and it is a common European custom to maintain the family circle with many rituals, such as visiting mothers and fathers every Sunday, without fail. The family, which may include numerous cousins, in-laws, and grandchildren, further helps the European to screen out the world. The American obsession with work and belief that things can be made better function like the enwrapping European family, which blocks unwelcome sensations, thoughts, images, and the fundamental anxiety of life. Relatives run interference for the Euro, and his world assumes, if not perfectly manageable proportions, then at least smaller ones.

A cognate defense is the clinging to a tradition of localism. Europeans pretend that things are as they were. In an attempt to strengthen the walls of their identity, they will tell you how they can't accept the notion that Europeans are one, or that even all Frenchmen are one, or that even all Frenchmen from a certain province are one; they will insist that people are different from town to town, even from neighborhood to neighborhood. A Dutch woman earnestly explains to me that when she moved from northern to southern Holland, a distance of a few dozen kilometers, "I had to explain my jokes." People will point with pride to the traditions of *their* valley or *their* village, drawing up imaginary bridges of local affiliation as if towns were still walled and international roads, railways, radio, television, and air routes did not penetrate old barriers. Theirs is an almost deliberate cultivation of an illusion of profound local difference, maintained in the teeth of modern universalism. This myth of the local (in Italian, *campanilismo,* "loyalty to the community," symbolized by the bell tower of the parish church) provides the European with still another bulwark against the unsettling flux of life.

But there is an underside to these stable interpersonal relationships. Sartre's famous remark "Hell is other people" describes a strikingly un-American idea. For us, other people are not hell but a diversion from a relative physical, social, and cultural emptiness. Other people are not contestants for a limited number of resources, nor potential enemies, but more or less friendly competitors in social and economic games at which many can do well. But not only does the recurrent horror of Europe's violent history make enemies into a hell, the defensive alliances mounted to meet these and other social challenges often make friends into a hell also.

We Americans are not locked into living with infernal neighbors or relatives; we can simply move away. But Europeans, even in these days of increased mobility, don't feel this easy freedom.

Once Jacqueline asked me why I had been hard on Harriet, an old colleague who had suddenly called from California wanting to stay with us during her upcoming visit to Florence. I had frankly told Harriet that she had been cool, even cold, to me in our brief contacts over the last ten years, and that her calling looking for a place to stay felt exploitative and annoying. She and I then had a frank discussion and she apologized, admitted I was right, confessed that she had always liked me but had been too narrowly focused on work to think of saying so, wanted to be my friend, and so forth. We agreed to pursue the conversation in Florence and hung up, feeling we might even make things right at last.

Jacqueline, however, felt she had to warn me, even after the fact. With European worldly wisdom she pointed out: "We might go back to live in California sometime, where Harriet is part of your old milieu and can spread a lot of poison about us among other people. I'm not saying that she's that kind of person, but one never knows." Boasting my manly American right to be free, I replied that I had known that might happen, though Harriet's reaction had seemed to me to obviate any real danger, but I had spoken nevertheless, "because you can eat just so much shit in life and I am forty-five and I have had my share." I spoke so crudely to my elegant wife because I wanted to emphasize my strong feelings about the subject.

She must have felt just as strongly because she replied: "No, you haven't. You don't know what it is to eat shit in life." I was shocked at her stooping to echo my obscene idiom, but her point went home all the more for it. As she spoke, I intuitively gave my assent. In the closed communities of Europe, where, as Sartre's phrase implies, there is no easy escape, one suffers indignities and worse from the boss, the boss's wife, whomever one has to be nice to, for a long time. And then it can burst out: someone goes screaming mad, or people start choosing sides and the usual civil war erupts.

Because he must be careful not only with strangers but also with intimates, the European defends himself from other people with masquerade. Europeans dress up and make up to face society, pushing this habit to the extreme of caricature found in the typical illustrations of any European fashion magazine:* the tortured and contrived poses, the defiant or seductive facial expressions, the infinite posturing. The private self will not be exhibited by Europeans. Bright young British professionals in their early thirties sit around a London pub table and talk with smirky knowingness about how much they like the "spectacle" of social life in Europe, compared to America: "The delightfully contrived touches in costume, bearing, even gait. We preen for each other. We are like actors going onstage. Generally, that is all anyone else is allowed to see."

One late October day, after pondering this masquerade for years, I have time before my train leaves Paris to sit in the Gare de Lyon café and write in my journal, to try to understand the theatricality and glimpse what lies beneath the disguises.

I sit and watch the people pass into and out of the station. They seem bundled up, vaguely shabby. It's a common French look. Is it the lousy climate that makes people look dowdy, creased, faded, mismatched, and old: like days of slush in New York? But there are many young men who wear thick, black, bombardier-style leather jackets, fists stuffed into the slashes of side pockets, shoulders hunched. I think of Jean-Paul Belmondo in the fifties. But who was *he* imitating? An American acquaintance who knows the French well said the other day that somebody had written an article in the *International Herald Tribune* telling them "to come off it. Not just the leather-jacketed bombardiers but almost all Parisians were pretending to be so tough and independent it was funny." People who had lost too many wars, I suppose: Algérie, Indochine, World War II, 1870, why even 1918 was only a technical victory; people who had seen shattered too many high ideals.

In Paris, one never sees the look of defeat, no ancient sense of being crushed or, rather, of life's crushingness. In Paris, in France generally, everyone is all right, No Thank You! They're in control. They've got it covered or, at the least, they can and are taking care of themselves. Their lives,

---

* Or, it should be added, their U.S. but un-American derivatives.

whether intellectual, executive, punk kid with a motorcycle, waiter, all are made to seem intact. You're supposed to think that no one has called for help in France since Olivier sounded his horn at Rouncevalles. In the Place de la Contrescarpe, even the drunks sit plastered on their sidewalks, legs spread before them in a V, wine bottles in hand, defiant. They stake out their urban turf. They even have dogs: pets for drunks! Why, in Paris, even the normally inscrutable Chinese smile sometimes. Everything's under control, No Thank You! Even the kids are O.K., No Thank You.

One wonders though at those signs everywhere in the subways for "SOS" hotlines: "Call twenty-four hours a day" if you feel desperate. Who's using them? Do they never ring? Do their volunteer operators just wait, playing cards, endlessly disappointed, thick cigarettes hanging from mouth corners, like so many lonesome Maytag repairman of yore? Of course, one calls confidentially, one doesn't need to leave a name.

In Italy, a different front, a gayer one, is usually kept up. But on the buses, people allow mere strangers to see the fatigue, the sag of steadily aging flesh on anyone over fifty. One asks oneself if it is defeat candidly made visible. Or is it not, rather, one among many tactics against bad fortune? For the old woman brightens when she meets someone she knows, she oozes affability, bursts into voluble life, a regular buck-and-winger of a dame. Almost as if she had learned to wear a certain mask of defeat for the general public. It says: "I haven't got anything, Mr. Purse Snatcher; no point in stopping at me, Mr. Bad Luck: I've already given!" But if the acquaintance asks directly how the woman is, she goes halfway back toward her slack, beaten look, no matter how well things are going. "How am I? *Non c'è male.*" "There's nothing wrong yet." Or, "*Si lavora.*" "One keeps on working." Or, even more portentously, "*Fino ad ora*" (pause) "*speriamo.*" "Up to now" (pause) "let's hope." As if to say: "Trouble or even the worst could happen at any time, so in case you're from the Cosmic Disaster Center, no need to envy me. Thank *you!*" No matter how well things are going, European pessimism is made palpable in such verbal and nonverbal masquerade.

Among the youth of Italy, current fashion reveals the same heavy defendedness. Time was, in the fifties, for example, that an elegant look was the defense. The Italian women of that era cultivated a demure front, turned out just so: heeled, girdled, stockinged, scarfed, hatted, and even gloved. All this is gone. Now we have a new breed that cultivates the worst aspects of youthful American sloppiness—*il look relax*—and carries it with a vaguely dirty, dissolute, hard, and all-knowing air. In the summertime, dark ringlets are chopped off in no apparent order, deliberately wrinkled linen suits are worn, a faded T-shirt underneath (the manufacturers made it to look faded from the beginning). They all look like Jane Russells mussed up on the outlaw straw. The slut look. As if they were to go nonchalantly from one gang bang to another. Of course, like their older sisters of the fifties, these girls won't give you the time of day, not even a serious glance. The point is the institutionalization of the dissolute—a tough, hard, pseudo-prostitute look that says: "Nothing can hurt or surprise me. I could sell myself and not get hurt in the process; I won't feel anything."

The exteriors of Europeans, whether dissolute or elegant, gloomy or vivacious, are so seamless that it is only by repeated analysis (often spurred on by irritation) that the American is able to penetrate at all. The European is deeply invested in his disguises. Whether in France or Italy, Sweden or England, masquerade is a defense against the opinions of others, their judgments, their "regard" or "gaze," as Michel Foucault might say. In a certain sense, the European is also defending himself against something more than his intimates or even the strangers he meets. Society itself is held at bay by dress, makeup, accent, intonation, gait, and the like. In the last analysis, the European defends himself against something even more generalized than society. The message he gives expands infinitely from "I'm all right, Jack!" to an "I'm all right!" addressed to the cosmos itself. It is the European equivalent of everyday American energy, boosterism, heartiness. "Great!" and "Terrific!" we say, with smiles, to almost anything from the timely delivery of a package to the victory of a Little League team to a supposed moral triumph in foreign affairs. The European masquerade is primarily social, but it is also a defensive apparatus against life itself—that is, against all possible failure, hurt, and death. How else would you expect people to behave in a society where everybody's watching, been watching, each other, small-town style, for thousands of years?

It is small wonder Europeans have trouble understanding Americans' lack of compulsion to construct similar social masquerades. This difficulty in understanding is often behind Europeans' routine accusation that we are "childish." They will tell you in French that *les Américains sont des grands enfants,* "big children," or *bon enfants,* "nice kids"; in Italian, they call us *infantile* and in German *kindlich.*

What they mean was well summarized to me by a Frenchwoman who had taught her native language for years to American businessmen and their families. She thought for a moment and then, in the organized fashion of someone whose mind has been French-trained, rattled off a list of subsidiary meanings:

"Childish? Yes. They laugh too easily and at anything.

"Americans don't know what to do with their bodies, how to hold themselves, how to sit. They sprawl, like children.

"They lack finesse. Like kids, they call you by your first name.

"They don't play a role—there is no theater about their behavior. At a public lecture, they are not embarrassed to yawn. Like children, they say what they think. They are simpleminded and natural."

This is another way of saying, as a San Francisco psychologist said upon visiting Europe, that "we are too much out there." In other words, we are not self-contained behind the masks of sobriety, careful gestures, formal family names; we "don't play a role," we say what we think. But the Frenchwoman went further by accusing us of being "natural." What could the implied praise of unnaturalness mean?

I got a clue from a venerable retired Italian diplomat when he too addressed himself to the subject of our "childishness": "Yes, Americans are not at all what the French call *malin,* cunning, clever, using their intelligence to personal, selfish ends. We

Europeans are more twisted, *contorto*. '*Timeo Danaos et dona ferentes*,' says Virgil—'I fear Greeks and especially Greeks bearing gifts.' You remember," he asks indulgently, "how the Trojans broke open their gate to admit the Greek gift of a huge wooden horse and then the Greek warriors stole from it in the middle of the night and slaughtered everyone?"

I am surprised he thinks me so uneducated, though it is not astonishing, given the image he has of us Americans as childish. I nod, indulging him in turn. I think that for many Europeans we are still dogface country-boy GIs.

As if he reads my mind, he says: "After the Second World War, look what our ten-year-old Neapolitan kids did to your soldiers! They gave them some story about taking them home to a sister. Then they got them drunk on cheap wine, robbed them of everything, even their clothes, and finally sold them, stark naked, back to the American army. Why, our ten-year-olds," he says, with evident satisfaction, "played with your grown men as if *they* were the children!"

When I ask an English publisher to give his perspective on our "childishness," his response shows how the European stance can turn in against itself. "With us, events are always analyzed and weighed. If somebody does us a good turn, we ask ourselves *what the person really wants*. If I sleep with a girl and it is wonderful, the next day I ask myself how many others she slept with before me, if she was acting, and so on—gradually, I can take this happy event and make myself miserable with my own analysis!"

As we have noticed, a watchfulness, a constant suspicion and motive-hunting, prevent easygoing, American-style intercourse in Europe. But because of their exposure to Americans, some Europeans regret their habits. A reporter for *Der Spiegel* who has manned a news bureau in the United States for many years complains: "The hardest thing to get in Europe is simplicity, people saying what they think and feel, openly and directly. *It never happens*."

My wife, who also hates European indirectness and loves straightforwardness, often likes to show me how Europeans cultivate their "devious" (Latin for "away from the main road") ways. It is good she does so, because, in my American simplicity, I often miss what's going on.

We have been staying for several days in Germany, at a

Fremdenzimmer in the Black Forest. Cleaning up after breakfast, the landlady, Frau Maier, who has been chatty and friendly, casually mentions that she wonders if other guests, the Kolbs, whom we have met at the common breakfast table, are "angry" at her. It seems that friends of the Kolbs' children arrived rather suddenly and Frau Maier could not find a room for them. "It is the busy season," she explains, apologetically, her red cheeks full of health but her black eyes small with worry. Unaware, I let it all go by.

Later on, irritated at Frau Maier's manner, Jacqueline explains. "Didn't you see what she was doing?" she begins.

I shake my head, large-eyed: "What?"

"It's that European complexity, their indirectness! Frau Maier is concerned that the Kolbs are offended. But does she go and confront them with that fear? Does she explain, as she did to us, that other people had reserved all her rooms from long before? Not a bit. No, she drags the idea across our eyes like a dead cat, first so that she will get our reaction—without asking for it, either!—and, second, since she knew we were having lunch today with the Kolbs, so that she can put *us* up to asking them. She could have gone herself and asked them what they felt, and then have expected they would tell the truth. But she was afraid to face them, and she wasn't sure they would, in fact, be frank with her. It drives me crazy, all this manipulating, touchiness, tentativeness, and zigzagging. Everybody here is Hamlet, Prince of Denmark: 'By indirections find directions out!'"

And yet even now, six years after our marriage, when I ask her a question, Jacqueline often still assumes I am making a hidden statement.

"Would you like some more steak?" I ask.

"Perhaps *you* would," she replies like a mind-reader. "Help yourself first," she says.

Or:

"Do you think we'll be on time?" I ask.

"Do you want me to hurry?" she automatically asks in return.

As an American, I generally make manful efforts to know and say what I mean, yet, sometimes, she catches me unawares. On the other hand, I have had to insist on many occasions that when I ask a question, that's all I am doing. Like so many Europeans who have learned to live with chronic indirectness, she is in her kind way a master psychologist, even an amateur detective. The European believes he knows by training and experience that people don't ask for what they want. At the very least, they are shy, cautious, too well-bred, or afraid of looking needy. So the Euro learns to scoop his way underneath questions and statements to find the unspoken, often buried, desire. He tends to assume that when someone speaks, there is always a motive, hidden or unconscious, which one must go home and think about. Automatically, he searches for clues to hidden meanings. Sometimes, when Jacqueline gets together with her good friend, Françoise, this educated will to penetrate to the other's real needs and desires gets so wrought up it spills over into nearly comic politeness:

"More dessert?" (One piece remains.)

"Help yourself."

"Oh, no. You always like profiteroles."

"Yes, but you said tonight how much you'd missed Belgian chocolate while you were away in America."

"Indeed. But I've eaten so much already and it isn't every day you serve these."

"To be sure, but I'm full myself."

"Please," proffering the plate.

And so on, and on, for many more rounds. Peter, an American economist who is Françoise's husband, and I frequently laugh at these charming Alphonse and Gaston routines. While we Americans are awed by the exquisiteness of such well-bred solicitude, we also have little patience with people's not saying what they mean and their assuming that others do the same—even when they are trying to be kind. Gradually, we learn to accept it in its various guises, whether benign like Françoise's and Jacqueline's or more obviously defensive and *malin* like Frau Maier's and the Italian ambassador's.

CHAPTER THREE

Survivorship

The European's intellectual and interpersonal defenses are complemented by another set deriving from his will and inner orientation, each of which evokes the other. Thus, a European's orientation toward the slowness of change is reinforced by his will to lead a slower-paced life than Americans. To take another example, the European's acute awareness of the past not only conditions his orientation (the direction he faces in life) it also conditions whether he'll take risks—a function of the will— or not.

To be an American is to live next to man-made things, most of which are no older than you are. You acquire the impression that the world began about the time you did, which in turn re-inforces the illusion that your mastery over existence is poten-tially without limits, almost infinite. The newness of things is emboldening and contrasts with the experience of European life, where one is surrounded by the evidence of history, ancient and modern. The daily evidence of the past reminds you often of the transitory, if not tragic, character of human existence. You will use these things; then, soon, you will be gone, but they will be here forever. Enduring monuments, the physical embodiments of tradition, help prevent the European, like many people from older societies around the world, from seeing himself or others as "going anywhere." So also does a past in which, for more than two thousand years, social and economic movement were utterly exceptional.

This orientation toward existence as a fixed entity, though it puts limits on dynamism and ambition, frees the European to take life's moments in a way different from the American. I talk with an American engineer-manager, a top executive at the Eu-ropean headquarters in Brussels of a major American company.

He's graying, fifty-two years old, and has had a triple bypass operation on his heart. He says that "every day" of the twenty years he has worked for the company, he's been "afraid of being fired." To conquer such free-market stress, he practices relaxation exercises, running, and meditation, and he pursues several hobbies, from collecting antiques with his wife to making wooden hunting decoys. It's all, he says, "an effort to slow down." He looks around the café in which we sit and says he has managed, after his emergency heart operation, to "still work hard; but, hell, I don't wake up at night thinking about the job anymore! Of course," he adds, "my illness helped a lot and also some luck in the stock market. It won't hurt so much if I get fired now." One can see, however, that despite his bravado, he's still worried, still in the grip of the Company and anxious about failing in his job.

Then he leans over and gestures toward another table. He lowers his voice. "See that Belgian guy over there across from us?" I look at a man with a florid, fat face. He sits in front of a partially emptied glass of beer in which occasional bubbles rise lazily; his wife sits beside him, before a similar glass; they stare idly into space or let their eyes follow whatever movement occurs in the room, a waiter coming, a patron putting on her coat and going. My American manager continues, full of admiration: "Look! He's just sitting with his wife and enjoying himself. He's not thinking, as an American would, of something else—getting ahead or getting laid or whatever."

Mark Twain, characterizing himself as an "innocent abroad," saw the very same contrast over a century ago:

> Afterwards we walked up and down one of the most popular streets for some time, enjoying other people's comfort and wishing we could export some of it to our restless, driving, vitality-consuming marts at home. Just in this one matter lies the main charm of life in Europe—comfort. In America, we hurry—which is well; but when the day's work is done, we go to thinking of losses and gain, we plan for the morrow, we even carry our business cares to bed with us and toss and worry over them. . . . What a robust people, what a nation of thinkers we might be, if we would only lay ourselves on the shelf occasionally and renew our edges. . . . I do envy these Europeans the comfort they take. When the

work of the day is done, they forget it. Some of them go with wife and children, to a beer-hall and sit quietly and genteelly drinking a mug or two of ale.

European visitors have always remarked on the restlessness of Americans and opposed it, implicitly or explicitly, to their more ordered rounds of life. One Briton I talked with, a bureaucrat in the foreign ministry who had been stationed in the United States, said, rather drily: "Americans are hoofers. Restless, agitated chaps." In his research on cultural difference, Edward Hall noticed that even people as time-conscious as the German Swiss made consistent observations about how Americans structure time very tightly and are sticklers for schedules. They observed that Americans don't leave any free time for themselves. When Hall asked what that meant, he discovered that "Europeans will schedule fewer events in the same time than Americans do and they will usually add that Europeans feel less 'pressed' for time than Americans. . . . Europeans allow more time for virtually everything involving important human relationships. Many . . . observed that in Europe human relationships are important whereas in the United States the schedule is important." One scornful Italian writer told me after a month's visit to the United States: "They are always in motion, the Americans. They are like sharks, who keep swimming even as they eat."

One thinks of those many busy Americans one has known, even of oneself: the empty focus on profit and winning, the mindless, machinelike energy, the infantile tantrums that even businessmen will throw when they feel frustrated, overwhelmed, or, as a recent expression has it, strung out. Activity fills every corner of American life and it frequently seems totally futile. I talk with a busy publishing executive who, at thirty-five, is a leader in her company and even her field. She has a trust fund from childhood, more than sufficient to support her in style. But like the much richer Jackie Kennedy Onassis, she feels the need to have a job, and in her case, she needs to work at it almost constantly. She tells me that she doesn't like the books she publishes: "I would never buy one of them myself." But despite her complete freedom to pursue other alternatives, she keeps working, always rushing to an airport, her college-girl kilts and white silk blouses a blur of purposeful motion. Her breaks from work are designed mainly to keep her going—she runs, plays racquet-ball, does aerobics. Her vacation travels are basically rest and re-cuperation. She is a soldier in the front lines of American activity.

Defending himself well, the European insists on his time off as time *out* of the race, but the American is compelled by different historical motives. For the Calvinist Puritans who first gave shape to the American experience, work, good works, could not save a person from the fires of hell, but they could give some reassurance that one was predestined to be saved. As Tawney so elegantly put it:

> For, since conduct and action, though availing nothing to attain the free gift of salvation, are a proof that the gift has been accorded, what is rejected as a means is resumed as a consequence . . . the Puritan flings himself into practical activities with . . . daemonic energy . . . Like a man who strives by unresting activity to exorcise a haunting demon . . . By the mere energy of his expanding spirit, he marks, not only his own character and habits and way of life, but family and church, industry and city, political institutions and social . . . it is will—will organized and disciplined and inspired, will . . . straining in violent energy . . . and for the intensification and organization of will every instrument in that tremendous arsenal of religious fervour is mobilized.

Take away the explicit religious reference to the sixteenth- and seventeenth-century Puritan and such descriptions fit well the American of our times. Though many Americans have forsaken all churches, they run as if the fear of God were in them still.

Historically, the availability of economic opportunity added secular energy to the spiritual forces driving Americans. Getting there first—for gold, for land, for water, for nearly anything that a new site or community could offer—became an American passion. The race was to the swift on many a frontier, and racing just for the hell of it, a generalized practice, often puzzled the European observer then just as it does now. In the nineteenth century, Baron de Gerstner remarked: "The Democrats here never like to remain behind one another; on the contrary, each wants to get ahead of the rest. The life of an American is, indeed, only a constant racing." In our time, we have largely secularized the Puritan idea of vocation and tend to believe, as I heard a businessman father solemnly tell his daughter, that "you can be anything you want to be." He yearns for the day when she will start hurrying as he does.

Lately, even economically secure Europeans feel pressured to give up the insulation of their spots of leisure time. A Dutch professor of English and American literature, the author of five books who now has senior administrative responsibilities within his university, confesses with bitterness: "I read books now, but with an effort. I used to spend four hours reading easily; now I feel some vague impulse that makes me need to get up every twenty minutes." He resents the constant interruptions of telephones, casual visits from other professors and administrators, and deliveries of regular and interoffice mail, all of which conspire to change his inner sense of time. But he resists the tendency. He scorns himself when he strays toward resembling the typical American business executive (who is interrupted, according to knowledgeable surveys, on the average of every eight minutes), and deplores the fact that his life is becoming so hectic.

Americans today are yearning more and more for that time-taking which Europeans use to meet and recuperate from life's assaults. I have been astonished to find how many American professional men and women between forty and fifty are dreaming of early retirement: a computer engineer who is forty-six wants to buy a sailboat, live on it, and cross the Atlantic; a forty-three-year-old technical editor says she and her stockbroker husband hope to retire in two years, at least half the time, and maybe open an export-import business and travel; a forty-eight-year-old university teacher, who just inherited his father's house, hopes he can open a sandwich store downtown and only work three or four hours a day. Modern American work life has lost some of its spiritual sanction without losing its demonic compulsiveness, and more and more Americans are hoping to get out from under and to put themselves on the shelf like Europeans of yore. When you ask them why, they explain, in a variety of ways, that they cannot stand the lack of dignity that attaches to work in a mass society.

More than the slower pace of European life finds its ultimate origin in the presence of the past in the European soul. In the

European family, and in the culture as a whole, for instance, the memories of the big defeats survive like glaciers. The time Uncle Georges lost his small shoe factory in the First World War and his son Rogier lost it again in the Second. The war, which made all the Hedrich family's savings worthless paper. The time a neighbor betrayed cousin Giovanna to the Gestapo or how Uncle Enrico was sold to the *partigiani* after that. Such memories of how society can turn upside down and against the individual make each European cautious in action. He pulls into himself. As I begin to tap this dreadful sense of history, I recognize the voices of my own immigrant parents and their extended family. I had thought their ancestral bad memories and consequent reticence were Jewish. I learn they are more properly seen as European.

The European sense of the past defends the individual by orienting, informing, and limiting his character, in ways that must often remain incomprehensible to us Americans, who often love to tear up our pasts. A dry English woman in a gray London square complains to an American visitor: "We had a great opportunity to set this city up in a logical way, but we didn't." "You mean after the Blitz?" "Oh, no! After the Great Fire, you remember—in 1666." Living with that much behind you is just different. Russians cry when they leave their country; Americans just move.

Some European psychologists will even speak of how the past "stratifies the unconscious" of their patients and of Europeans generally. As the therapist watches the gradual opening of the person, he becomes aware of layers of collective history embedded in each personality. Thus, for instance, the therapist encounters the layer corresponding to the Catholic church, one that often carries terrors for the individual at an unconscious level but that in his conscious life he will laugh at. Frequently, these have to do with sex, shame, and guilt. Someone who lives in areas that were ruled by the Bourbons is almost bound to pick up, at least in the unconscious, attitudes which that family's domination made common in the people: corruption, a sense that a crime is not a crime unless one is caught at it, a disdain for work, and so on. Someone who has heard tell since he was a child, or seen the ruins that prove it, of the cracking and breaking up of three empires, for instance, will tend, unconsciously, never to think about doing things in a big way. This layer of the unconscious will demand that one have only modest aspirations so as to avoid disappointment.

Unconscious European memories, because of their collective origin and social shaping, may be very hard to get rid of, even when the person is a middle-class professional with a scientific education. One German psychiatrist told me of an engineer who discovered after two years in psychoanalysis that he carried with him a literal fear of hell—flames, chains, torture in perpetuity—that he had acquired as a child from his Catholic education. Several long sessions were spent exploring it, bringing it to catharsis, analyzing the key incidents in its formation, and otherwise ridding this man of a piece of emotional baggage which, rationally, he looked upon as unnecessary and harmful. After the last of these sessions, however, as the patient was leaving the office, his hand still on the doorknob, he turned and asked—or rather one part of himself asked his rational part—"But what if hell really *exists?*"

Americans are also shaped by history, but their unconscious is not stratified in quite the collectively enclosing and defended way of Europeans. After all, America was the land where trying new things and looking forward often brought sensationally impressive results. Because of this special background, our orientation is toward the future, and we face it with openness and hope.

The European, however, lives a mentality like those who suffered the Great Depression in the United States, but to a much greater extent than we can easily imagine. When I was a child growing up in the forties, American memories of that disaster were still fresh. Moreover, times had always been harder than they are now because there was just so much less. I recall that my camp counselor, a man in his late thirties who was a teacher during the school year, advised me in 1947, when I was ten: "Whatever you might want to do eventually, get on the civil service lists as soon as you can. You never know when it might come in handy. During the Depression, when thirty percent of the people had no jobs, some city schoolteachers came to work in chauffeur-driven cars! It was because *they* were working. Think about it," he solemnly suggested.

But I never did. To me, this was the defeatist mentality of

what seemed, already, a long-past episode. It was only the anxious talk of tired middle age. I knew that to be an American, to live, was to aim high, to risk. Signing up for government jobs primarily because one wanted assurance of a steady income seemed to me to be giving up before one tried. One was bound. to go for greater things. Fame, success, I didn't know in what, in politics or scholarship or science or business, must be my goals. At the least, I would do better than my parents.

In Europe, such an up-and-at-'em mentality is uncommon. Our endless ambitiousness, the desire to be a free electron flying out of ancestral orbits into pure space, is not the norm. In contrast, European lives are more stable than ours. My friend Piero Ferrucci, descendant of a legendary freedom fighter of the Florentine Renaissance, tells me that when he was a child, he thought that "your house and your job were both given to you by law and you couldn't change them. I admire the States so much, where you can change careers easily."

Not only can't you change careers so easily in Europe, most people don't even think of it. Mainly, the European becomes tired at the very idea of risk. He wants security. He gets no big thrill from freedom, opportunity, energy, and change, the way we do. Or, if he does, often he thinks of emigrating to the United States. As an American, I find it shocking, for example, that 70 percent of the generation of Italy's famous economic boom, the kids born between 1960 and 1965, albeit coming on the labor market during a time of national budgetary cutbacks, have the following aspiration: they want to find a *posto fisso,* a permanent government job, the kind that cannot by law ever be cut from any budget, even if society doesn't need it anymore.

People may not always get much money for doing these jobs, but they want them. They want things quiet and steady and are willing to pay with boredom of almost infinite dimension. The Italian kids know very well that all 70 percent of them can't get government jobs; instead, almost none will. But they rarely dream of going into the new private sectors where jobs may be available: financial and insurance services, consultant services, travel, and computers. They don't even know about the existence of such jobs. Their education, already out of date by the time they leave school, is given by public employees, who, you may be sure, are not sweating to keep current. Like their parents, who could give them guidance, European kids have their own eyes squarely fixed on yesterday.

Thus the European, though now a modern, resists the new and unknown and tends to be Epimethean: his orientation is backwards in time. He associates himself with the lore of the past and, insofar as possible, is conservative and traditional. Americans, on the contrary, have always been Promethean, foreseeing, future-oriented. The American still speaks the tall talk of the frontier, the language of the perennial booster. Now, just as in the nineteenth century, we use words of mere aspiration for new institutions. Then, as Boorstin shows, a new small town was called a "city," and "university" designated an institution which in Europe might have been called a mere "college," and "college" became a synonym for almost any educational enterprise however small its resources. When we continue to do this sort of thing, we don't think of ourselves as exaggerating, just anticipating. The whole world is our canvas. To the European, his meager portion of canvas has been handed him by history, and generally speaking, he wills himself to accept what he gets and to cling to it. He finds meaning in this act of will and protection from a big, shifting world.

An essential technique for bolstering the will is the cultivation of personal pride, because pride is very close to the self-esteem that has helped the European deal with his difficult world. The defense of pride says: "No matter what may happen to me, I am worthwhile." A willed attitude, it is very close to being will itself: I am that I am. Christianity has always hated pride because it puts a man's importance in the place God should occupy. But in societies where life has been as hard as it has in Europe, the individual is driven to feed on the primal energy of his own individual existence and to affirm it.

Hence the French peasant who has not money enough to buy even a horse, who has barely enough food to eat, can willfully assert his sense of personal being and worth: "Since I am too poor to buy any other horse, at least the Horse of Pride will always have a stall in my stable." This kind of defiance of circumstance and all others is common in Europe. Sometimes it verges on hauteur.

In America, by contrast, it is hard, especially nowadays, to have personal pride. The doors of opportunity in our country are, supposedly, open to all. Therefore, one is always inclined to question oneself and ask why one isn't rich and famous, or richer and *more* famous. A German executive resigned in disgust from his American firm when he realized: "In an American company, being number one is the *only* thing." Richard Sennett and other sociologists have pointed out that in the United States, the whole blue-collar class suffers hidden injuries to their sense of dignity because of our ideology or illusion of meritocracy. In fact, as we have seen in the case of the top executive in Brussels, every American suffers such injuries. Because the European comes from a tradition much more closed to opportunity, the farmer, the working man, even the middle-class person, inherits centuries of institutionalized difficulty in social mobility. Against the ceiling on his progress he cultivates his pride in himself.

Europeans who know Americans well are shocked by our lack of pride. An Italian journalist who dated American college women in Rome during his twenties says, with pride: "And even though I ultimately married an Italian, those girls are still my friends. Because I respected them. What I did, mostly, was just listen. Often, they shocked me with their *crudezza*, the rawness of their complaints about their 'weakness,' their confessions of little sins, big self-doubts, self-hatred, really. And these were privileged, intelligent, attractive young women, the 'best and the brightest,' you might say. Their American male counterparts were somewhat more restrained but it was mainly the same. An epidemic sense of unworthiness. A European would *never* share such feelings. Our pride goes a long way toward preventing those feelings from arising at all."

The European's willed personal pride helps him to meet the most severe blows life can dispense. He cultivates his pride under all circumstances, even when things are going well, in a kind of preparation for the worst that is sure, sooner or later, to come. While this habit encourages more useless intellectual combat and increases the distance between people, Europeans boast that pride combined with cynicism and their "twist" makes them better able to meet certain difficulties. A group of Parisian doctors and lawyers agreed one evening at dinner that while Americans see things simply and are direct in addressing them, this approach doesn't work when life is complex. "When things get complicated, we Europeans are better, because of our complex history and the mentality we inherit. When the going gets tough, we can't simply move on, the way Americans do. Our skills are sharpened not only by our lifetimes, but by the lifetimes we inherit, to face difficulties, both external and internal." As an Illinois manufacturer who has worked extensively on the Continent says: "I respect their grit, their adaptability, the way, for instance, they are survivors in wartime." Indeed, even their ability to survive each other's complicated defenses and machinations during peacetime is admirable.

To me, Italians have always seemed prototypical in this regard. One night in Perugia, a man who could be nearly sixty and who is sitting next to me and Jacqueline in a crowded trattoria explains: "We've been invaded for thousands of years: the Phoenicians, the Greeks, the people who became the Romans, the Ostrogoths, Vandals, and Visigoths, the Huns, Lombards, and Franks, the Arabs, French, Spanish, Austrians, Germans, and the Americans, not to speak of Italians from other parts of Italy. You have to learn to live with it and to be happy despite everything." He laughs for a long time, a few gold teeth adding extra sparkle to his heartily felt affirmation. Because he has learned Jacqueline is Belgian, he adds admiringly: "The Belgians are good survivors also, always being bounced around by the English, Dutch, French, and Germans. They are a tenacious people and have learned to cope."

This precious survivorship can also be seen as a habit of the will, which says: "No matter what happens, I will endure." Europeans learn to toughen themselves with this continually renewed decision. If the American would be the adventurous traveler through life, the voyager and conqueror, the European would be, at a minimum, the immovable rock.

Aspects of the European character, like survivorship and taking time for life, are wholly admirable. And the European defenses as a whole have a function and a historical excuse. Moreover, there is much to learn, if one can, from people who have struggled for centuries with adversity and human cruelty. It is certainly a pleasure to meet, occasionally, the cheerful European who seems to rise so well above daunting circumstances.

But as an American abroad, I increasingly find myself disappointed with much purported European wisdom. In the defended character structure of the present day, Europe has lost too much of its traditional self. Defenses become ends in themselves and cover emptiness. We Americans may look to Europe for what Europeans say they have to offer, such as that much-vaunted *savoir vivre*. From a psychological point of view, we are seeking feminine qualities, in the archetypal sense of that word: art and culture, good food, gracefulness, courtesy, civilization, warmth, and depth. I will comment later on these aspects of contemporary European life. Here, however, to begin an evaluation of European defenses, I suggest that it is the essential sourness, the deadly realism and dirtiness of the European character that is contemporary Europe's latest lesson. It is a continent full of a chronic and subtle pessimism, which prevents its citizens from standing up forthrightly to the corrosiveness of the modern world.

If one lives long enough in Europe, one can even be corrupted by their complex defenses. One day at the Gare du Nord in Paris, I wait patiently in a long line of people trying to get something to eat at a hot dog stand (!). The line has bent itself outward into the shape of a J, but I and others move slowly and obediently along it toward the food. Then I notice two young men, about eighteen years old, who ignore the eight or nine people waiting and dart right up to the counter.

My suspicion of such behavior has become instinctive. I go up to them: *"Italiani?"*—"Are you Italians?"—I ask. The darker, taller one answers yes.

"You've got to get in line," I declare, an undeputized enforcer of international order. The two hesitate; then, the smaller one leading, they move toward the end.

Midway there, the taller one stops and turns to me: "You have something against Italians?"

"No, but the line forms over there."

"You think too badly of Italians," he asserts. "We were only going to ask prices, not to buy." He takes a high tone with me, mildly outraged. Automatically now, I back down. "I'm so sorry," I say. "I *beg* your pardon." Then, he and his friend go and return to the head of the line.

But I don't really believe him. They only pretend, I think, to ask the short-order cook about prices, which are already clearly posted on a signboard above her head. I believe that, having been caught, they are playacting in order to save face. I congratulate myself that I have turned them back from crashing the line. And, suddenly, I look at myself. I see how I have been distrustful, prudent, indirect, and meretricious. Even though I am certain they were trying to crash the line, I don't simply say so. Perhaps they weren't trying to crash the line at all. I observe that I have become a searcher after motives. I am, if not *contorto,* then enmeshed in imagined complexities. And to top it off, I have lost my natural American straightforwardness. I smirked my real message at him when I said, "I beg your pardon." Sure, I'll let him save face, but I can see he's a liar and I'm going to let him know without daring to say so.

I think, this must be what it's like to be European. In the States, in such confrontations, the truth will out. Here there is manipulation, distrust, *double-entendre,* caution, masked aggression, but never the stated truth, the direct accusation. I am falling prey to the Great Twist, the *malin,* of European character. It's eating me up.

When I go back to America for a visit, the affliction stays with me. In Los Angeles, I rent a car from Hertz. I need it immediately, so once I get the papers signed, I jump in and speed off the lot. As soon as I'm on the road, I notice that the side mirror is broken, useless. But I haven't time to stop and do anything about it. A few days later, I call Hertz about getting the mirror repaired or getting a new car of the same kind. After I tell the man what the problem is, I say: "I didn't break the mirror. It was broken when I got the car."

"Oh, of course," says the cheerful telephone voice. "Sorry about that. No problem!"

The American believes me! I don't have to insist on my innocence! I am astonished. I'm not used anymore to people trusting each other that way. And I realize that the European defensive disease has gotten to me.

It is helpful to imagine much of the European character as a prince (or princess) in a castle, surrounded by rings of fortifications and moats: the well-worked-out personal philosophy, the eristic intellectual style, the money quietly put in the mattress, the house registered in the name of a cousin, the protective family, the group of acquaintances and friends from school days, the buttress of memories both good and bad, the shrewd pessimism, the cynicism, the motive-hunting, the social role-playing, the secrecy, even a certain resignation to whatever life may bring. Within these defenses lives his personality, but it is difficult to tell whether there is real depth to his being or only fear, whether his face is reflective of an inner profundity or is merely a mask.

One thing is certain: the tensions of contemporary life, the assaults on stability caused by the rise of new occupations, ever more new people in their growing cities, and the opening of opportunities to people in all social classes have worn away at the European defenses. In many cases, not just the outer perimeters have been breached, but the citadel of personality has been attacked and badly damaged. Formerly, being in psychotherapy was utterly exotic in Europe. But now, from literary friends all over the continent, I hear that "everybody is in therapy or analysis." Naturally, they don't literally mean "everybody." They mean a small trend-setting group of intellectual and professional people. But if these cultural leaders, who until a few years ago scorned psychotherapy as being an American fad, have submitted themselves, it must be because the traditional European defenses of character are under tremendous assault. One of the main functions of psychotherapy is to provide an affirmation of self; to make the isolated individual seem, by virtue of the therapist playing audience, significant. Expect to see more Europeans in therapy.

Moreover, the spread of the scientific spirit makes intellectual dogmatism, even that of the salon, seem ridiculous, and even the European intellectual style, as we have seen, is yielding. As the need to meet competitive initiatives in every kind of business grows, friendships and the stable network of family will decline, and their place will be taken by teams formed at work where colleagues must, at least to some degree, disclose themselves so that they can trust each other. As an upward-driving and expanding urban population lives more and more in modern housing developments, barren and barely distinguishable from those in another European country or even in America, the ties with the past will be destroyed. As education becomes more technical, the continuity of great cultural traditions will also be cut. As the pace of life requires more and more flexibility of character, of manners and habit, the traditional armor will have to melt. Then the faces of those Europeans of yore will disappear. Expect to see more faceless Europeans.

PART THREE

RULE OF THE LORDS

LORD

From Old English *hlaf-waere* = *bread-keeper*. Thus, *master* of a *household* with *servants* who eat his *bread*. *Waere*, from Old English *werdian* = to *guard, protect*. Compare: Old High German *Werre* = *strife*, akin to English *war*. Used to translate Latin *dominus*, from Sanskrit *damanas: he who supplies*, hence *master, possessor, ruler, lord, proprietor*. Compare: Latin *domus* = *house*, from Sanskrit *damas*. *Lord* is also used for *God* or *Jesus Christ*.

SIRE

From Old French *sieur, sor* = a *knight*. From Sanskrit *sana* = *old*. From Latin *senior, one who is older;* from *senex*, a man over forty = *a father of a family*. Compare: *senatus,* modern English *senator*. Used in addressing *God* or *Jesus Christ*.

MASTER

From Latin *magister* = *the greater one*, the *bigger, commander, leader, teacher*.

ARISTOCRACY

Literally, *government by the best*. Since the French Revolution, *contrasted with democracy*.

NOBLE

Illustrious by *position, character,* or *exploit; titular preeminence over others;* of *birth, blood,* or *family;* having *high moral qualities*. or *ideals,* of a *great* or *lofty character;* distinguished by *splendor, magnificence, or stateliness of appearance; surpassingly good.*

HIERARCHY

Originally, *each of the three divisions of angels, every one comprising three orders*. Later and more generally, *rule* or *domain*. Still later, *a body of persons, ranked in grades, orders, or classes one above another.*

CHAPTER FOUR

Hierarchy

Violence and blood, castles and defense, are two sets of ideas and images which, when illuminated by history, describe and explain much of European behavior and being. The idea of hierarchy and the ancient image of aristocracy, rule of the lords, will help in similar ways. There is a general causal logic to the sequence: violence necessitated defense, defense led to rule by a class of armed men.

In Florence, where I have lived several times now, there is a splendid bookstore on the Via Tornabuoni, the city's best shopping street. Large windows display new books in many languages. They are placed so carefully and exhibited with such art that passing those windows I have always experienced a visceral anticipatory pleasure, the kind one feels in front of a candy store. An old place, within, but inviting—walls painted a soft yellow, high white ceilings, dark wood shelves, and airy aisles with room to browse at leisure; a distinguished, Old World emporium of the mind.

When I first came upon it, more than a quarter-century ago, I was a Fulbright student. Italian libraries were inefficient and books hard to get on loan. So each of us had been given three hundred dollars, a large sum at the time, with which to buy books. The local Italian teacher who took care of us had told me that we could get a 10 percent discount at this splendid store I had already noticed. Accordingly, I presented myself for the discount in halting Italian and with some youthful diffidence.

But the reaction to me was more than the cordiality I was used to in American shops, even those which saw the chance of getting a good new customer. "*Certo, professore, certo,*" said the middle-aged man who was the manager. He bowed his gray head and shoulders a little, several times. "If you need any help," he continued, "at any time, I am always at your service." He bowed again and—it is not the wrong word—retired.

Courtesy, consideration, and deference from a well-dressed, graying, middle-aged man to a twenty-year-old foreign student. More than deference—a title. For some unknown reason, I had become "*professore*," and not only the manager but his clerk, even the knockout blond girl at the cash register would thereafter smile and exclaim as I entered or left: "*Buon giorno, professore! Grazie, grazie, professore!*" Not merely deference but a sort of institutionalized affection was mine. Many visitors to Italy—indeed, to many parts of Europe—before that period and well into the sixties will have had exactly the kind of experience I am talking about. We saw the end of the old regime. On occasion, we were treated like lords.

Nearly every society is hierarchically ordered. Verticality is one of the ordering principles of mind and perhaps one of the categories of existence itself. Yet the notion of a stable schematic hierarchy into which not only men but all things fit is not essentially American. Class consciousness has always been muted in America; social position has been not strictly inherited but relatively fluid. But to this day in a great many European countries, when you walk into a café, shop, or pub, the locals look you over as if they are estimating your place. And when you get into a discussion of American politics with a European, he will express astonishment at the kind of people who head our government— a haberdasher, a peanut farmer, an actor—people not suited for the top.

To truly understand these and other attitudes and behaviors of the contemporary European requires some patience and work. We need to examine in detail what the linked historical phenomena of hierarchy and aristocracy really were. And we need to imagine how they marked the European mind and soul.

Rough meanings are easy. Hierarchy was the fixed, severe, vertical structuring of European social classes over thousands of years and especially from the barbarian invasions on. Aristocracy was the legally and hereditarily dominant group formed in the

Middle Ages at the top of the hierarchy. Dictionary meanings also help a little. But to really grasp the mystery, we must go deeper.

One has to search hard in the American experience for analogies that can help us elicit some of the character that typified the ancient European verticality. It was a social order that, in its strictness, was nearly military. Or, one could say, it was like a highly bureaucratic corporation with no chance for promotion and no freedom to change companies or careers or even place. In European society, one was born to a place on a ladder of wealth, prestige, power, influence, opportunity, and cultivation. With only the rarest exceptions, one stayed put, looking up or down, for one's whole life, without hope or fear or even thought of change, not only for oneself but also for one's descendants in perpetuity. In America, only slaves and their owners knew something of this condition, though even here the system was in doubt and owners had to institutionalize military measures, like the infamous "patrols," against their constant fear of slave revolt. The European order was much more long-lived than American slavery, infinitely more accepted by all parties, and during most of its existence more stable.

The European hierarchy had its gradations: within the nobility, as time went on, there were in Germany, for example, the princes, the Electors, all the way down to minesterales or servile knights; in France, the hierarchy within the nobility ran from king to peers, to counts, to knights, to an intermediate class of chamberlains, supervisors, local experts, state officials, artisans, domestic servants, some of noble birth, some free, and some serfs. The hierarchy was often insisted on. A high lord could summon his vassals in peacetime to his court, and men of high rank would have to perform public gestures of deference, acting as squires or cupbearers. Marginal differentiations of rank were extended even to dress, severely regulated by law lest someone pretend to the appearance of a higher station.

But the fundamental distinction was the more abrupt one; the social distance between the vast bottom and the small top is the essence of the old European mentality. Even as late as the time of the French Revolution, twenty-five million Frenchmen were dominated by 120,000 nobles who owned three-quarters of the land in what was an almost totally agricultural economy.

At the bottom, the mass of country people were found, the serfs and peasants, the average, described in a famous passage by the seventeenth-century writer Jean de La Bruyère:

> One spies certain wild animals, males and females, scattered across the countryside, black, livid, burnt by the sun, attached to the earth that they search and they turn over with an invincible tenacity; they have a voice and when they rise on their feet they show a human face, and in fact they are men; they sleep at night in holes in the earth where they live on black bread, water and roots.

As a picture of the general condition, this is perhaps somewhat exaggerated, but not utterly. As late as 1900, country families in France typically wintered around a fire in a stinking single-room house, thronged with children, pigs, a cow, and, if they were lucky enough to have one, a horse.

At the top, on the contrary, was a class whose near monopoly of the preponderant goods of life—wealth, power, culture, taste, and even the expression of what is considered virtuous and good—was routinely impressive to those below. From the top, as a general attitude, came contempt for those below: in ancient phrase, "a cascade of disdain." From the bottom came fear, dependence, veneration, and a wish to imitate in any allowable way. From the top, at best, came a paternalistic affection and acceptance of responsibility for one's own "people"; at worst, an attitude typified by what a French abbot said of his serf: "He is mine from the top of his head to the soles of his feet!"

Like violence and defense, hierarchy was embodied in the human landscape of monuments and exerted its impress on local minds living under the domination and protection of an infinite number of fortified towers, castles, and other strong places.

One day, seeking cool after the blinding summer heat outside, I wandered into the Romanesque cathedral of Fiesole. It is a building I had thought I knew well, but I noticed for the first time the two marble funerary sculptures on the north wall. One, placed by a Corsini in the nineteenth century, commemorates the four-hundredth anniversary of a family member's birthday, a saint. The other remembers Francesco Ferrucci, the Florentine patriot who fought and lost defending the Republic's liberty at the beginning of the sixteenth century. In Florence today, I know a Corsini princess who has fallen on un-princess-like times: she rents the large family palace down the hill in Florence to various businesses wanting offices at a prestige address. And my friend Piero Ferrucci, despite the differences from past times, still leads a life like the princess, redolent of continuity. Though his father is only a pharmacist, the pharmacy has been in the family for more than two hundred years.

What can it be like to grow up, if one is a Corsini or a Ferrucci, and know that these monuments, and others scattered around Tuscany and the rest of Italy, celebrate your line? Surely it gives one a special feeling of backing, of a support in time that is nearly timeless. And in the old days, for those lower on the social scale, what must it have been like to meet a Corsini or a Ferrucci, to see their family monuments in the churches, their blazons on the façades of magnificent residences and public buildings, and later, when some could read, to find their names in the history books? Surely the effect was more powerful than that of a family who merely had great wealth. They must have been regarded as Special People, Big People, Aristocrats, who might, as in medieval paintings, tower over the lower orders who surrounded them. These are people big by virtue of an abiding institution, their family. Their ancestors have a place even in the Fiesole cathedral, where the ceiling soars to heaven and where, on the west wall, della Robbia made the likeness of one of them, a Corsini pope, stare on the same eye level at the even more ancient fresco of God the Father on the curving apse of the east. It must have seemed as if God the Father, that pope, and the totality of the high families were all equally high: elevated to form an axis of divinity, of beings sacred and eternal.

Part of the permanence which lent such dignity to the nobility was fastened in the family's land. Aristocratic families were organizations of men and women forever settled on estates which others worked. With rare exception, by rule of primogeniture, the land was passed down to the first son, undivided, unchanged, generation after generation. The other children more or less found their place around this heir, or in the Church, and the family's dominance found physical expression in their land's permanence. The land recalls the past and promises an unending future. It gives confidence to those who own it and reminds those who work it, generation after fixed generation, of their subordination.

Against such a background of familial, landed, sacred permanence, American distinctions of wealth seem flimsy. In the United States, with its more mobile social ways, money took the place of land, and this is one of the reasons why there are only a handful of distinguished family names in all of American history. Fluid cash, stocks, and bonds do not lend themselves to the building of dynasties.

The old European hierarchy, however, was built on more than family, tradition, respect, and land. It was founded also on the legal structure of society. Slippery money can put an American and his family more or less temporarily in what we informally call a high social class, but the old European system went beyond class. It was an order of civil "estates." Sometime before 1250, membership in the European nobility became a legal and hereditary matter. Beyond the informality of custom or de facto power, the top was defined in law and had all the force of law to support its elevation and exclude others. One group of people was, by blood, now legally better than another. Used as we are now to the idea of all men being equal before the law and having the same general status, rights, and duties, it takes some effort to imagine the full force of such distinctions. Ours is now the "common law," but under hierarchy, the legal privileges of the aristocratic top weighed heavily on consciousness and behavior, making indelible the notion of vertical distinction.

A privilege was not what we Americans now think it, an informal or temporary advantage, as when we say "the rich are privileged." All we mean is that one group of people can afford what another group can't: tuition at private schools, houses in low-crime neighborhoods, access to the ear of a public official or a highly effective lawyer. While these are important advantages, in one way or another the common law has tended to work toward their elimination; at the least, there is the constant threat that the law will overturn these distinctions. Those who don't enjoy these advantages are ever full of hope and even of some reasonable expectation that the unfair differences will be relieved. Our American privileged are, therefore, an uneasy group who tend to feel their distinctive position constantly in doubt. But in the old order, privilege was literally a *privus lex,* a private law for a hereditary social estate. Social advantages were established by it. True, in American history at its most vertical, white men in the Old South were legally distinguished from black. But within the larger white group, there was no true aristocracy. Despite the dominance by certain families of wealth and political power, one law applied to all.

The legal privileges of the European nobility were far from trivial. The aristocrat was exempt from taxes and had the further privilege of imposing a private taxation on those around him, and to the limit of his wishes: *le serf est taillable et corvéable à merci,* reads the old law. The landowner legally took what he wanted of a harvest or its proceeds; and he also took for his own construction projects what time and labor of his inferiors he wished. As for self-defense, only the noble had the right to bear arms during peacetime; he carried a sword; *you,* at most, had a stick. Later, under centralized monarchy, the noble was exempt from service in the local militia (in which *you* had to serve), but in the king's army only he and his kind could be promoted to positions of even minimal importance. In the long centuries of uncertain food supplies, poor nutrition, and endemic shortages of protein, only the noble had the right to hunt, while anyone else could be hung for poaching. This privilege, like many of the others, was also replete with emotional meaning. Among a rural population, more attuned to nature and the ways of animals, the hunt is always something that distracts from boredom and stirs the blood and soul. In sexual matters, the *droit du seigneur,* or the *droit de cuissage* ("the right of thighs"), as it was sometimes called, legally put the master into a special, nearly divine relationship to the deep human worlds of desire, love, and family solidarity. If he committed a crime, he could be tried only by his peers, and if he were sentenced to death, it was not for him the struggling, kicking humility of hanging: he was legally privileged to suffer only the axman's quick, sharp stroke. For centuries, the private individuals of the aristocracy raised and maintained soldiers, administered justice, and often interpreted and even made the law in their localities. They were, to some considerable extent, not just privileged by and before the law, they *were* their own law. Taking into account all of these weighty privileges, it is safe to infer that the aristocrat not only behaved differently, but also *was* a different sort of human being from those beneath him.

   The status of the aristocrat at the top of the hierarchy was further defined by a number of characteristic personality traits and ideals. They set the tone of the old order, and many of the manners and behaviors were increasingly accorded prestige. Though there were always brutal, crude, foolish nobles, certain norms and values of the nobility were generally admired. Understanding these personal differences, attached to the old high social station, helps one to know today's later Europeans.

   The aristocrat saw himself first as a knight, a social being whose personality was shaped by the military origins of his class, which arose by defending local populations from the chaos of the barbarian invasions. The knight's primal social function as protector of those who surrendered their land to him, his ability to fight, and his willingness to fight marauding barbarians legitimized his dominant position, and this sense of social legitimacy lived on for many centuries.

   Originally, fighting was the whole purpose of noble life, yet even as the aristocracy continued into more peaceful times, the ideals of strength, vigor, courage, and love of combat fixed themselves as the basis of personal values at the top of the European hierarchy. Nobles moved to the country not only to occupy their fiefs, but to exercise their martial skills as well. They cultivated vigorous country amusements: hunting and tournaments, play and combat. A man who added to his wealth by sudden feats of arms—whether in jousts for entertainment and practice or in actual warfare—was not interested in the prudent calculations of profit and loss. His creed, at least, called for him to risk, to get, and to give away with a free hand. Useful manual work, and later on work for profit in commerce or industry, were despised, and an ideal of leisure was cultivated. The knight had to be above mundane concerns lest his warlike character and bravery be undermined.

   With time, this fighting self became codified into what was supposed to be a morally superior self. In chivalry, the knight's role as a servant of numerous good causes (the defense of the widow, the poor, and the church, and the pursuit of the malefactor) took a prominent place. Consequently, aristocratic dominance, originally justified by simple physical defense, now became justified by the defense of high values, nobility came to be seen as entailing not only many privileges but many obligations, the fulfillment of which strengthened the claim to superiority. The noble became supposed to be morally better than others.

These ideals in the dominant class had an impressive effect on lower orders, and this was also the case, as can easily be imagined, with other traits of the normative aristocratic personality. At the top of the society, the noble had a strong sense of self-worth derived not only from the ideology of knightly courage and service but also from other directions. From an early age, nobles were inculcated with a belief in their general apartness. As the schoolmaster-priest says to his aristocratic pupils in Michel de Saint-Pierre's novel, *Les Aristocrates:* "The elite is not only superior, it is different." A collective distance from others, not founded merely on merit or accomplishment but, he is led to believe, on the nature of things, helps shape the noble personality.

This sense of apartness, which encases personality and makes it steady and secure, is further reinforced by a social role that he is taught is at once superior and, most important, assured in its superiority. The aristocrat is *born* into a role and educated to occupy it. The aristocrat knows who he is. So does the serf, of course, but he is as conscious of his inferiority as the noble is of his superiority. For most of those at the top and bottom of the old order, existentialism would be a philosophy without meaning: essence preceded existence and one tried to fill one's role with as much worthiness as one could.

Necessarily, then, those below the top of the ancient social pyramid worked deliberately to cultivate dignity. They strove to be who they were, to fill their role fittingly, rightly. Peasant or carpenter, milkmaid or wheelwright, they were taught to be conscious of their goodness in their role and to found their self-respect upon it.

The aristocrat had more than dignity and self-respect, however. He had the personal pride (French, *fierté*) that came from a certainty of the worth and "cleanliness" (French, *propreté*) of his distinguished family line, that came from the fabled deeds of the founder, who won the nobility, and that was carefully preserved and cultivated through the intervening generations. Transmitted to him, this certainty strengthened his personal identity even more, with a result radically different from what we think of as personality in traditionally democratic America. We Americans are chronically in doubt. We have little sense of family tradition and still less of an assured superiority and worth running from the depths of time to the present moment when they are embodied in us. We may be certain of our right to try, to experiment, and even to struggle for what is good. We may be daring, even dashing, in certain ways. But we don't have the firm interior structure, inherited dignity, and absolute belief in our own worth that is part of the European tradition. We feel that we must earn our way.

The noble's social place and family traditions gave him advantages that expressed themselves in habits and aspirations also foreign to the American. The nobility had the time and wealth to develop increasingly refined tastes in every possible domain of human experience: art, love, horses, tapestries, song, gardens, architecture, furniture, poetry, prose, food, wine and ideas. Not hasty practical production but grace, elegance, and exquisiteness became important values. Local craftsmen were encouraged to surpass each other in satisfying those demands, which, over the centuries, drifted higher and higher. If the aristocrat happened himself to be an artist or an intellectual, he could take many years to pursue a project, immune from the hastening exigencies of the marketplace. If he were simply a consumer of culture, his taste was firm and fixed by tradition—it didn't change quickly but tended toward the increasing development and elaboration of what had gone before. His was not, for example, an interest in how the story came out, but rather in how it was told: in cadence, style, and subtly complex variations of old themes.

Extend this attitude to life in general and you begin to grasp what was so dear to the aristocratic imagination: the possibility that man himself—his manner and experience—could be elevated above his animal proclivities to a general fineness that nearly transcended the human. Even in violent warfare, such transcendent refinement was cultivated. As one aristocratic soldier says to another in *La Grande Illusion*, that elegy for the First World War's devastation of the nobility: "*Si on veut faire la guerre, au moins on peut la faire poliment*" ("If one wants to make war, at least one can do it politely"). One thinks, too, of those First World War aviators who, machine-gun ammunition exhausted, pulled close their planes of sticks and paper so as to salute each other in midair.

The secure and stable aristocratic self was trained to reach higher still toward a fully formed personality that was exalted, even imperial, in its mastery of the ordinary. The aristocrat aspired to a definition of human possibility that was nothing less than personal greatness.

This is a concept remote from our democratic American consciousness. There is a difference between the aristocratic aspiration toward greatness—when it occurred—and the democratic aspiration toward "excellence," "quality," or "achievement." Excellence is seen in achievement but greatness is seen in personal being itself. Not the product but the man is the focus of the aspiration. *He* is seen in his actions. Rather than his actions being seen to be excellent and reflecting credit upon him, his excellent actions are seen to reflect who he truly *is:* in himself excellent, great.

In fact, logical analysis cannot do justice to the concept in which the ego was raised to such a high pitch, for it is impossible with the instruments of reason neatly to separate a man from his products. Similarly, one cannot say that "greatness" is entirely separate from "goodness" as a category of praise or aspiration. Few men in the European tradition could be considered great who did not do deeds which had effects that men must consider, at least in part, good by some ethical standard.

To explicate the aristocratic understanding of the Imperial Self, we do well to take a counterlogical route and try to penetrate the meaning of another one of their characteristically un-American words. The aristocrat, when he did aspire, was after "glory." This word means "fame," of course, but it is fame surrounded by light and color, a vivid, visible splendor. The colorful accoutrements of war in the officer class reflected this sought-for personal radiance. In one European library where I sometimes work, there is a simple still life which passed unregarded by me until a day when, trying to penetrate this foreign notion of personal "glory," I caught its import. The background is dark and colored somber gray, green, and brown. One sees on the table that occupies the foreground the accoutrements of the Napoleonic cavalry officer. They emerge from the somber background, shining: a burnished helmet with its brilliant white plumes, the old hilt of a cavalry saber that catches the light, three silver buttons on the scarlet jacket shoulder, a brass trumpet gleaming behind the helmet, the white gloves, nearly luminous, free from any speck of dirt or contamination.

By the time the picture was painted—around 1915—these objects were antique and already representative of a heroic warrior culture which was being eliminated by trenches, barbed wire, and poison gas. And yet this painting symbolically represents that fixation on personal distinction carried to the point of splendor that was the old ideal—just two generations ago. It implies the routinely probable existence of a man who in his duty and bravery shines with an interior radiance symbolized by his costume. Now, properly, we despise war. Its gradual massification has drowned ideas of military glory in a sea of misery. No one can now believe that real war can carry a man to the heights of human dignity and greatness. But these are recent developments and not the perennial experience of the aristocracy and those who admired it.

The warrior class could wear the costumes of splendor because those accoutrements were intended to help lead them to incandescence in act and being. The aristocrat could aspire so high, because he had not his living to make nor his role to establish. Because we must do both, our energies are always distracted and ambiguous. In general, the most we hope for is not glory but rather a brief celebrity, which we spend as so much capital in further maintaining or advancing our economic and social position. Contrast instead the aristocratic individual at his best, a man capable of enormous personal potency. Lord, baron, count, or king, the man on horseback followed by his private army, the man who cultivates the terrible military virtues of daring, will, exertion, personal honor, personal grandeur, and the virtues of great men—generosity, largeness of spirit, elegance of manner, the obligation of nobility to give and in giving to be the best. Such a man could seem touched with divinity. And it is from these qualities that heroes like Ferruccis and saints like Corsinis can be made. It was part of the ethos and the ideal of traditional Europe that such mighty realizations were attainable by mere men. These prestigious possibilities were in the collective air and depended upon the existence of a class who started at the top and who could push the top higher in their individual case.

We, by contrast, living as we do 'in a massified, more democratic and practical way, are liable to suspect such notions and believe them to have always and everywhere been mere fantasies, if not simply self-serving lies. We see ourselves by comparison as mere Don Quixotes. At worst, we dream schmaltzy dreams in a musical comedy version of the novel; at best, we tilt but only at windmills. We sometimes dare to hope for personal goodness, and perhaps even for usefulness and a major accomplishment or two. But none of us dreams of that rounded greatness of being which drove, toward the beginning of the end of the aristocratic tradition, a Don Quixote mad with pursuit of the knightly ideal. We may believe in personal progress but feel ourselves hemmed in by a crowd. History seems an accumulation of billions of which we are one. Mysterious forces push men and deflect our energies. The individual can make only a slight difference. Such is our view of personal possibilities: shrunken, tragicomic, antiheroic.

It is true, of course, that the old glory could be sought with a wicked disregard of others. One thinks, for example, of the devastations wrought by Louis XIV's pursuit of glory in attacking the Spanish Netherlands or of Frederick the Great's enormously destructive efforts to win Silesia. There was often great harm in the ideology of personal greatness. But such high aspiration could also raise the sights of certain privileged men and even of those around them to a transcendent, generous view of things. It could also cultivate deep convictions and lead the way to acts of profound devotion. An utterly unmodern conception of the personality, the belief in an individual's conquering glory partially captured the imagination of the aristocrat and through him of the whole society over which he presided.

Having come this far, we must now deal with a common objection. Some people point out that every society has a hierarchy and a top, including the United States. Moreover, despite historic differences from America, Europe had nothing like the petrified order of such ancient dynasties as the Chinese, the Egyptian, or the Mayan. The argument intends to show that because there was movement and fluidity in the hierarchical tradition of Europe, it was a society more or less open and, therefore, much like our own.

That there was some mobility must be admitted. In France, around 1100, a few families owned all the land and ruled the inhabitants, but by 1270 the first ennoblement took place and nobility, which was formerly something without price, could be bought. With time, other fluidities came to exist in the system. A serf could become a priest and, on those occasions when clerics of aristocratic origin did not totally dominate all promotion, he might even move upwards and briefly take precedence over nobles and kings. As society became more ordered and complex, lawyers began to appear at court beside the knights. As trade developed, men living in free towns were able to accumulate wealth. The richest, the Fuggers of Germany, despised but flattered by royalty, had the power by lending him their money to help Charles V buy the election to the throne of empire. As money became a source of power, land could be bought and not simply inherited by feudal tenure. As society became more and more civilized, artists, thinkers, and various technical professionals developed; mind became an element in success, gradually empowering even the poor.

And yet if we look closely at such a late and comparatively volatile period as the sixteenth century, we see that changes are accommodated by the fixed pattern of the older order. Though the dramatic rise in trade of that time is often seen as a watershed period in the overturning of the old European aristocracy, the complex facts tell a different story. True, Turkish victories in the east cut off old trade routes and made western cities like Lyons and Antwerp boomtowns. Also, the discovery of America brought immense quantities of gold and silver into Europe, creating inflation and further stimulating commerce.

But the old hierarchy adapted rather than fell. Many nobles kept their stations and simply went into business. Italian and German Renaissance merchant families were, in many cases, of noble origin. More importantly, the new class of rich bourgeois tended to intermarry, first among themselves, then into the old, landowning, military caste, creating an oligarchy of crossed alliances in which genealogy influenced business. The richest penetrated into the highest aristocracy. Landowning was a way of stabilizing the investment of a fortune, aristocratic alliances a way of supporting and increasing it. These alliances gave access to local and national governments, to the vastly useful information of the clerical hierarchy, to the protection of the aristocratic international community.

So tenacious was the hold of the old system and its concomitant ideas that even the French Revolution did not utterly shake it. Though legal privileges had been struck down, Napoleon when he became emperor tried to marry his generals into old aristocratic families all over Europe. He even thought that what was needed in France was not a complete upheaval of the established order but a king like himself, who would emerge from the Revolution. The Restoration after his downfall brought back most of the old families of Europe. In France, probably only one in four noble families had been affected by the revolutionary emigration to begin with. Perhaps not more than a fifth of noble lands there—the economic, social, and psychological basis, as we have seen, of the old order—passed out of aristocratic hands during the Revolution. In many regions of France, it was another century before nobles ceased to be the largest landowners. The new Napoleonic aristocracy merged by marriage with the old. The new class of industrialists and manufacturers, tried very often to do the same and consciously imitated the ancient habits, tastes, manners, ideals, and myths of the aristocracy. Though industrial capitalism tore the serf or tenant farmer from the land, creating a huge underclass of proletarian wage earners, still the hierarchy held. True, the ancient sentimental ties of affection, loyalty, and paternalism were broken into a new, impersonal, and fluid urbanism; but the hierarchy kept itself in place and the aristocratic personality continued to be produced and admired.

Indeed, though Europe is infinitely more democratic now than it was and, in many ways, is even socialistic—important developments with which we will deal later—both the old hierarchy and its aristocratic top survive in certain important ways. As Talcott Parsons explains: "In contrast to American and Soviet societies," the democratic countries of northwestern Europe "continue to permit aristocratic elements to share in defining the establishments." He gives Germany, Sweden, and Britain as examples and notices that in France, "aristocracy . . . and other ascriptive components of society remained prominent after 1870." Even in such a democratic country as Holland, I hear the word *eliter* (pronounced *eLEEtaire*). This I am told means the "high middle class." As one Dutch sociologist explains it to me, "there is a very large group of *nouveaux riches* in Holland and they try to get into the high middle class, which includes by marriage the nobility. But money is not enough. Birth counts, being members of the titled nobility or being bourgeoisie of good family background. And, also, culture, education." Access to this education is considerably restricted according to class lines. An American sociologist who has studied Dutch society tells me: "It is still a place for a tiny group. I find the rags-to-riches story much more common in the U.S. The students here don't work very hard, they come from a self-conscious '*elite*,' have good government scholarships, strong financial backing from parents, and nearly assured prospects afterwards."

Though deprived of the dominant social role they once had, aristocrats all over Europe still transmit their ideals of character and behavior to modern European society, not just by means of history books and innumerable monuments and memories, but also by personal presence and contact. I have felt the force of this transmission many times, as will any visitor who lives in Europe for a while.

A Belgian count, old, portly, but red-faced, lived next door to me for two years in Brussels but never greeted me on the street. Neither did his silver-haired wife. That's nothing unusual: Belgians do not acknowledge each other unless they have been introduced, and I soon learned to suppress my outgoing American ways. But one night the doorbell rings, and I answer it to find an elderly woman who breathlessly explains that she is the count's cousin, that she's just arrived from England, that no one answers her ring next door, and that she would like to use the phone. I invite her in and she phones; no answer. Dismal, she goes to open my front door and looks out. Then she brightens. "They are here," she calls as the neighbors' car pulls up. I help her down the front stairs with her bag, which she then takes from me, murmuring a thank-you. I nod, smiling to her, then nod to the neighbors who are standing a short distance from me, waiting to receive her. But they look away.

The incident shocked me and I had to ask European friends what it meant. Some opined that the neighbors were just awkward people; some said they were stupid; but all agreed that their drawing back was simply an automatic class reaction. An American might try to find a functional explanation: that in these fluid times, an important and rich family must be careful lest it make casual contact with people who would try to profit from the acquaintance, whether financially or in some other up-and-coming way. But, I come to see, that is not what is finally at work here. They may have forgotten their manners, but I suspect they have deliberately snubbed me. I don't belong. And I and others who don't belong simply don't exist for them, even if I am clearly seen doing a favor for one of their own. "The elite is not only separate, it is different." As an American, I am annoyed mainly at their lack of simple courtesy, but a European would also be painfully reminded of his place. As an American, I wish I could simply tell them to get off their high horse, but the European, instead, would hear the tolling of old bells ringing changes on ancient disdain.

In London, another time, I meet an English baronet in his modest apartment. I already know a little about him. As the senior male heir of his family, he inherited many square miles of precious English farmland. During his twenties, he raced airplanes and won some national championships. Then, with knightly abandon and sense of mission, he gave his energies, his money and land, to a small group investigating psychic phenomena. The goal was to communicate with extraterrestrial intelligences who were, according to a well-known medium, preparing the group to save the world from nuclear war.

He lost everything. Now his Connecticut-born wife, a junior executive, supports him and their daughter while he busies himself, for no pay, with more orthodox attempts to promote the cause of world peace. In the corner of their small living room, he has a large glass case full of family memorabilia going back to the 1400s. Not precious things, he says, just family jewels cut in old ways, of little market value, medals gained in various wars, a parchment with the family motto, *Semper Fidelis,* like the U.S. Marines. Like them, he continues faithful to his traditions. He clings to his sense of mission and an inner assurance, his from birth, that he has the right and duty to do so, despite the fact that he is financially dependent on another and that he lives in much less comfort than would be the case if he got a regular job. An American might think the man absurd, not only because he threw away an inherited fortune but because he has such continuing self-assurance. One looks for some middle-class self-doubt, some agonizing confrontation with conscience, with an idea of reality that encompasses prosperity, money, and the market. The European, instead, even if he has some of the same critical thoughts, can be impressed by the *fierté,* the sense of personal right, the attitude of *noblesse oblige.* On one wall, a painting of the baronet's blond mother in blue silks; on the other, a photograph of his father in the leather-belted, khaki uniform of a First World War cavalry officer, immaculate. *Semper Fidelis.*

I meet a sixty-year-old German countess who lives in a shabby modern house beside an old stone *Schloss.* The family, whose fortunes are in leisurely decline, can no longer maintain the castle and has deeded it to the town for use as a museum. But when we talk, the countess doesn't dwell on her financial condition. She discovers that I am a writer and reveals that she, too, writes, and, after asking me about my work habits, says: "I wish I had more energy. I work every morning. That's the best time, I think, don't you?"

"Yes," I agree, "but what are you working on, Countess?"

"A novel."

"How interesting. And how far have you gotten?"

"Oh!" she complains with a sigh. "I have written fifty-six chapters and the end is not in sight! It is a book my father began. He died fifteen years ago at eighty and worked on it most of his life."

"But he never finished it?"

"That's right."

"And you have been working on it for the last fifteen years?"

"That's right," she says, a little wearily. "I'm not sure I will live long enough to finish it myself. It's quite a complex affair."

Later I learn that one of the daughters—now reduced to working as a secretary in Munich—also thinks of herself as a writer, and I am told that after the mother dies or gives up the project because of old age, the daughter will take up the work, unto the third generation. The American in me is astonished at such rampant impracticality. But a European, whatever his modern doubts at the family's never having finished the book, much less having sold it to a publisher, would likely be impressed by the time-honored habits, the aristocratic disdain for product and audience, the unbending dedication to the work itself.

CHAPTER FIVE

Tradition and Character

As long ago as 1916, D. H. Lawrence evoked a changing idea of hierarchy among the European masses. He describes the two opposing views of a married peasant couple, Paolo and Maria, from San Gaudenzo in the north of Italy. Paolo has worked as a laborer in America. Returned home, he is, for Lawrence, the noble but unsentimentalized peasant of the best old tradition, a figure with the hard dignity of Mantegna's humble people. His wife, Maria, however, is of another kind. She has been in domestic service in Venice. Now, she has come back to the country and transformed the couple's tiny house into a sort of inn where Lawrence is staying with his wife. She is the harbinger of the European mass which had reached and would continue to reach upwards in a new spirit:

> In her soul she was in a state of anger because of her closedness. It was a violation to her strong animal nature. Yet her mind had wakened to the value of money. She knew she could alter her position, the position of her children, by virtue of money. She knew it was only money that made the difference between master and servant.

Lawrence contrasts this fluid, modern, almost "American" view of things with Paolo's more fixed, complex, and traditional outlook:

> Paolo was untouched by all this. For him there was some divinity about a master which even America had not destroyed. If we came in for supper whilst the family was still at table he would have the children at once take their plates to the wall, he would have Maria at once set the table for us, though their own meals were never finished. *And this*

was not servility, it was the dignity of a religious conception. Paolo regarded us as belonging to the Signoria, those who are elect, near to God. . . . His life was a ritual. It was very beautiful, but it made me unhappy, the purity of his spirit was so sacred and the actual facts seemed such a sacrilege to it. Maria was nearer the truth when she said that money was the only distinction. But Paolo had hold of an eternal truth where hers was only temporal. Only Paolo misapplied this eternal truth. He should not have given Giovanni [another peasant] the inferior status and a fat, mean Italian tradesman the superior. . . . But Paolo could not distinguish between the accident of riches and the aristocracy of spirit. . . . He would have given me anything, trusting implicitly that I would fulfill my own nature as a Signore, one of those more godlike, nearer the light of perfection than himself, a peasant. (Italics mine)

In contemporary Europe, Maria's values have largely won. But not entirely. The old continent was too infected—or too uplifted, if you prefer—by the old traditions of hierarchy and nobility to change utterly. Something remains in the blood, mixed in confusion with other values and ways.

Most fundamentally, the ancient social hierarchy of Europe, surviving intact until very recently and now existing in a debased form, provided men with a continuous visible model for the hierarchy of worth in all things. This order was an ancient view of the world in which there was a natural, fated, and right elevation to all beings. In society there was the ascending order of peasant, artisan, merchant, and lord. In the kingdoms of creation, it was the hierarchy of mineral, vegetable, animal, and human. Even in the kingdoms of the supernatural, there was a hierarchy of saints, angels, and archangels, all leading up to God Himself.

This sense of an inherent, proper, vertical scheme to everything, with an established aristocracy at the top of the human social order, so un-American, still runs like a current of influence and meaning in the European character. It is too mixed, nowadays, with other contrary movements of thought to lend itself to perfectly systematic description. Rather, one must discover it in small subpatterns, almost like cultural slips of the tongue.

The most obvious psychological survival of the old order is

the European's acute consciousness of social class. A Japanese-American student, majoring in physics and passing the summer in France, runs into a French girl of Algerian background at a café. They get to talking. It is one of those romantic moments: the student is smitten and the girl is also. He accompanies her home on the Métro and they agree that he will pick her up the following morning. They only shake hands at her door, but it is a touch full of meaning.

When the student rings the bell the next day, the girl's older brother answers it. He looks the American up and down, defiantly, and after curtly introducing himself says: "Yvette cannot go out with you. I have forbidden it. It is clear what you are and what you are after." The student is shocked and uncertain; it rushes through his mind that he may be dealing with some kind of racist, but he instinctively feels this is not the case. Perhaps prompted by the boy's wondering expression the brother explains himself: "A person of your social class could not be seriously interested in a girl like Yvette, from a working-class background. All you could possibly have in mind is some fast, casual sex and I am not going to let you lead her on and exploit her." So saying, he shut the door firmly in the American's face.

Sociologists and some popular writers pretend that class is as real in America as anywhere else. Certainly Americans are imperfect democrats, but there is a wide gap between Europeans and us in regard to class. It is hard to imagine the incident with Yvette's brother happening in the United States. It has an old-fashioned quality; there is something medieval about it. But it happens quite normally in France. Vertical class divisions are not only still in place in Europe, they are on people's minds. For example, while recurrent attempts to get American workers to think of themselves as a sociopolitical class and to organize themselves accordingly into a political party have been utter failures, in England in the 1980s a major labor leader, threatened with jail by a court injunction, roared his defiance at a mass meeting of workers, promising: "I will be loyal to my *union,* and loyal to my *class!*"

While it would be wrong to conclude that today's Europeans are totally ridden by such hierarchical class consciousness, its presence is strong and nearly ubiquitous. In Great Britain, that cradle of democracy, class consciousness is stronger than almost anywhere else in Europe. The reasons for this have to do with the relative lack of centralized administration in British history, a lack that left the landholding aristocracy in firm charge of their districts. The gentry collected the land tax, commanded the militia, administered the poor law and justice, and virtually monopolized parliamentary representation for centuries after the continental hierarchy had been partially undermined by centralized monarchy.

Because they are almost hyperaware of class difference, the British (and other Europeans) exhibit a great deal of caution when they first meet strangers. In *The Kingdom by the Sea,* the American writer Paul Theroux, who has lived in England for nearly fifteen years, describes an encounter on the cliff near Dover:

> Ahead on the path a person was coming toward me, down a hill four hundred yards away; but whether it was a man or a woman, I could not tell. Some minutes later I saw her scarf and her skirt, and for some more minutes on those long slopes we strode toward each other under the big sky. We were the only people visible in the landscape—there was no one behind either of us. She was a real walker—arms swinging, flat shoes, no dog, no map. It was lovely, too: blue sky above, the sun in the southeast, and a cloudburst hanging like a broken bag in the west. I watched this woman, this fairly old woman, in her warm scarf and heavy coat, a bunch of flowers in her hand—I watched her come on, and I thought: I am not going to say hello until she does.
>
> She did not look at me. She drew level and didn't notice me. There was no other human being in sight on the coast; only a fishing boat out there like a black flatiron. [She] was striding, lifting the hem of her coat with her knees. Now she was a fraction past me, and still stony-faced.
>
> "Morning!" I said.
>
> "Oh." She twisted her head at me. "Good morning!"
>
> She gave me a good smile, because I had spoken first. But if I hadn't, we would have passed each other . . . in that clifftop meadow—not another soul around—five feet apart,

in the vibrant silence that was taken for safety here, without
a word.

Theroux goes on to explain that "talk or chat was not in itself a
friendly gesture in England, as it was in the United States. Speaking to strangers was regarded as challenging in England; it meant
entering a minefield of verbal and social distinctions." In short,
the English are conscious of class differences that can hurt when
they are inadvertently pressed, so they approach new people with
fear, shyness, and caution.

Even in Holland, which is notoriously right-thinking and
progressive, which makes enormous efforts to be democratic and
to share decision-making, where the queen rides a bicycle, and
where the landed aristocracy long ago merged with the upper
bourgeoisie, the old pattern of vertical class consciousness persists. It is true that there is a tradition of democratic consultation
with all ranks of employees—long and frequent nighttime meetings called "*vergadering*"—to the point where an American psychologist at a Dutch university complains to me that he has to
take advice from everyone in the department he chairs in order
to hire a secretary. But the Chair has come to know, as he explains, that "here one is much more conscious of the social hierarchy. Lip service is given to the idea that nobody takes the inherited hierarchy seriously, but it is only lip service." One young
woman from Amsterdam tells me that when she was growing up,
she would be routinely questioned by people she was introduced
to for the first time: "Not only 'What does your father do?,'
'What street do you live on?,' but 'What was your mother's
maiden name?'"

The examination that is routinely conducted in an effort to
place you on the hierarchy extends to the tiny details of appearance. When Euros look you boldly up and down, as they do in
many countries, they are not just making a vague survey. They
are judging you by your shoes. Yes, shoes. I am friendly with a
Belgian count (not the one who snubbed me), who is a true
gentleman in the best aristocratic tradition—full of *gentillesse*,
that untranslatable French word for the best behavior to others.
It signifies a mixture of kindness, gentleness, thoughtfulness, delicacy, and polish. Because the changes of modern life have made
it impossible for him to stay home on his estates, he must go out

into the great competitive world as a stockbroker to make the money that will support his five children in the old style. One day I went to chat with him in his office. After our meeting was finished, when he began unaristocratically rushing to get to a luncheon meeting with a new client, I saw him stop in his tracks, plunge downwards to open the bottom drawer of his desk, pull out a kit, and begin furiously to brush his shoes. He apologized for having to withdraw his attention from me, saying with mixed embarrassment and annoyance: "There are some people who judge you only by your shoes!" Weeks later, I ask him what he meant. He explains to me that the cleanliness and shine of shoes, their quality and price, their appropriateness to the season and the activity, and even their color all count. There is a social language of hierarchy that is spoken sometimes by one's accent, sometimes by one's shoes.

It doesn't take much historical imagination to understand how shoes became such important symbols on a continent where strict class barriers long endured. The lord could afford to be well shod: he had people to clean his boots and he had many pairs for different purposes. In the days when the streets of cities were open sewers so noxious that one could smell eighteenth-century Berlin six miles before getting there, the aristocrat was above the muck. While others walked, he rode, first on horseback, then in coaches and sedan chairs. Peasants or even bourgeois would be dirtier, their shoes of poorer quality or more worn because they were the only pair. Indeed, until well into this century, many of the European rural masses had no shoes at all, or they had one pair reserved only for feast-day wearing. Accordingly, now in many European countries, people who would escape the harsher glances of vertical social estimation will busy themselves in an immaculate conception and reconception of their feet. Even counts from old families who have been forced into trade do it. And, as an American living in Europe, I have been driven, with coaching from European friends, in the "right" direction. I have given up that Bohemian, college-boy habit of buying one pair of loafers at a time and wearing them until they give out. Now I buy expensive, solid, British clumpers—of evident quality (at least it is evident, I am told, to those who care) and impeccable lineage. I keep them clean and brushed shiny, and alternate them so they look lively. My Euro friends and family have told me these habits will keep certain people in certain countries, from hasty bad judgments of me. I can report that the tactic works.

The ancient cascades of social evaluation and disdain only strike the American who stays around for a while. Europeans, at first, cannot fit us into their hierarchy and don't even try to examine or "place" individuals who are plainly ignorant even of the importance of shoes. But, eventually, they will try to fix you—not all of them by any means, but a surprising number who are at once victims and practitioners of the old ways.

The longer I have lived in Europe, the more I have felt it. I have, for example, an acquaintance, a physician in Germany. In his provincial city, Heinz is *the* doctor, as far as the American consulate is concerned. They send him all the ailing tourists, students, and traveling businessmen. He jokes with mingled pride and scorn: "They have appointed me 'Official Local Medical Officer.' They even gave me a certificate so I could prove it." (Understood: "As if a respectable person like myself, from a good, old, bourgeois family, has need of such proof.")

When I first met him, years ago, he treated me with great respect and sweetness. He prides himself, rightly, on what he calls his "humanitarian attitude." As the years have gone on, however, he confesses that he has "soured on people"—he hates the new "rushing, the bad manners, the erosion of privilege among the professional classes, the disappearance of what I will call 'society' in the new and ever more democratic Europe." Perhaps it is only this general disillusionment that has affected his attitude toward me, but I think not. I have felt the nets closing for some time. His wife, Magda, who was always cynical and disillusioned, has also changed. Over the years, they have taken my social pulses: money, fame, power, acquaintance. Once, Heinz says jocularly: "I am a snob." But despite his chuckle at assuming what must be thought of as an attitude, it is in fact no joke. His contempt toward me builds until it is the reciprocal of what he divines to be my social weight. He becomes less available on the telephone, his wife more easily bored. Gradually, she gets more obvious. One night at dinner at their place, she wants to know *where* exactly my house is in San Francisco, even though she has never been there. I become certain she will check out the neighborhood with other Germans who know the city. When a highly favorable review of the German translation of my last book appears in the city newspaper, she wants to know: "How did you manage that?" Jacqueline, perhaps rightly, finds the question insulting. My own analysis is more neutral: "I think she's just still collecting information. She's double-checking to make sure she's got me pegged rightly, that I don't, for example, know people in this town who might be more important than she is." As long as we live in the city, like careful spies, Magda and Heinz continue to collect background information on me, to check and double-check and eventually to consign me with obvious contempt to some social lower depths once they learn that, in their terms, I am not more potent than they.

Because of the hierarchical tradition, with aristocrats being absolutely supreme, the European has different feelings toward his own and others' social station than Americans do. A lower-class child grows up to have contempt for himself and comes to want to stay in his own safe place, down there at the bottom; were he to challenge traditional social ordering, he would risk the contempt of others. Consequently, the European worker is not as ambitious or restless as the American. He expects, in return for his work and humility, to be taken care of by someone—nowadays the government, in the old days the *seigneur*—a reward for his docility. He, in turn, has contempt for the bourgeoisie, whom he judges by the old aristocratic standards. The bourgeoisie frequently shares this contempt for itself, viewing its own trappings of aristocracy—a concern with refined eating, for instance—as "bourgeois," a pretension. Though the bourgeois and the lower-class person also, at times and paradoxically, express contempt for aristocrats (as being themselves no better than they should be, arrogant, effete, stupidly outdoorsy, unproductive, and so forth), they are nevertheless imbued with a belief in the rightness of some old, known, and predetermined social order.

This belief explains the scorn, bizarre to an American, that one still encounters toward the "self-made man." Take the case of an Italian whose father was a letter carrier and mother a housemaid. He left school at fourteen and entered the army, making sure he survived his occupation service in France. When Italy surrendered to the Allies, he enterprisingly bought himself civilian clothes and filtered past Gestapo checkpoints in the Milan railway station to get back home to safety in Perugia. The rest of the war he spent in prudent hiding, and then he emerged to make a small fortune in earth-moving equipment.

He is, like many self-made millionaires the world over, radiant with energy. His face has the high color of a man whose blood courses easily. He is not nervous, but there is a constant agitation, a habit of motion. Even now, in retirement at sixty, he never stops. He still keeps an office in the giant depot where his daughter and former colleagues manage the old concern. When there is little for him to do, he prowls the countryside in an old Mercedes looking for real estate deals. He has bought the land next door to the depot and installed an immense series of hot-houses. Let other men stoop to cultivating the proverbial small garden of the retired. At night, or during the long afternoon lunch breaks, he bottles his own oil, makes his own wine, and displays with pride his enormous *cantina:* a half-basement with sturdy bars on the window, packed with brimming wine casks, terra-cotta vats of oil as big as Ali Baba's, giant tables at which to entertain his family and acquaintances. Felled by a heart attack, he looks healthier a mere three weeks later than he did before.

In America, such men are admired. A little larger than life, and a lot bigger than other mortals who strive in an open society for fortune, they are even slightly feared. In Perugia, people defer to him because he is rich. But there are few, even those who have made money as he has, who will not also reveal, some of the time, a certain scorn: *"Corrado, lui è un 'self-made man.'"* They say it in English but with a little contempt. For them, like the majority of Europeans, such people are just a little amusing. They are still partly viewed from the perspective of an old Europe nearly gone, in which it was right to keep one's place faithfully, doing the job that God and society had assigned you: nobles to fight, clergy to pray, others to work. Corrado is automatically suspected of pretension, because in some vague way he has risen against the laws of custom and, perhaps, even of nature.

In developing his threefold typology of character—tradition-directed, inner-directed, and other-directed—sociologist David Riesman, seemed most American in admiring the inner-directed quality of the nineteenth-century entrepreneur. This is the man who set his internal compass himself and who heroically charted his course and followed it: the Christopher Columbuses of commerce. For the tradition-directed European, on the other hand, I observe that heroes are more likely to have aristocratic qualities. Even when he is openly impressed and deferential, secretly the European is likely to view the successful entrepreneur as a low type who is not, as we see him, a man who made both his fortune and himself but is, instead, a creature made by the market. Corrado's ilk are seen as shifting, bending types, agitatedly trimming their sails to every change in the winds of commerce, every whim of other merchants and of consumers, every fad and fashion. The "self-made man" is viewed then as if he were a crafty *pícaro,* a kind of low rogue, almost a servant to the fickle vectors of survival and prosperity. Instinctively and subconsciously, he is unfavorably compared to the true lord, he who was constant because he inherited a tradition that trained him to be only a certain way: *Semper Fidelis.* The entrepreneur—and the more successful he is the more he is submitted to such stereotypes of judgment—is shifty, a slave, a man who will do anything not for an old inwardly held class ideal but for money. In the English mind, he is a "bounder," someone who will use any means to bound to the top, to get to the head of the line.

Americans generally are seen as people without real loyalties in existence, people who are obsessed with profiting from circumstances rather than with living life according to real values. Of course, there is often some truth in this. Nevertheless, European contempt for us, and, more importantly, their contempt for themselves and for one another, is cancerous—it clouds the vision and eats humanity.

What is ultimately behind this contempt is the belief that hierarchy is not, as it is thought to be in the United States, functional. Americans will let him be on top who does best what it takes to be on top, whatever the game being played may be: baseball, business, politics, and so forth. Europeans take a more formal view, as if they were saying: We know what kind of person is a top person, and such a person is tops in general. That is, his topness partakes of that diffuse superiority of the old nobility, including not only wealth, power, and prerogative but attributes of mind and being. So, for instance, an old Italian friend, a long-time professor of classical archaeology, let slip a telltale remark when I told him about a new acquaintance, a professor of modern history. "Yes, I know him," says Rodrigo, "at least I have seen

him at the university. But he is not a great one—*non è un grande.*"
Now who, I wonder to myself, asked Rodrigo whether he
thought Marcello was "great"? *I* didn't. But Rodrigo, like many
Europeans, is applying and defending a rule of the vertical order
of men that includes "greatness" among its criteria for social elevation as, for instance, to a professorial chair. If you are important, then you should be great.

In the old aristocratic notion of glory, a true knight was not
just a man good with a sword; according to the older notion, he
was also a glorious man—a paragon of many virtues, who legit-
imately and intrinsically towered over others in his very essence.
According to such a notion, it is not enough to be an adequate
professor, or even a good professor. A professor should be splendid, glorious, like God, just as anyone at the top of any hierarchy
should be. Behind this notion again is the idea of the single chain
of being from rock up to God, with a human hierarchy in the
middle where all individuals have their precise rank and no
changing places is allowed. According to such a way of looking
at things, people are born generally superior, inferior, or in the
middle. Accordingly, Euros, much more than we, attempt to
identify talented individuals early and to support them and pre-
pare them for their place in the hierarchy (which, from a certain
point of view, they already occupy). These individuals acquire,
therefore, certain general qualities of character, intellect, and
manners—a style of being which includes the air of superiority.
This style of being may involve, naturally, a fair amount of condescension toward inferiors. Corrado, our self-made man, has
money, but he should have something more: he should bear the
traditional marks of a high person and, because he made himself,
he doesn't. He has been rough, rude, pushing himself forward,
and he remains rude, out of place in a preformed scheme. Similarly, as I have mentioned before, no European I have ever met
could fully understand or accept the fact that "in the United
States even an actor can be elected President!" Even in a democracy, only those of a certain kind, by talent recognized soon after
birth and then by training, should be important leaders.

As an American, I always feel pride in conversations about
our presidents. Unlike Europeans, I was brought up to feel a
certain democratic satisfaction that someone not a politician, not
born into high social class, not born rich, and not selected for

early training to be a member of an administrative elite could be elected president. The European, on the contrary, feels that there is something inexplicable and wrong here. When a European political leader is not of high social class, it is assumed he will have been chosen early for his leadership qualities and groomed accordingly to look high class. The American, however, is virtually trained to feel uncomfortable with the presence in high office of high-born people, fancy people, people too well-spoken, too well-educated. We prefer a rail-splitter for president, someone in whom we can see the manners and qualities of a regular guy. People had to adjust to Franklin Roosevelt's patrician accent and aristocratic cigarette holder, and as for John Kennedy—well, he worked in shirt-sleeves, was an honest-to-goodness war hero, spoke with a regional, not a class, accent, wouldn't wear a hat, had a father who had probably been a bootlegger, was the first of his minority group to be elected, and so, in a way, still had to work his way up. In Europe, on the contrary, politicians of all political persuasions tend to have similar elite educations, accents, manners, clothes, and other tokens of class.

The old leveling tradition in America is falsely democratic in the eyes of many Europeans, who believe it impedes the full expression of innate superiority. It pretends too much that everybody is the same, whereas, in theory anyway, everybody only has the same opportunity, not the same talent. An American acquaintance of mine was dazzlingly bright as a child, one of those children who answered the most recondite questions on radio and television as a Quiz Kid. From his earliest years, he had read widely and remembered it all. He went to a decent regional private elementary school, his parents were a well-educated lawyer and a writer, he had a number of what we Americans would call other advantages. But, like other American prodigies, he feels he has been frustrated. He now occupies a chair at a major university and has achieved an international reputation as a historian, but he believes that he could have gone much farther. His old Viennese-born psychoanalyst, a good European, though long transplanted to the United States, agrees with him: "Had you been born in Europe, yours would have been a higher destiny. You would have received special coaching from the beginning. Instead of having to start learning Latin and Greek in your prep school, you would have started as early as possible; in your case that might have been age three, even two. You would have had the same backing for any talent you showed, for example, in mathematics, about which you have continued regrets that you didn't go further. You started too late and are right to feel resentment toward your parents. But you must forgive them. They couldn't have done better. They were Americans and here, even among the high bourgeoisie, there is no understanding of such things."

In Europe, still, the image of hierarchy extends to the family, which, despite many changes, as we have noticed already, is still stronger than in the United States. Individuals maintain ties to their kin, and these tend to be hierarchical.

Women are still more or less ranked lower than men. Even when wives are working professionals in two-career couples, as is often the case, role differentiation between the sexes continues to be prevalent and at least a formal subordination of women obtains. Many European women accept this situation for a number of reasons. First, the continued existence of a feminine role and a woman's world gives them prestige if not symmetrical equality or dominance. Secondly, despite formal subordination, women have preserved many traditional ways to exert influence and power. Finally, the accepted legitimacy of the hierarchical idea makes them more content with their position than American women would be.

Though there is much variation from country to country and, above all, from south to north, respect is still extended by children to father and mother and to the oldest people in the extended family, including ancestors. Persistent European habits of saving in order to leave inheritances to their children tend to justify and reinforce this hierarchical ordering of the family by age. Parents believe they have the right to make their kids do as *they* wish and, so, European children are still generally much better behaved (the old word would be *disciplined*) than American children. Little Mark or Marc or Marco or Marcos is taught to behave like a well-mannered adult when in company. When you arrive, a five-year-old boy solemnly comes over and shakes your hand or gives you a ritual kiss on the cheek. Then he goes back to sit quietly on his chair—for what seems a miraculously long time to the American visitor. Even European dogs fit the picture. They are much less unruly than American dogs; they too are taught their place.

The hierarchical ordering by age practiced in family life is reflected out of the clan in a more general attitude I shall call *seniority*. Euros are much more conscious than we are of the privileges of age. Generally, their old people are better taken care of by the state and other public organizations than ours are. In many European countries, an older worker applying for any job *must*, by law, be paid more than a younger one. Naturally, this often means that if he leaves or loses his job after a certain age (in some countries as young as forty), an older worker is never hired again; young people are so much cheaper to hire for the same work. In Italy, I find a particularly striking example of the principle of un-American seniority. Franco Morelli is thirty-one years old, bright, big, handsome, and energetic. Like some Europeans of his generation, he has a certain American-style restlessness and drive. He has asked me several times how the sales of my last book are going. Though naïve about the world of writers and publishing, he feels the impulse to encourage and even push me. He says: "You'll become very famous! You'll become very rich!"

"Oh, no," I say. "I'm no longer interested. Besides, I'm forty-seven, too old now for all that. I don't even think of such things. They say that if you haven't made your millions by the time you're forty, you never will."

He looks at me with a surprised air and asks: "Who says that?"

"Well, they say that in America," I reply, puzzled at his surprise.

"That's not the way it is over here," he says, with bitterness.

"How is it?"

"I can't get anywhere in business yet. I'm too young. You can't begin to think of promotion even to moderately high places until you're fifty. My whole generation is frustrated, because all the top posts and even the middle ones are occupied by older men who will stay there or get promoted higher until they die or retire."

After a moment's reflection, he resumes: "You know, if you apply even for a government job here, your age counts decisively.

My cousin just took a competitive exam to become a school teacher. You get 'points,' formal *punti,* for various things—education, experience, having to support children. Four hundred people took the test for three jobs. She scored as high as another person at the top of the list, but he got the job. You know why? Because he was born in the same leap-year year, on February 28, and she was born on February 29! Can you imagine such a stupid way of selecting people?"

Verticality also influences social behavior wherever leadership is involved. A New York psychiatrist who has worked in Paris for years says about the French: "If you want to play games here, *act* like an authority." Whereas Americans are inclined to question authority, Europeans, after all the grumblings and contentions, have a strong need to give themselves over to authority. The American sociologist in Holland observed to me: "There is much less skepticism about authority or high position here. People feel that the member of the elite truly *merits his position.* Consequently, though he must go through all the motions of consultation, the *vergadering,* the man of the *elite* (one who has an elite position) "must act like a true authority. The man should exercise his power delicately but carry an aura of entitlement and prestige that to our eyes seems quite undemocratic."

The respect for leaders is a deep reflex in the European character and embodies the ancient belief that some people are rightly born to rule, a belief that crosses all political lines. The wife of an acquaintance of mine from graduate school often feels driven to speak about her problems with working in Italy. She and her husband, Lawrence, have lived there for nearly fifteen years, she working as a physiotherapist. A serious professional woman in the American mold, Ellen is dedicated to the service of her patients. For years, she complained about being exploited and unrecognized while working as a teacher under a full professor (informally, they are known as "*baroni,*" barons). So she quit. Now, we are talking at a café about her new job in a small rural city, a center of cloth manufacturing in the north of Italy.

"I thought I had found something unusual in this country," she says, "a place where I could work in a truly effective way." As so often happens in Italy, she tells me, a group of local communists got elected to municipal government and then tried to root out antique corruption and set community affairs on an efficient and fair basis. "When they came in ten years ago, they put young leadership in office, started many new projects, reached out to include the people and to serve them. I'm not a Communist, of course, nor does ideology enter into my choice of living here—which is very inconvenient for Lawrence, who has to work an hour away. It's just that the general atmosphere was so progressive. The people here created their own way of socializing, for example, and not just at *carnevale* and *feste* either. They organize trips to the mountains just to fly kites and eat together; or they organize dancing lessons for old people. It's the kind of imaginative, aggressive, community activism that sometimes you have on a volunteer basis back home. It extended to setting up the job I have—they invited me here as part of a new, small, community health care team they wanted. All this helps people to deal with or get away from difficult, tiring, and boring jobs. It enriches their lives, cares for their bodies and even their souls.

"But despite all these efforts and the family feeling which has arisen among much of the population of Vincenzi—about nine thousand people—everything and everybody is totally dependent on their leaders. It's the same in my health care team. Everything depends on the doctor, who's only there two days a week. This drives me crazy. There's no real cooperation with me from the psychologist, or the learning specialist, or the nurse. Nor among themselves. I thought I was going to have real colleagues. I'm very disappointed."

She goes on to detail how, despite an attempt to enlist active participation among the people themselves, "they all look to the new community leadership that replaced the old leadership of the *padroni,* the Big Daddies, the landowning masters. If it weren't for Roberto, the mayor, and half a dozen other enthusiastic public officials, all reform would stop. And new people don't join the leadership. Oh, they discuss, argue, debate: they wouldn't be Italians if they didn't. But it disturbs me as an American how they are happy to leave things to these few energetic men. It's as if they believed that others, especially certain others, must always lead and they follow. They just cross their arms and go along for the ride."

An American journalist who worked for the Spanish subsidiary of a multinational corporation recalls his astonishment when, as editor of the in-house paper, he attended many meetings of the president and vice-president, five divisional managers, and three regional managers. "They were all Spanish. Following the parent company's American management style, if there was a problem of some sort, they would go around the table and discuss it. But the lower people just wouldn't talk. They'd back off, try not to answer questions. After a little while, only the two chief people ever spoke, although everyone came."

He muses for a moment, searching to find an explanation: "I come from Florida, a long time back. But this happened in a modern European country only a couple of years ago. Yet it was like the Old South, asking a black to sit down in a white's house— 'That's all right, ma'am. I'll just stand.' And those junior managers were all very successful guys, they drove Porsches and Simca-Matras!

"Once, they got this group together because the head of the whole multinational came for a visit. The subsidiary manufactured and sold manure spreaders, harvesters, and so on. The CEO wanted it to be a brainstorming session about how to get Spanish farmers to buy larger machinery even though the farms are smaller here. The American felt that European farmers could be induced to buy this stuff. He wanted to know: 'What's the situation like in your territory? How should sales be approached?' The Europeans, all of them, especially the three most junior guys, wanted to defer to the guy above them. They were very uneasy and they wouldn't say much of anything.

"At last, this guy from the States got angry. He leaned over at one of them: 'Listen, fella, don't you *know anything* about your district?' Finally, the Spaniard talked, but with great reluctance."

All the many reasons for such behavior revolve around a collective agreement about what is proper to hierarchy. A strong fear exists that the higher-up will get you if you seem to move in on his perch. *He* believes he has the right to do so. The fear is increased by the knowledge that to make a mistake even in the appearances of precedence would be to risk perpetual vengeance, for in Europe people tend to stay in the particular hierarchy to which they belong. Managers, for example, like members of other groups, don't generally jump from one organization to another, as people more often do in the United States. Thus, even if your angry boss gets promoted, word will be passed down about you, the uppity subordinate, and appropriate measures taken by the hierarchy, forever.

The subordinate's reluctance to step out of place, even by answering direct questions, has even deeper roots in the feeling that *the higher person* is supposed to know and to answer. Still more profound is the feeling that each person has his own level and competence. It was astonishing to me, as an American, to realize, even in these late days, when the old ways of the kaiser are so long gone, that sober, critical, and even self-critical West Germans—a schoolteacher-painter who votes for the Green party, a socialist nurse who survived the Second World War but lost her father and husband—would tell me that in their country, despite everything, the old Prussian watchwords of *Pflicht und Gehorsam,* "Duty and Obedience," still had a deep place in people's souls. They even admitted, with a certain bitter melancholy, that these words still mean something to them personally, rebellious types though they are. It would be foolish to maintain that West Germans are old Prussian soldiers of yore, or that the various European nationalities resemble Germans in the degree to which they are inclined to follow authority. Nevertheless, as a consequence of motives ranging from functional fear of reprisal down through deeper-rooted responses to notions of propriety, reverence, and competence, Europeans will often show themselves willing to be what seems to us subservient and even craven. For them, rank is right and helps give order to the world in business as in the family and government.

In the most subtle ways imaginable, the old hierarchical idea runs like a figure in a carpet, ever more worn and faint but still part of the pattern, through the European's mentality. I think it not fanciful to suggest that the greater European tendency toward abstraction is tied up with the collective memory of an unchanging hierarchical order. Reality, in William James's phrase, is a "vast buzzing confusion," but the ancient social structure of Europe made a clear human order. That orderliness gave Europeans the habit of seeing people and things in abstract classes, and in so doing gave them the desire to approach the human preoccupations of art, politics, philosophy, literature, history, with the abstraction of "isms": Futurism, Impressionism, Fascism, Symbolism, an ism for every need and moment. As is well known, Americans are much less inclined—although there are many exceptions—toward this kind of thing.

Then, too, the lingering memory of the church-blessed hierarchical order in human life accounts in part for the European tendency to love "tradition." That is, to cling to the old when possible. What was done, like the social structure within which it once took place, comes to the European trailing clouds of inevitability, depth, honor and glamor. Viewed anew from this perspective, the European attitude to time and things past is not only a functional method of slowing up and thereby more effectively dealing with an ever more hurried world. It is also a product of the long experience of a relatively unchanging vertical system. Ask a European to explain why he loves "tradition," and chances are he cannot do so. An American is even harder pressed to understand this European love, though we maintain some collective traditions of our own still. Americans tend to indulge in what seems, to others, a lawless impulse to make everything new.

Because Europeans tend to feel every person is hierarchically in his right place, they also tend to believe in the "rightness" or "wrongness" of many things. Accordingly, a greater intellectual certainty and a drive toward ever more certainty will often erupt in Europeans, aspects of intellectual style that go far beyond any American hankering after consensus. The mass movements of fascism and communism are only the most extreme and destructive examples of how this yearning for rightness and simple organization can surface from the depths of a culture which has known, for long centuries, such clarity.

These tendencies to classification, abstraction, traditionalism, and rightness make a clump of qualities in the European mentality which derives from a tradition-directed past not long gone and whose vestiges, as in the survival of the aristocracy as a group and of kings and queens, continue into our day. Traditionalist cultures like the European will naturally have, even in modernist phases, remnants of old ways of thought. Obviously, these traditionalist elements will be much greater than in countries like our own, of refugees, immigrants, adventurers, cultists, and seekers of every kind, where traditions of all sorts were constantly being challenged.

Less obvious is the connection between certain other aspects of their hierarchical past and the way Europeans are nowadays. Earlier, we talked about aggressive intellectuality as a defense. One could also see it as a transfer to the mental realm of certain aristocratic norms of old: the cultivation of strength, the joy of combat, the assertion of personal honor, the prestige of fighting and victory, and, finally, the formerly close connection between fighting and truth—as among knights who were pledged to the defense of the church. One should also make another direct connection with the old noble custom of ritualized combat. Gradually disarmed and democratized, the modern European transfers such exercises in bellicosity to the domain of argument. No wonder, the schools have prepared him to do this. Children rehearse for lifelong intellectual jousting in such school exercises as this one from Germany (its parallel exists nearly everywhere else): "Helmut, stand up! Please talk for five minutes about why trams are better than busses." (He talks, confidence increasing with the passing minutes). "Now, Helmut, please talk for five minutes on why busses are better than trams." What is this but the intellectualization of a squire's training with lance, broadsword, and ax? The violent background of the highest in society helps set the tone for some of current intellectual style.

Similarly, a number of other traits which we have considered from the viewpoint of defenses of personality also look backward to the old aristocrats. Certainly, the European taste for leisure is one. Besides, in a hierarchically ordered society there was no point in working much because you couldn't get very much for it. Also, the whole drama of self-presentation and the general sense of social life as theater have some of their origins in the leisured playful activities of an upper class seeking imaginative ways to affirm its difference from those who were only concerned with the utilitarian and the necessary: those obsessions with work and reproduction which even from before classical times have distinguished slaves from free men. Likewise, traits of pride, privacy, and a sense of personal dignity, while serving good defensive functions for the personality, acquire some of their coloration and importance from a process of imitation of the aristocratic higher-ups with their *fierté* and *orgueil*. When the miserable Breton peasant said, not long before 1900, "Since I am too poor to buy any other horse, at least the Horse of Pride will always have a stall in my stable," he mounted his steed like a knight.

Even a generalized European rage for social order comes from the hierarchical tradition. Europeans are often disturbed by the lack of a centralized administration for all political and legal matters in America. They don't really like the differences in local and state laws which seem to them to complicate American life and make it messy. Though they complain about their governments much more than Americans do, they would be profoundly uncomfortable if their centralized administrative hierarchy of bureaucracy was removed. They like the fact that there is a system, just as they like to bend their energies toward ingenious individual combinations of both joining and beating it—as, for example, the man who gets a safe but low-paid government post but works on the side secretly, avoiding paying taxes which, ironically, could raise his salary on his government job.

Going over the list of character traits in the chapter on the defended European personality, the reader can easily think for himself how many of these are in part derived from and shaped by the tradition of hierarchy with aristocracy at the top. The very image we have used for the defended European personality—the prince in his castle—is itself derived from those same traditions.

Happily, old aristocratic habits also influence European life in high and noble ways, as, for instance, in manners at their best. A view on this subject is opened by the comments of a fortyish Belgian physicist, Roland Dupont, with whom I have occasionally sought some truth on matters European. We are riding one day to Paris, alone in a compartment on one of those mournful trains which speed across the bleak Belgian flatlands to France. He is balding, but there is still something childlike about him. I know he comes from a "good" upper-middle-class family, that he had two servants in the house when he grew up, plus a governess whose sister was, by marriage, a "countess." More than many of his class, Roland is a man who has a deep interest in the *ancien régime:* he loves to relate anecdotes about the court of Louis XIV—the striking *bon mot,* the impressive pose. One of Roland's most winning characteristics is his availability to others. Despite the press of his own affairs, and though he is by no means affluent anymore, he is always ready to do a favor or answer a need. He is one of a great many people I have asked about aristocracy in the old and new Europe and about how they would explain it to Americans. His answers to my questions are revealing.

"*Les autres existent,*" he says, "'other people exist.' I would suppose that here is the essence. The aristocratic temper requires that one recognize this fact. Of course, this is just common sense and a basically ethical attitude. But there is a particular charge and character to it. Others exist, including people who don't have the same opportunities. My parents, and my governess, always said, 'Don't forget you've been privileged.'"

It is not clear yet what the charge or character is, but as he goes on to talk about his Dutch governess, some of its meaning emerges: "She had a great sense of caste. Her uncle had been president-general, the English would say 'governor-general,' of Jakarta when Indonesia was the Dutch East Indies. When a tradesman who entered the kitchen treated her familiarly as a servant, she dismissed him: '*Een echte proletariër,* a real proletarian; he doesn't see the difference.' She taught us: '*Quant-à-soi!*' That we weren't supposed to be familiar, to have tea with anyone, for instance."

"Do you have this sense of castelike separation?"

He thinks, then admits: "Perhaps. In a certain way. I feel that there are differences in people's education—not formal education, rather what the French mean when they say a person is '*bien*' or '*mal éduqué.*' You could call it a difference in manners, but it's more than that. Deeper attitudes are implied. I have a great pleasure being with someone who has what we call *l'exquise courtoisie,* for instance. This comes back to my original point. It means avoiding hurts, making things soft. There is a code of a gentleman: *dignité, tenue, courtoisie*—a universal *bienveillance* for everyone. One should never hurt people. For instance, even if you're rich or educated, when you meet others, you are conscious of such norms and that your privileges demand courtesy. This is different from being merely 'nice.' It requires a thoughtful interest in the other and deciphering his desires and needs and doing your best, within moral limits, to fill them."

It is interesting, as our exploration of these concepts continues, to note how, not only old aristocratic ideals, like courtesy, but a prevailing wish for elevation appears in much of what Roland says. Roland mentions a colleague who is proud of an old aunt, a village notable, who with "force, an awareness of her difference, and a sense of command and obligation, walks the fields and points with her cane, in regard to a public construction project, 'Here is where the new road will go.' Many people are very proud of such aristocratic relatives."

"Why?" I ask.

"Because there is something heroic about it." I am pressing Roland and his physicist's mind is trying to do logical work on a subject that doesn't have quite a linear quality, even though, as he speaks, the underlying themes reveal themselves. "I was also taught you should never be *petit,* small. There are equivalents to the phrase I am about to use, I think, in all European languages, and everyone who understands aristocracy I think would say, one should be *grand seigneur,* a great lord. That is, one is not small and one is so in a fashion that has the self-regard of theater.

"In a subtle way, one is always reaching for a higher level. So, someone who has absorbed this attitude would say, at least in the old days, *'Je suis votre serviteur,'* 'I am your servant,' and the other would probably reply, *'Non, non, je suis le vôtre!,'* 'No, no, I am *yours!'* A generous, magnanimous, noble liberality. An attitude which comprehends both the need to give and the superiority that comes from giving: attention, favors, courtesy, even material largess. As when we entertain people at home, spending so much to make them feel comfortable, to feel honored, to meet their preferences in food and drink, to serve something exceptionally good so that they will have a pleasure from it. Or, at a restaurant, when we Europeans *always* insist on paying the bill, with us there is this rivalry in being large of spirit and gesture. Or, since the time when dueling was outlawed, the habit of never returning an insult, being above that. When my colleague—the one with the aunt in the village—and I talk about physicists, we automatically put people on levels according to these values. We'll say, 'You can't imagine Professor X doing something like that.' 'Of course,' the other will remark, 'he is too much *grand seigneur.'*

"Another word is *mesquin*—a hard one to translate: it doesn't only mean *petit,* small and small-minded. It means 'cheap' in one's attitudes and behavior, 'low,' 'shabby' in a moral way and in one's whole way of being. It's reflected in the man who never tips because it isn't technically necessary when there is already a service charge in a restaurant, or the man who doesn't try to pay the check in company, the man whose life is a calculation of profit and loss to the nearest sou, not just in money but in everything. Or, to go back to what I said at the beginning, that lack of considering others first: *courtoisie*. In many Europeans, even when they are *petit* or *mesquin* by nature, there is a part of them that rises up inside, like some old count to do battle."

As he says this, I notice that we have arrived: large, tenementlike apartment blocks, modern, new but already shabby, have begun to appear outside the compartment window, mile after mile of them, announcing that we have entered the edge of greater Paris. For twenty minutes, the facts of modern massification and then the arrival in the dirty, cast-iron, Gare du Nord seem to mock Roland's visions of elevation even in the small details of human relationships.

And yet my experience is that in manners, many Europeans of all classes are still often influenced by the old figure of the *grand seigneur*. I think of the Belgian accountant, intensely practical, who complains with exasperation that her brother-in-law, an attorney, continues to lavish hospitality on his friends even when, because of business reverses, he cannot for the moment afford it. I think also of the old psychiatrist, Roberto Assagioli, whose psychological institute was wracked by the intense quarrels of different factions, much like Freud's before him. One day, after watching the heavy exchange of accusations and counterclaims among his agitated young followers, he retired upstairs to his study and remarked to his assistant: *"Hai visto, come al mercato!"* "Did you see, just like at the market:" haggling unworthy of that image of nobility still carried by many Europeans.

Here is the opposing counterpart of the old ambassador's quality of being *malin*—of that foxy shifting taught by having to survive, of the practical shrewdness, the watching out for number one, the doing what is useful and productive above all other values. When, as so often befalls the hapless American visitor abroad, a European acquaintance will have mysteriously, imperiously, firmly commandeered a check at a restaurant, it is the *grand seigneur,* in charge and still riding.

One wishes that he would ride through more of contemporary European life—yet perhaps, in a way, he does. A clue is provided me when a French count of very old lineage (Leonardo da Vinci died in the family château) remarks: *"Le ciment de l'Europe actuelle c'est la bourgeoisie qui fait semblant d'être aristo-crate"* ("The cement of present-day Europe is the middle-class people who act as if they were aristocrats"). I think then of my friend Jean-Louis, in whose family home are no ancestral suits of armor, who has no patents of nobility, who works hard for a good living as owner-editor of several magazines. But he is, in so many ways, an aristocrat: from the leisurely way he puts on an expensive glove, reflecting calmly on both the act and the subject of conversation, to his extraordinary generosity of attention and wealth. When I ask him if he thinks of himself as an aristocrat, he first makes sure that I understand there is no blue blood in question and then adds: "But in another way, perhaps. Since you insist on my saying what that means, it means faithfulness to a family name, a willingness to have discipline and courage and to give service to what is important. And teaching these values to your children." I have seen him behave accordingly—*grand sei-gneur*—mocking a crypto-fascist politician in a television debate by opposing his own severe humanism and elegance of manner to the other's rabble-rousing racism. Even his consenting to de-bate with this particular politician is dangerous for Jean-Louis and requires an elevated principle and courage, because the other has many thugs in his entourage who would hurt their leader's antagonists without even being asked.

Jean-Louis is an example of a man who, having become one of Europe's important people, naturally takes on the mantle of its aristocratic traditions. Such individuals—and they are impres-sive—tend to assume that their privileges are deserved, that they justifiably assume an elevated attitude, that they must be con-scious of their differences from others, and, finally, that they must take care of others: *noblesse oblige.*

I think of a man I often consult about developments at the Common Market, one of its most senior civil servants. He is a tall, lean political scientist who stutters shyly and politely in the Oxbridge manner. His personality, however, is a strong one, and he lets you know it when he says, for example: "The European political and administrative elite now coming into power—people between forty and fifty—are determined, one way or an-other, to stitch Europe together: there *will* be a true European community." We had been talking about the seemingly hopeless cause of European integration, and I had pointed out how most people generally shrug their shoulders with contempt at the whole subject, and that the newspapers are constantly reporting crises and blocks. But he lets me behind the scenes to look at it from a privileged point of view not at all public or even democratic. An "elite," the chosen few, have already set a course for the continent. No longer aristocrats by blood, they have slipped, nonetheless, into the old high niches in the grand old ways. They too feel themselves heirs to the rights, privileges, power, and duties of the *grands seigneurs*.

So the great chain of being survives. Anyone who lives with Europeans will meet it at home in myriad small ways. My wife is in many ways an old-fashioned woman. She dresses with exquisite care, her manners are sublime and elevate those with whom she comes in contact, her sense of aesthetic delight in the things of everyday is acute and charms others—despite the fact that she is trained as a lawyer, has traveled widely in the modern world both in Europe and North America, and has lived in several countries on the two continents. Nevertheless, because of her deep sense of tradition, often she seems to make manifest the very core of the old Europe that still remains. Sometimes this extends to little prejudices that an American will find amazing but also charming. Such was what I have come to call in my own mind the "silver spoon episode," a momentary event but revelatory of how deeply, among Europeans, the old sense of vertical order in all things will sometimes still prevail.

One day, troubled by a succession of colds, Jacqueline went to her doctor and then, cheered by hope in the new liquid medicine he has given her, to her mother's house in Brussels. "I've got to take it three times a day," she says. "Because Stuart and I are driving to Florence right away, I should borrow a silver spoon from the house."

"Of course," her mother agrees. "I'll get you one."

I say, "Jacqueline, if you take one of those old silver spoons, we might lose it on the trip. Take a stainless-steel one, or one of those plastic spoons we have for picnics."

"Oh, no, I couldn't do that," Jacqueline says.

"Why not?" I ask.

"The stainless-steel surface might come off the spoon and what's beneath could contaminate the medicine," she says. "And the same is true for the plastic one. No, for something important like making sure the medication is really allowed to work, I have to be careful. It must be silver."

Her mother produces the spoon. "Here," she says, handing it over. Jacqueline beams with the air of one arming herself against disease with both the right medicine and the right accessory equipment. A tiny surge of confidence that cure will come passes between mother and daughter, the hopeful medical moment. It is unspoiled by the rejected American suggestion and its pretense, patently ridiculous, of reasonableness and practicality.

Some Americans and even certain new-fangled Europeans would dismiss Jacqueline's and her mother's insistence on silver as "ignorant" and "superstitious." To do so would be wrong. In the first place, Jacqueline, the only child of an engineer, knows something about chemistry and physics. In the second place, to look at the incident in purely practical terms is to miss its real meaning. I myself learned only much after the silver spoon episode what really took place there. Modern materials such as stainless steel or plastic and old ones like tin or wood are useful, but to Europeans who retain a sense of the old order, silver is better, higher, more noble. If Americans also retain traces of such activities—because actually they are archetypal in the human psyche—we do so much less. One cannot imagine modern Americans as educated as Jacqueline and her mother insisting on silver. But in the heart of the traditional European, for certain high purposes only silver will do.

PART FOUR
THE SOUL BESIEGED

When standards of equality have resulted from a long struggle between the different classes of which the old society was composed, envy, hatred, and distrust of his neighbor, together with pride and exaggerated confidence in himself, invade the human heart and for some time hold dominion there. That fact, without reference to equality, works powerfully to divide men.

—Alexis de Tocqueville

Hurrah for Revolution and more cannon-shot!
A beggar upon horseback lashes a beggar on foot.

—W. B. Yeats

The Revolution is like Saturn—it eats its own children.

—Georg Büchner

CHAPTER SIX

The Reign of Nastiness

Though the image of a strictly hierarchical society lingers in the European psyche, other realities have been pushing themselves forward for centuries. Regarding the recent past, a Roman physician of old family, who still lives in a seventeenth-century villa on one of the famous hills, tells me: "The biggest change in the last twenty years has been in the way people feel and behave everyday. Go into a shop; before they were glad to see you; now the salespeople ignore you, insult you, do you a favor by waiting on you—they have their strong labor unions and their guaranteed salary. In the streets, courtesy is forgotten, people are rushing, tired and unhappy. It is very different from what it was; and yet everyone is rich, by comparison with before—at least the mass of people are. They have cars, fancy clothes, and now it's even boats they are after! It is a paradox, this increase in general wealth and decrease in courtesy and good humor."

A Milanese manufacturer of export gifts, who is also a journalist, echoes the thought: "There has been a decay in manners, people are brusque, rude, insulting in their casual interchanges."

In Paris, I hear over and over again the description of a new "aggressivity" in the street, the Métro, shops. In Portugal, so far removed in distance from either Italy or France, and so different in economic development (the average wage is one-sixth that in France), the people have always prided themselves on their *branduras dos costumes,* I am told; that is, on the blandness or softness of their customs and manners. One night, far out of the capital, the car of my Portuguese hosts nearly out of gas, the gas stations all closed, we stop by a small clump of men gathered beneath the blue light that marks the volunteer fire department of provincial Sangarém. The chief, for so he reveals himself to be, offers to sell us, at cost, twenty liters of diesel. Afterwards, smiling to herself, my petite hostess in the front seat turns back toward me and says: "That's very Portuguese." "Are people, then, as nice as they seem?" I ask. "Certainly. But it's changed in the cities now since the revolution of 1974. People are aggressive now." Same word as in Paris, same word I hear in London, where a publisher tells me: "Oh, yes, people are much more rude than before, aggressive."

Even an American friend, a psychologist who has been working for years in Germany and Scandinavia, says: "It's just a symptom, but it means something. I find European people increasingly rough, brusque, full of resentment, and unwilling to change. When I get back to America, though, the customs man smiles at me and says: 'Welcome Home.' In Europe, he glowers, tries to look menacing, pretends to be important. Just little images but they add up."

I would be inclined to dismiss all this as mere griping, the invidious comparison of present with past by people who tend to romanticize the past as they get older. But I cannot. My own experience confirms what they say and comes to illuminate it.

One hot September day, I enter the Florence railroad station to take the evening sleeper to Paris. I am something of a nervous departee and have learned to ease my tensions by arriving early. So it is that I have more than an hour to wait. My plan is to do some last-minute errands, in as perfectly calm a mood as I can muster, and to first deposit my four heavy bags with a porter, a *facchino*. (The Italian word has a violent sound and lends itself to the shouted calls of arriving passengers needing help with their bags and leaning anxiously out of windows: Fah-KEEE-no! Indeed, the word has something of the quality of the old French expression *laquais*, English "lackey," though its connotations are even worse, as shown in the proverbial expression *È un mestiere da facchino*, "It's work for a mule," or *Si comporta come un facchino*, "He behaves like a porter.")

My *facchino*, faded-looking in his old blue smock—the nearly extinct uniform of the traditional, lower-class, manual laborer of Europe—is not coarse and harsh but rather straightforward and accommodating. I am so early for my train that by rights I should deposit my bags in the storage room. But to do so would mean that, in a mere half-hour, I would have to go back to stand in line at the storage room, nervously hoping to retrieve them in time, and then having got them, rush to find porters at the very moment when they are most in demand. My *facchino*, however, leaning on the handles of his ancient cart and chatting with others of his kind, is agreeably willing to do me the favor; he smiles and nods reassuringly, saying he will bring the bags to me at the sleeper car—the number of which I give him—in thirty minutes.

That off my mind, I proceed to the station pharmacy for some last-minute purchases. When I enter, it is mercifully empty of other customers. Three young women pharmacists, wearing the white coats and little lapel insignia of that profession to which sexual and economic democracy have recently given them access, lounge, alert and intelligent-looking, behind the counter. I cast them a simple American smile of greeting, but they all seem to draw back and their happy chatter becomes transformed into nearly forbidding professional coolness. One radiates suspicion, the other hauteur, and the third a vague discomfort. I remember that years ago everybody would smile when you entered a shop. They get me my purchases but hold tight to their unwelcoming expressions.

Feeling slightly ill-used—the prevoyage mood I am in makes me, like all travelers, more than usually sensitive—I move fast to the tobacco stand to buy a pack of cigarettes. (These long European train trips lend themselves to meditative smoking.) Mercifully, there are only two young women, a pair of Americans from their accents, in front of me waiting to be served. The tobacconist, a middle-aged woman of the petite-bourgeoisie school, hardworking and slightly severe, is trying to deal with their English. I dislike her patronizing manner but am working hard on maintaining tranquillity before the long trip and trying to block the mounting annoyance that has been planted in my upper back and shoulders by the pharmacy reception. At this moment, a tall young man in a long coat rushes up in front of the Americans, thrusts fifteen hundred lire at the tobacco shop owner, and demands his *"pacchetto di MS."* My self-control fails me and—as in the Paris incident I related earlier—I erupt. "I'll break your arm!"

I say in English, and as I say it (comes from seeing too many cowboy movies when I was a child, I suppose), I place my arm between him and the counter.

He cringes. Or rather he pretends to cringe. Despite his height and youth, despite my spectacles and tie, he backs off, saying: "*Certo! Scusi! Prego!,*" a certain smile of mock apology mixed with spite playing on his lips. My having spoken in English has been half-deliberate, and it has helped to make him retire so automatically, for though he doesn't understand the slang, he understands the tone, and it acquires more force for his lack of comprehension.

I am quite pleased with my spontaneous defense of right and self; manly, I despise his cringing lack of old-fashioned dignity. But it is a fleeting pleasure, for the tobacco woman, ignoring not only my precedence but that of the two Americans who have not quite finished their own transaction, abruptly takes the part of the interloper, hands him the pack of cigarettes, and allows him to retire with his cheap victory—a collaborator with disorder. I am so nonplussed that I cannot think of a word to say, either in Italian or English. I wait my turn with a mixture of resignation and mute anger. Then, when I finally get to the counter, she hands me my purchase and says: "*In Italia non si fa come all' estero.*" "In Italy, we don't do things the way they do abroad." Meaning, we give way to disorder rather than trying to correct it. It is a worldly wisdom which, amidst the new daily chaos, may have its cheap though prudent point. But at the moment I am angry enough at her endorsement of social confusion that I say some John Wayne thing like "*Lo faccio io!*" "I do!" Ever the embattled but defiant sheriff.

Trying to calm down, I take my cigarettes and walk toward the train. There, before my car, I see the porter, patiently seated on his cart, like some loyal peasant of old, my baggage carefully piled beside him. But I must give my attention to the brown-uniformed man with clipboard, some sort of *wagon-lit* steward I suppose, who stands at the entrance to the car. He has a semi-professional air, and I automatically deliver my ticket with a friendly smile. He ignores both the ticket and the smile. Instead, he checks something on his board. I wait and continue to smile my polite greeting. But when he finally takes the ticket, he merely looks me up and down, unimpressed and unmoved, making me conscious of my old raincoat, and of his spic-and-span French (I can tell by the accent with which he asks, in Italian, for my passport) neatness, a momentary charge of *sine nobilitate* projected toward me. Coolly, he checks my name off, then jerks a thumb toward the train car door.

The *facchino,* however, is ready, accommodating, and pleasant as he grunts the heaviest of the bags onto the platform of the car and then onward to my compartment. With quick intelligence and care, he places each of my bags neatly and securely in the overhead racks. I am grateful for his earlier favor in guarding the bags, his promptness in being on the spot. I am grateful for his simple service. I give him the usual sum for handling the number of bags and add an unnecessary and uncustomary tip of 25 percent. He smiles with natural gratitude but without servility and leaves me with a polite "Grazie" and his wishes for a pleasant trip.

Later on, I reflect on the incident and on the hundreds of daily insults I have suffered in casual intercourse with today's Europeans. I think again of the many complaints I have heard from Europeans themselves about the bad treatment they daily receive. The *facchino* has behaved the most correctly, the most "simply," many Europeans would say. The others have behaved in ways that seem determined by causes which do not reside in the situation itself. For when they are not actually fighting about something, men, whether in civilized or aboriginal societies, are friendly. Certainly in times of peace this *was* the usual way Europeans behaved until recently. Courtesy was the usual mode of an aristocracy secure in its power and privilege and sufficiently rich and leisured to develop refined and even delicate manners. Lower orders imitated them, down to the peasantry. Despite the undeniable exploitation of one group by another, because competition was limited by the high and seemingly permanent barriers between fixed classes, a mutual cordiality and even love could be regularly cultivated. With strangers, notions of courtly behavior ruled the upper classes, and ancient notions of simple hospitality for guests ordinarily ruled the lower ones. And for all classes, the stranger offered a grateful escape from the narrow rounds of limited lives.

But as anyone who looks at the glossy, rich, modern surface of today's European cities can see, there have been big changes since the Second World War. Particularly since the early sixties, there has been an enormous increase in general wealth, enough to call it nothing less than a "revolution." And here is the main reason for the reign of nastiness in European social relations of everyday.

A process started before 1789 has come to fulfillment, and all across Europe the ancient hierarchy of old that served, among other things, to shape the relations between men has come crashing down. Though certain remnants of the old order remain, as we have seen, vast masses of people have left immemorially fixed places and climbed out of the peasantry and even out of the working class. Where before social hierarchy ruled absolutely, now there is much more equality, much more social mobility, and much more confusion in men's souls.

People no longer know how to behave to one another. Moreover, since hierarchy tumbled only after a long revolutionary struggle—two hundred years of episodic revolt by those lower alternating with counterrevolutionary repression by those higher—now, in the triumph of egalitarian revolution, the bitterness of the old conflicts seeps into everyday life. A lower man who has risen against opposition, even against repression, is proud of himself. A higher man who has failed to repress this rising is suspicious of the other, angry, watchful. Each man is uncertain of what the future will bring to him. Each man is free to be full of envy for what others may have. Each man is anxious to prove that he is at least as good as the next man, probably better.

Except the *facchino*. He is not part of the new progressive spirit. Socially and economically on the bottom, he has no big plans, nothing to prove. He can afford to be courteous and even friendly. The European revolution that began with the violent taking of the Bastille and Versailles, that was put down over and over again in such terrible episodes as Fascism or National Socialism and that was only truly completed by the peaceful upheaval brought by large-scale prosperity in the sixties and seventies, has passed the *facchino* by. But not the pharmacists. And they are proud of having arrived at their situation. They are also frustrated that, because of many reasons, including parts of old hierarchical traditions that survive, they can't rise farther. They are not sure how to feel about themselves. They are uneasy with others. The young man who cuts into the line? In this new Europe where hierarchy still penetrates but no longer commands, he's got to get his. So, too, the tobacconist: she instinctively backs disorder, because in it she has herself thriven. And the sleeping car steward, lower-middle class, he wants to make sure that you esteem him at his own valuation.

In such an atmosphere, all men pretend to worth they do not have, all are jealous of their prerogatives, and no one has any longer a sure sense of his place. People are engaged in a daily, quiet, nonviolent civil war. They have all the desires that democracy excites but never enough satisfactions, so they run after more and resent those others have managed to get. A mean-spiritedness reigns, especially now that the great economic boom has slowed into more limited opportunity.

The rule of nastiness in European life has been highlighted in recent years by a contrast which Americans and Europeans both make. Americans are always asking: "Why are they so rude?" and Europeans, on the contrary, ask: "Why are they so friendly?" Indeed, though the competitive conditions of American democratic life continually create uneasiness and frustration, here the rule is that one ought to behave in a pleasant and warm way to other people. Many European visitors to America remark on the easy manners, the quick hospitality, the proverbial (even to new acquaintances) "Help yourself to anything in the refrigerator." One visitor to San Francisco, a person of the old school, mindful of bygone ways back home, was moved by recurrent cheerful hellos, smiles, and warm thank-yous from shopkeepers to blurt out: "Why this is the most civilized country in the Western world!"

For this considerable social blessing, we owe thanks to several unique historical circumstances. First, unlike Europeans, we did not have to win our democratic conditions the hard way, over centuries of conflict and in the teeth of counterrevolutions. The American colonies were, by any historical standard, already democratic when our revolution occurred. Indeed, that uprising and war were not a product of class enmity and conflict but of the will to continue already well-established colonial self-government. The richness of the country made men much more easy with one another than in other societies. Just as we never had hierarchy, in the traditional sense, so we never had revolution.

To these economic, social, and political blessings were added others. The Puritans who gathered to come on the *May-flower*, and whose ways gave a definite shape to so much of American civilization and manners, were pledged not only as particularly devout Christians to love all men but also as members of a more or less hastily assembled group to love each other. Wilderness circumstances led to the repetition of this pattern of warm affiliation. Total strangers gathered together to make up the wagon trains. After going as far as they wanted, individuals would break away, but they would preserve the habit of joining easily with others. The American frontier has never closed in certain ways, Americans taking advantage of their continent-size civilization to churn around the country, moving in search of a better apartment or house, or a better job, or a new horizon. We must learn to be friendly. Preserving this value from the past is useful to Americans in the modern world, with all its uprooting mobilities of place, career, social status, economic prosperity, and psychological and emotional development.

But Europeans, burdened as they are with the legacies of hierarchy and bitter revolution and counterrevolution, are not yet able to enjoy such ease. Despite efforts in many societies (Holland and some of the Scandinavian countries, with their relative isolation and strong racial and social homogeneity, are good examples) to make peaceful mutuality and citizen participation prevail in government and in every organization, Europe is not at peace. The protest against hierarchy, ancient and modern, the rebellions against the reaction to the revolutions, in simple and homely ways on the everyday level of manners, spoil the texture of social existence and make it, as the Europeans complain, "aggressive."

CHAPTER SEVEN

Change and Terror

Indeed, poverty was so obsessive that people expected to encounter it, at any turn in the road, in the form of a raw-boned, shaggy bitch, its chops curled back showing yellow teeth. . . . The poor people who worked for others during the day would group together and figure out ways to clear their own uncultivated land at night, by the light of the moon. . . .

This time, the revolution of the world has been so colossal and so profoundly unsettling, while the dread of the future is so great and the present so precarious, that men are clinging to the last stable values they had once lived by, understood, and sometimes repudiated, and which they have just come to acknowledge—that is, to accept as a means of taking refuge in the context of today. . . . Now in today's folklore festivals, what we see are images of a time when the hand prevailed over the machine, when you could drink river water, when trees were felled only to make roofs or fires, when you could be distinguished from others by your costume. Even in this century, folklore festivals were spontaneous events. Today they serve only to recall certain values that we are in the process of losing and which, as we have come to know, are essential. . . .

Nothing is left of my civilization but wreckage.
—Pierre-Jakez Hélias,
The Horse of Pride: Life in a Breton Village

The decay in European manners is profoundly unsettling, but Europeans' complaints about their present existence go far beyond the everyday surface of life. A Dutch textile manufacturer remarks: "You Americans must defend us from the Russians." "Why can't you do it yourselves?" I ask. "Oh, we are too tired.

We are finished." A major French publisher surveys the contemporary scene and snaps what he sees into one hard word: "Decadence." An acquaintance, an old Italian physician of great culture and dignity, says to me: *"Oggi, c'è qualche cosa di corrotto nell'anima italiana."* "Today, there is something corrupt in the Italian soul." He emphasizes the word *corrotto*, rolling the *r*'s with a large open mouth and nearly spitting out the *t*'s. The statement, and many others like it I have heard, strikes me as old-fashioned, moralistic, not in the contemporary line at all but something from very far back: ancestral voices prophesying doom.

No search of daily newspapers, no attention to the surface of current events, will easily clarify for Americans wishing to understand Europeans today what giant thing it is that bothers them so. Though a few European intellectuals began commenting on the continent's decline two centuries ago, now the idea is in the mouth of Everyman. It is particularly odd, however, that at the moment of their greatest material prosperity and greatest popular political participation, Europeans should so often feel bankrupt, decadent, helpless, and rotten. To comprehend this turmoil in the soul, one must look at what else besides manners has perished with hierarchy. For when hierarchy fell, and in a very real sense that has only happened since 1945, a world died.

As children, the Europeans who now complain were inhabitants of a different continent, one governed not only by ancient hierarchy but also by countless other ways of being associated with it. True, by the outbreak of the Second World War the Industrial Revolution had affected large numbers of people. But while many had left the land and were pursuing life in the shadow of machines, both in the country and town, an ancient life still held the main sway. Hierarchy was only the largest element in an embracing pattern which gave men a sense of meaning and luster in their lives. A continuity gripped each part of daily life in an immense web, and in the large design thus formed, men lived with what will seem to us now, only decades later, an astonishing certainty.

Fully to summon up that other world and the felt perception of its destruction would require nothing less than a time-machine that could take us backward. Even Europeans themselves, living as they do in the very stream of time that descends from those days, have little conscious clarity about what has happened. They mutter words like "finished," or "corrupt," or "decadence," but their experience of a massive and bewildering event is seldom given adequate utterance. From a foreign perspective, however, one can see the process pretty clearly.

In Italy, for example, a mere twenty-five years ago, the old pattern still presided. One could as well pick nearly any other corner of contemporary Europe, but Italy's changes have symbolic importance beyond themselves. After all, for millennia the peninsula was the very center of European civilization. It was the place from which Roman, Christian, medieval, Renaissance, and Counter-Reformation Europe all came into being. Though later Italy was on the margins of some great movements, this fact is a further advantage, because one can observe there, nearly as in a laboratory case, the swift development of trying conditions which have accompanied recent revolution in all its many aspects.

Even today, most Americans and many Europeans still imagine contemporary Italy as it was: slow, dirty, and smiling, a country of gnarled peasants, colorful donkey carts, folk festivals, little old women in widow's black and creased leathery faces. They imagine an essentially rural society, as from time beyond memory, supporting some picturesque but decaying cities, these decorated with splendid monuments built by lords who preside over the people. They imagine, that is, the Italy of hierarchy.

In fact, until a few years ago, that was the way things were. The integrating pattern of that old world—leave aside for the moment the terrible sufferings which poverty, exploitation, and backwardness visited on the majority—penetrated everywhere. As late as the 1960s, on city or village streets, you would see walking the men and women of holy medieval orders: Franciscans with their brown robes, Dominicans in black and white, priests and seminarians, varieties of nuns, attendants, sacristans. Mother Church exhibited herself. Moreover, she was available. Her brothers handled the business of schooling, her sisters tended you when you were sick in hospital; other representatives of God and Peter dispensed charity, organized religious festivals, called you to account when you strayed, and prayed over you when you died. There was in this clerical presence an implicit reminder of a nearly primitive, cosmic, holy order, visible in the streets and on the roads, intermingled with all of life. Now the monks and priests and nuns are gone. I almost never see them. When I do, they look like everybody else. The nuns wear skirts and show their legs, the priest wears a suit instead of a long black cassock. One is inclined to ask, if one is not too preoccupied with his daily tasks, in a mood as if pinching oneself and rubbing one's eyes: "What happened? Where did they go? How did what was so permanent and so portentous with human and even cosmic significance dwindle so fast and seemingly disappear? How could those old antagonists of modernity be so suddenly swept away?"

That sacred order of old, once visible in the persons of its numberless clergy, is mute now; it has no easy answer to give the spirit which poses such questions. And the European spirit, albeit distracted by busy modern errands, does unconsciously pose them, broods on the sudden transition, the dismemberment of a body social. Just as I, walking back of Fiesole down the blacktop of Via Giovanni Dupré, near the Roman amphitheater, wonder on my little road what has happened to the sheep, the sheep which when I lived here only twenty-five years ago used to come home at twilight, fat, wooly, and puffy with rose-colored dust from the old earthen road, driven by the shepherd. He was the husband of Richetta, the *contadina* who made a few extra lire every morning by coming and straightening up the house I rented here. Where is she?

I went looking for her in her old *casa*, but a Swiss couple was there instead. They were on holiday, they told me, using the British word for vacation, and, no, there was no Richetta there. It had been a long time, they laughed, since peasants lived there, and they invited me to look for myself through the door at a remodeled interior which could have come out of some slick decorating magazine: a thick white rug, a bright stainless-steel lamp, a shiny glass table. By some bizarre automatism my mind at the moment remembers the eggs: splendid eggs with red yokes that Richetta would bring some mornings for breakfast. She would fry them in her husband's own thick, green olive oil and they were delicious, mighty creations, eggs with all the natural consistency and nourishment of two hefty steaks. For years, far away, I longed for them. Our own modern American eggs are so yellowish, watery, and tasteless by comparison. Now, in Italy, I can't get eggs like Richetta's anymore, no matter where I look. The chickens that used to lay them, white-feathered, red-combed, proud and cantankerous birds, were fed on the leftovers of Richetta's family's meals: sheep cheese rinds, pasta, olive oil, the bones of a roasted homegrown rabbit, garden tomatoes put up last summer, and bread home-made in an outdoor oven whose old shape recalled Roman tombs. . . . Maybe, my mind thinks, these health-food people are on to something, and it really makes a difference what you eat because food like that . . . the chickens were very happy . . . they laid those fantastic eggs . . .

Embarrassed, I catch myself and stop my reverie, and thank the Swiss. And shrug. I know very well where Richetta and her husband have gone. Just as the visible sacred has been removed from the old order that one knew those few years ago, so has the culture of the land. Nowadays, sheep come slaughtered, cut up, and frozen from a supermarket, and shepherds roam these hills no more: the lambs arrive in plastic sleeves, pieces in container ships, dead and meaningless, from New Zealand and America. Richetta and her husband, almost certainly, have joined the urban masses down the hill in Florence, in Turin at the Fiat plant, in Milan. They make better money, get better access to doctors, accumulate old-age pensions—maybe they are spending them by now. But that old order of land, sheep and shepherd, cock, hen, and precious eggs—it's vanished.

Let us not seem sentimental about the past. Not all the changes are bad. Then Italy was poor. The day I first landed in Naples in 1958, I was eating under the dark green awning of an outdoor restaurant when two ten-year-old boys, eluding the waiter's haughty surveillance, stole the extra bread right off my plate. There were beggars everywhere. Today, there are no true poor in Italy. Prosperity is normal, wages and savings are high and social welfare agencies provide for all. The only beggars are a few stubborn gypsies—ancient professionals, artisans of importunity, among the last workers in the old spirit.

But then, traditional poverty was part of the nature of things: hierarchy rested on it; in many ways, the Catholic Church with its promise of redemption in the hereafter rested on it; and household agriculture rested on it. But as part of the total old order poverty also had other meanings and functions. It pushed people to extraordinary means to survive so that the famous Italian ingenuity was cultivated in poverty. And some people developed marginal approaches to making a living that were touched with magic. I remember one morning in Perugia, two months after the Naples beggars had taken my bread, being awakened by bagpipes. These were no Scotch bagpipes. As I later learned, pipes and the tartan are native to the Mediterranean. The Etruscans had them before the Romans came. The tunes that echoed in the stone streets that morning were deliciously sad and thrilling. I opened the shutters and looked down at two men, one holding cap in hand, the other blowing on a contraption which, despite its bellows being the remains of an inner tube, was giving out skirls that seemed to come from the spirit of Pan himself.

Now, in Perugia's piazzas, American teenagers with electric guitars and portable amplifiers earn a summer's subsistence between college years. No Italian has to make real music in the streets to get by. You never see the strolling singers with mandolins and guitars in the restaurants anymore; half-mendicants they were, to be sure, but they brought something extra to a meal. Common people who used to discuss the merits of tenors with passion and be able to hum and even sing whole operas seem to have vanished. Even the more casual singing for which Italy is proverbial and which northern peoples imagine is a spontaneous expression of the Italian character—as if song were as natural to humans on that peninsula as to birds—is gone. Italians don't sing in the open air anymore. In the last six years, carefully counting, I have heard a total of four people sing. But under the old order, in a squalid Roman trattoria near the *stazione,* around nine-thirty at night when everyone had finished eating and the old railway workers, pensioners with their canes and missing teeth, lingered before going home to cold rooms, you might catch the grace. One man would wave an arm and start to hum. Another would take up the melody, closing his eyes to feel the music more. A third would break open the words, in the strong, male, Italian roundness which can fill a room. Before long, the men would be singing joyously, those on the left side alternating with those on the right, like aged monks facing each other in the stalls of a choir.

I ask a prosperous factory worker what happened to the singing and he says: *"Per la musica, ci vuole la miseria"*—"For

music, you need poverty, destitution, suffering"—as if the tradition of folk song was, like homemade clothes, a beauty possible
only when people had less.

Who would have believed that in getting affluence, we Romans, we Europeans, would have to give up music and singing?
Who could have imagined that the old culture—which did more
than relieve suffering, it embellished life—would perish with
prosperity? It puzzles the mind, it makes one restless with doubt
and wonder. God and good eggs and song were, apparently, all
connected in the old life, along with poverty and begging. It is
not easy for the mind to understand this. The roiled spirit, which
would not go back because of the price to pay, finds itself, paradoxically, with empty pockets anyhow. So the spirit broods on
loss and contradiction.

Of course when one contemplates that old world, one is not
always driven to gravity, because so much that one recalls was
simple fun. I think, for example, of such an apparently trivial
convenience as the automobile. A mere twenty years ago, most
of the main highways of Italy were paved-over Roman affairs.
Museums, really. Slow, curved, hand-built, and with the most
regular rhythms to their windings, once you got the hang of it.
Such roads made driving itself an art that demanded great skill.
Now, there are super highways: the same anonymous, mass-
produced roads you can find in America, or anywhere in the rest
of Europe for that matter. They are less crowded and faster but
their straight lines are monotonous and driving on them is a
bore.

Then, driving was heroic adventure. Italians worshipped the
bravura of the automobile driver and even the cars themselves.
The great road races, the *Mille Miglia,* and its drivers (*piloti*), were
celebrated, as were the car makers; one thinks of a Nuvolari,
whose name is associated with great driving as Stradivarius with
great violin music. Then, all driving, on or off the track, was
sport, but in a society where hierarchy has long reigned, as Johan
Huizinga said of the aristocratically dominated late Middle Ages,
life itself can become art, and the concept of the "art of living,"
of putting art into life, was central to the old civilization. So, the
driver of any car was expected to be and strived to become an

artist: in his reflexes, his timing, his smoothness, his ability to evade the most pressing dangers. I got my first driver's license in Italy back then, and I was, for an American and in my day, not bad. But I was nearly worshipful in admiration of my Italian compeers. They lived a tense harmony with the car, a verve and supple athleticism that were truly life as art. At the same time, the Italian driver, surely the best in the world, was a *grand seigneur*. Not a heavy, clumsy, charging churl (the best that most Europeans can do nowadays at the wheel), rather he combined the chivalric virtues of courage on the one hand and finesse on the other, a credit to his heritage.

What must it feel like then, when all this is gone? Become a bitter chore, driving is spiritless and merely aggressive. Driving now expresses the revolutionary condition before a society moving toward true democracy has managed to come to some collective and personal harmony and peace. As a consequence, a Swedish executive, no mean driver herself, remarks the change in Italians and cites overwhelming personal evidence to prove that their driving, which was once much racier and *apparently* more frightening, has in fact become slower but sloppier and, consequently, more dangerous. "Watch out!" she cautions. "Once they were princes and artists at the wheel, now they are ham-fisted shopkeepers and proles."

Because there were few cars then, those with the money for one had the cachet of *signori* of old. Anywhere in Italy—in all Europe, for that matter—you could drive your vehicle, no matter how humble, up to the ancient cathedral you might want to see and be certain of finding a parking place in front of it. *That* was luxury. Awaiting you and your vehicle, wearing a dusty uniform and a peaked cap, was the parking attendant, a man usually belonging to a society of veterans, many wounded in the war. This poor fellow doing rough work in all weathers not only wrote out the receipt for the trifling sum you had to pay him but would insist on guiding your car with the seriousness and precision of one waving pilots of great planes into the narrow bays of airline terminals: "*No, dottore! A destra, più a destra! Venga, venga, dottore! Va bene, spenga il motore. Perfetto!*" "No, *dottore!* Turn to the right, more to the right! Come on, come forward, *dottore!* Good, turn off the motor. Perfect!" He had his dignity and he recognized yours. Indeed, he saluted you when you first approached the parking lot, and saluted you again after he handed you your claim check. He was, in his job, like so many then even without military background in other jobs, faithful, the soldier, a man of respect.*

These days, the parking attendants are still there, but they have been banished along with cars to less dignified places: new, modern, boring piazzas. They care less about what they do. You park the car yourself. They watch but do not guide. Unless you are heading straight for a collision, they have no interest in you or anybody. And they don't salute. Why should they? In revolutionary times, no man is deserving of honor, and least of all oneself. One cultivates, the parking attendants cultivate, instead, a certain resentful defiance. It is the right of a newly freed man, of free men everywhere, but it is not pleasant. The sacrifice of so many daily meanings and pleasures presses added weight on the worst sides of the European character. Each small loss exists not only in its own right, it also represents all the complex power an old civilization had to dignify and delight. The deprived European spirit feeds itself with cynicism, with pessimism, and once more anger finds itself, in unseen but daily ways, stoked, excited, aroused.

One could itemize a thousand other parallel changes in a hundred sectors of European life, each one of them expressive of an integrating world broken. One could speak of death and the difference between being driven away in a black carriage drawn by immense black horses whose heads nod under ostrich plumes, and being carted away to the cemetery in a sensible Fiat hearse. One could speak of sociability and difference between the old *passeggiata,* the strolling back and forth of couples, friends, and relatives, looking at each other, recognizing and being recognized, and today's evening "shopping" (an American term they have imported), when people descend in a frenzy to the same streets, only to be insulted in the shops. One could speak as well of the difference between peasants who had left school at age ten yet could still recite to each other whole cantos of Dante's *Com-*

*With amiable exaggeration, it was assumed that everyone who had a car was a university graduate and due, at a minimum, the title of one who was *laureato,* entitled to wear the laurel leaves of the hero-scholar, a learned person, *dottore,* a doctor, originally from Latin *dux,* a leader. Thus did tradition embrace the automobile even in the order of its language.

media, summa poema, and pages of Manzoni's great novel *I pro-
messi sposi,* and the mesmerized, exhausted, postindustrial workers
who nightly watch local, American, and Japanese TV programs:
quiz shows, lessons in hairstyling, cops and robbers, Westerns
and sci-fis, and absurd vaudevilles in which short-legged Italian
girls try to pretend they are doing the real thing in Las Vegas.

A Florentine man I know, who apprenticed for ten full years
to become a deft wood-carver of life-size Roman statues (a
mythic faun, a togaed Caesar), tells me that he and two friends
are giving it up to buy a pizza parlor to feed German tourists, a
story that typifies the death of the order of the hand, the handmade and homemade, true manu-facture yielding to machine
production and quality declining everywhere.

Like so many other aspects, the family was possessed by the
interconnecting ordering principles of the old life. Hierarchy?
Certainly. The family was large and ordered according to seniority. Not only did Father rule his brood, Grandfather ruled collective broods that he had spawned, until, naturally, he became in-
competent. Such principles gave the possibility of existence to
the clan, which was able to imprison each of its individuals in its
collective wishes, on the one hand, and on the other hand
to commit formidable human resources to the support of each
person.

The order of hierarchy was interpenetrated by the order of
"gender." This was a principle so old and basic that it was reflected
even in language itself. As nouns in most European languages
divided by gender, so the worlds of men and women were dis-
tinct. As the household was the women's, the cafés were the
men's. In Italy, through the mid-sixties, women and men were
almost two separate tribes. One couldn't expect the same things
of either. In towns, for example, girls and young women were
supposed to be frivolous, even stupid, and they obligingly behaved accordingly; young men were supposed to be intelligent
and to be preparing themselves for concern with the important
things. On the other hand, because the order of the holy also
penetrated here, the pregnant woman was a being transformed.
Proud though fragile, she was the first in any company. A pregnant peasant girl would momentarily eclipse the mayor or a vis-

iting cardinal: all had to give homage to the living image of the Mother of God.

Furthermore, young women were formed by rich definitions of feminine style. Out of doors and in the public eye, always chaperoned, they were soignée, tailored, elegant. They would stride like full-blown Venuses of Titian, of the Greek and Roman sculptures one would see in the museums. Their hips and breasts were ripe with life and power and by some mysterious magic, they wore their hair like crowns: full, radiant, splendid. The men cultivated a style which has been too belittled by the word *macho*. Perhaps that expression is appropriate in Latin America, I am not sure, but in Italy, even fifteen years ago, strength, dignity, mastery, were the qualities which a man was supposed to emanate; not a tensile bullying sort of thing but a hefty, grounded force that besides belonging to the order of gender also had its affiliations with that of beauty. You would see it in the handsome lounger outside a café, his pants pressed and shoes shined, his legs planted solidly on the ground, his pelvis drawn back, ever so slightly cocked, his jacket worn over the shoulders like a matador's.

The separation of the sexes gave to their domains and to their interactions a quality of theatricality which Luigi Barzini, in *The Italians,* generalized to say was characteristic of all Italian life. The intense looks of flirtation during the *passeggiata,* brown eyes meeting brown eyes in deep but momentary stares, the intense arias of courtship, hot with the desperation which separation excited, the plots of seduction, the deadly scenes of jealousy, the crimes of passion, a weeping husband and a smoking pistol being a daily item in the newspaper, all this was life lived with the intensity of drama and with its certainty. People knew who they were and what part to play, for the drama's main lines had been laid down millennia before they were born.

Naturally, the child participated in this drama, especially its sacred aspects. Any young child, male or female, was adored. The cult of the child derived from the order of the holy: if mother was Madonna, the child, especially the male, was Savior. Moreover, in the order of poverty, the child was precious as another worker at seed and harvesttime, a support in old age. And in the aesthetic order, that world within a world in which everything, every thought and experience, was divided and appraised according to the incessantly used adjectives of *bello* and *brutto,* beautiful and ugly, the child with its soft, blushing skin and big, round eyes was a gift of beauty which every family, no matter how poor, could enjoy.

Like the rest, all this is finished. Oh, should you need a job or an apartment, the family survives as a loose network of support, but the tribal reality and all the rest of it are gone. Now, nuclear couples dwell apart and grandmothers survive alone in solitary flats. After marriage, brothers and sisters seek their own places to live and the clan doesn't assemble, regularly, even once a week. Women still get pregnant, of course, but even that is much more rare. There are fewer children and many more pets in revolutionary Italy. And when women do give birth, nobody makes the old fuss; a woman can't be a Madonna anymore, her destiny has been torn from the sky. Instead, she gets to go to work, nearly all jobs routine ones, and to keep house, both. Even though her husband now helps a little with the housework— itself a deep shock to sensibilities still touched by ancient norms—it is not the same as when sisters, female cousins, and your own mother were part of an immediate solidarity of gender. On the street, one still sees good-looking and flirtatious women, but never a Venus. And the men are still handsome—that is, their faces are still handsome—but they seem glum, the old confidence is gone, the full certainty, the poise of that Bull which could be Zeus. Gender is broken. The old theater, the show which characterized Italian life, is mainly finished. The curtain has come down on all that and risen instead on a unisex world where people are pale and isolated.

How can anyone worry about the family whole and its appearance before the audience of the world? The family was itself an order in life, holding its members in safe, well-known paths. Once everyone in a family knew what to do about everything; right and wrong held no mysteries. Superior, they laughed at Americans who produced and read child-rearing manuals: "As if such things could be *problems!*" Europeans had, from tradition, all the knowledge to live that was needed. But now, Dr. Spock and his various followers are to be found, translated, everywhere, even in the bookstore on the *signorile* Via Tornabuoni. Minds once certain have to grasp for directions.

Once, only ten years ago, drug abuse was scorned as "an

American problem, particularly of your oppressed Negroes." The family knew how to manage the young so that no individual, much less a child, could stray out of the order. Children were neat, conventional, and obedient. Now teenage drug use is common enough that people shrug: "The piazzas are covered at night with used syringes; the kids shoot up right out in the open." Drunk with the revolutionary future, Italians skipped marijuana and other less dangerous alternatives and passed directly to heroin. Newspapers no longer feature ancient crimes of passion but drug busts, suicides, overdoses, and the anxious conferences of helpless modern experts. No one knows what to do about the problem.

We can never for a moment, whether in the family or in other aspects, ignore the many deficiencies of that old world gone. It had a confining quality, boring routine, narrowness. But it also had lift. When it transformed a car and parking attendant or relieved poverty with the saving graces of music and song, it gave to life not only design but also *Dasein*—energy, vitality, being.

To lose all this and more is to lose a great deal indeed. Now one sees to the bottom of the European soul. There is the widening gyre of which Yeats wrote: the center not holding, the spirit dispersing itself along with society and its traditions. And it has happened very quickly. One can find specific parallels to the Italian example in Scandinavia, England, France, Germany, and Holland, among other countries. And there are still others where even more profoundly rapid and revolutionary changes have shaken people—Spain, Portugal, Greece, and, again, in certain ways, Germany. One begins to understand the epidemic discouragement, the murmurs about "corruption" or being "finished." The people of Europe are demoralized.

Some will still demand: "But why? The United States is changing also. We suffer from 'future shock,' too, if you will, but we're not demoralized."

The kinds of changes that have happened to Europe, however, are not the same as the "future shock" which our own society has undergone. The challenge to personality caused by our rapid technological progress and changes of manners is one thing. Revolution in the bases of the social and psychological order is another. People in American society have certainly had to stretch. In only a few decades, for example, our sexually repressive culture became the most permissive on the globe. However, American women were *always* freer than Europeans. Early nineteenth-century visitors were amazed at how New England girls were allowed to take long, very-late-night summer walks alone with their boyfriends. American women were never really segregated into a gender-enclosed world of their own. From Molly Pitcher and the frontier women to the audacious heroines of James's genteel novels and beyond, they lived in a world essentially fluid, not fixed; modern, not traditional; secular, not sacred.

More broadly, ours was a culture of dynamism, of *movement* founded by people who had emigrated out of the older pattern; never was it a culture committed to ancient rules and detailed notions of right and wrong, everything in its place. In this sense, we have not had to struggle with the consequences of profound revolutions in our national life, because we were founded on the revolutionary. The break of Pilgrim immigrants with the past was renewed and reaffirmed by the Founding Fathers. Again, the *Novus Ordo Seclorum* on the reverse of the Great Seal of the United States is no casual phrase: the country was dedicated to a new order in the centuries of time. We have had no Roman roads, no ancient farms, no strict hierarchy, no universal church, no Madonnas, no tradition of artisans and artists, no poor peasant class giving birth to song. Thus, though "future shock" strains us, we basically like it. We are adaptable and change exhilarates us. Europeans, on the other hand, suffer "future shock" as we do but with no habit of pleasure in change and, in addition, they have revolution—the collapse of ancient hierarchy followed by a sense that a natural cultural order which was seemingly as firm as the fixed stars has been painfully broken in nearly every detail.

Perhaps the best way to understand what goes on nowadays in the European, far beneath the often dull, empty, and nagging surface of everyday, is to look at a baffling development that may at first seem far removed from these concerns with Europe's heart and soul: political terrorism. I do not mean those violent movements with specific goals—the IRA, the Basque separatists, the Corsicans. Those are part of the perennial tradition of European civil war and are neither new nor baffling. I speak instead of the more diffuse and ambitious terrorism, like that of the Red Brigades and the Baader-Meinhof. Near the gas pumps on every German *Autobahn* are posted the faces of major leaders still at large. So great is the danger it is felt they still pose that the whole society must be mobilized against them. In Italy, the story is the same. The newspapers daily report the trials of captured terrorists as they drag on for years. The terrorists—let us speak only of the left for the moment, much the largest group—continue their occasional kidnappings of the rich, their executions and maimings of public officials and industrialists. All who symbolize the modern age are attacked and people live in a diffuse fear.

Only a few years ago, the fear was more widespread and deeper. Terrorists seemed to be everywhere and no one able to stop them. They captured, tortured, displayed, and then killed the very head of government, a man who—in revolutionary fashion—was engineering the reconciliation of traditional enemies, the Communists and the Christian Democrats.

People's fear was exacerbated by their fruitless searching for logic in a situation where there was none: the terrorists had no program, no clear vision for the future, no clear goals. Because these left-wing terrorists clearly carried no agenda for any suppressed underclass of proletarians, because the terrorists themselves tended to be children of the new middle-class society, the newspapers called the movement "senseless."

In fact, however, there was sense: the terrorists represent the essence of a society already sensitive to being terrorized. It had been terrorized by broken traditions and cut roots, by the violent rejection of old customs and even of the rules laid down by God's Church, by too much opportunity. The people themselves were already terrorized by revolutionary shock on top of "future shock" and they didn't know how to handle the new freedoms that succeeded hierarchy. Awakening from the sleep of tradition into the bright light of modernity, they were terrorized by the need for achievement, the need to define themselves by themselves. Suddenly they inhabited a space without limits, a life no longer classically controlled, a romantic world in which they could live out their individual and collective fantasies, or hope to, but in which they encountered on every hand frustrations of the very dreams that same world engenders. It is a world where the very definitions of the simplest old ideas—mother, father, wife, husband, priest, neighborhood—were suddenly problematic.

In such confusing circumstances, one easily feels crazy. So, for everyone, the terrorists are acting out pain and anger, and that is cathartic. But they are doing more. At the height of the terrorist menace, it was commonly said that the terrorists, never a large group, were stronger than all of society: too clever to catch, too purposeful, too well supplied with outside funds and information and weapons, more intelligent and better organized than the police. There is no doubt that for a long time they had a formidable solidarity. But the real reason they weren't caught sooner was that *people secretly liked what they were doing*. The society as a whole resonated with an obscure motive in the movement. In the vast majority of cases, this approval was not conscious, but I did meet a number of rather ordinary individuals who would confide: "Perhaps what they are doing is not so bad."

For people understood that the terrorists were all essentially *counter*revolutionaries, wanting to stop the new world and get off. Despite their rhetoric, the terrorists embodied any number of traditional values. Like Europeans of old—village folk and the old tight family—they were united. Moreover, they were willing to risk and to act, they had courage. And even if they had no precise program, they radiated higher purpose. All these were qualities of the top of the old hierarchy, which, despite its many defects, nearly all Europeans, at least in part, regret. Terrorism posed as anarchic revolutionarism, but the people correctly felt it to be another attempt to halt the disruptions of modernity and to restore some version, however uncertain, of the old order's human quality.

Looking at the traditional past and the loss of its order and looking at the recent terroristic present both help give the American access to the European self in this tortured moment. But the painful passing of the ancient wholeness, within society and the souls of people, is also something the visitor can and will feel for himself. Whoever stays long enough—a few weeks will do—so that the intoxicating spell of the old monuments wears off and one can see them as they are now, will have the experience.

One day, when I was casually walking in the very center of

Florence, my eyes by chance lifted to see the Palazzo Strozzi. I took a moment to look at it. I know something of its background. It was one of the first important monuments of Renaissance architecture. And, as was always the case, it was also a fortress for a powerful family and an ostentatious display of their power and wealth. But, as an early embodiment of certain Renaissance ideals, it is justly famous in art history books for displaying Nobility, Dignity, Proportion, Balance, Order, Harmony, Beauty, and Life (after all, the palace was mainly designed to be a home) as Art.

But, as a resident, I realize that seldom if ever do I encounter these qualities in the new revolutionary Italy. My dealings with the *facchino* furnish a tiny example of rare and very partial exceptions. I am suddenly filled with sadness. How paradoxical, tragic, and even infuriating to find myself living in a country and on a continent full of the most beautiful monuments to the highest values of the past, and yet, now, those monuments have almost *nothing* to do with the human life which circulates around them. No longer a mere tourist, I cannot any more ignore the life of the moment. I can no longer pass with easy historical reverie into that magnificent past and, indeed, into that timelessness of value represented by the *palazzi*, the splendid churches and gracious villas, even the landscapes of pines and olive trees sculpted over centuries to make lovely hillsides ever more exquisite.

These remnants of an old order and its highest visions still exist, but I find myself looking at them less and less often, because they make life worse. They stand there for me, not, as many Italians remark, as exhibits in the "gigantic museum" that is Europe or Italy, but as too vivid reminders of a great, wonderful tradition now dead. If this sense of contradiction and loss, this pain, continues while I live here, I shall come to hate that old beauty which so dramatically serves to set off the present confusion and social ugliness. The shadow it casts is part of what is "*corrotto*" in the soul of European people today.

CHAPTER EIGHT

Boxification

Despite all the tearing up of their old world, the loss, and the resulting confusion, Europeans still don't have a sense of practical freedom. Often, they complain that they can't move, that they don't feel free even to dream, and that optimism, dynamism, and "punch" (they have adopted the American word) are lacking. Observers say Europeans also lack the feeling of responsibility for their own destiny. Even economic resources seem blocked. In fact, 10 percent of Europeans can't even get jobs, although their more or less socialistic countries constitutionally guarantee full employment.

It has been said the American revolution was the only successful one. What is meant is that ours emerged into a single clear victory. Elsewhere, and particularly in Europe, the results were more equivocal. When hierarchy came tumbling down during the French Revolution it splintered into dozens of shades of political opinion. Society and consciousness, once arranged on a vertical axis of hierarchy, now became arranged on a horizontal one. The institutionalization of the fixed political poles of left and right—hardly an American phenomenon—created a permanent divisiveness in society that persists to this day. Moreover, revolutions alternated with successive waves of counterrevolution. This had two effects. First, the vertical principle was repeatedly reerected in society. It came to coexist with the new horizontal one. Second, men became radically unsure of the benignity of government. One year it was on their side, the next it was against them. In addition, these alternations frequently derived not from mild successions or evolutions of power but from bitter and violent contestations of faction, and often of government against the citizens and vice versa.

The organization of society and even consciousness along

two axes, a vertical one of hierarchy and a horizontal one of programmatic struggle of left and right in politics and the street, created a social matrix which results in what I will call, with mocking intent, the "boxification" of European life.

Compartments became the human rule. The horizontal axis is usually defined by a large number of well-organized political parties fighting for control of the whole: radicals, communists, socialists, liberals, fascists, etc. But there are also many other durable organizations that compete, for example, commercial and industrial associations and many trade unions. Each organization occupies its box in the matrix: the steelworkers are low on the vertical axis and toward the left on the horizontal; the association of antique dealers is far to the right and medium high; the association of banking employees is high but in the center; the association of industrial managers is very high and middle-right. And so on. Each such organization is rather closely allied with one or more political parties and each is jealous of its vertical position and seeking to better it. Thus, each group is in a fixed conflict of interest and ideology not only with all other groups but also with the whole matrix—with society itself. American life has its pressure groups, to be sure, but it is much more ad hoc and flexible, much less divided into this angular organization of fixed competing boxes.

The compartmentalized arrangement of European society has been felt to be necessary in the revolutionary and counterrevolutionary circumstances which typified the last two hundred years. Each man has been uncertain of his present standing and future possibilities, and so he has joined with some others and enclosed himself. The castle of his personality is thus enveloped by the fortress of his group.

Resisting the state has been part of the motive for these arrangements even in peacetime. Historians have observed that the French Revolution arose, in part, from the king's curtailing liberties by centralizing state power. Certainly, no subsequent European revolution has reduced centralization. Despite endless attempts at democratic reforms in numberless republican constitutions, the Code Napoleon, a dictator's law, still governs most countries. To this day, in a Paris bakery or a Milan café or a Munich hotel, the price of a baguette, an espresso, or a *Zimmer* is regulated on a *national* basis. In Greece, not the Greece of the colonels but socialist Greece, three taxi drivers have been jailed under a law forbidding insulting the prime minister, other cabinet officials, and even key opposition leaders. In the habit of taxi drivers everywhere, they were shooting the breeze with the passengers in the backseat. Their numbers were taken and the government machinery brought them to trial and prison. Now, cards have gone up in each taxi forbidding conversations with the driver about anything but the trip. Even in supposedly democratic England, one hears the same complaints about central government power. Press censorship exists and strict laws prohibit many types of printed statements about public individuals and, above all, as in Greece, officeholders of the state. As a British publisher puts it to me: "You Americans have no idea of the liberties you enjoy. If you were to publish here what is routinely published in your own country, nearly half the editors of your newspapers and the heads of most of your publishing houses would find themselves in jail. It is the ancient libel laws effectively used by the modern state to suppress certain kinds of information. We do not have real freedom of the press in your sense."

No wonder that European political parties, labor unions, farmers' organizations, must be much more active, ambitious, strong, and hard than ours. No wonder that in such embittered historical circumstances there is a stupid tendency to ignore the interests of other groups and get what one can. And no wonder that individuals, when deprived and even punished for their group memberships by competitors, seek to identify ever more closely with their group. The two world wars arose, in part, from such conflicts. Now the conflicts—except for the terrorists, the Catholics, Protestants, and English in Northern Ireland, the various separatist movements, and the occasional intergroup street fracas—are largely peaceful.

To the American mind, the pervasiveness of boxification can seem grotesque: a woman friend exclaims that her Italian "PTA is just a waste of time." I ask her to elaborate and am shocked by her reply. "Last week," she says, "at the kindergarten meeting with the other mothers, we got nowhere, because, after an hour's discussion about the curtains, the Communist mothers all walked out!" It is as if, in our peacefully revolutionary times, the European mind has fallen back upon images and habits from a violent past. All those ancient enclosures of town walls, moats, ancient hedgerows, and stone dividers of fields have been resurrected in the boxes of social life. That rigid division of medieval town life by group—the guilds of joiners, butchers, bakers, carpenters, masons, blacksmiths, tinsmiths, and so forth—has been revived in new ways in the revolutionary present.

The following example is taken from the world of trade unions, but those, apart from the political parties themselves, are only the most obvious compartments in a boxified culture. In a major European capital, where business failures and unemployment have been punishingly high for years, the Dutch head of the AP bureau, a man Americanized by ten years' previous service in the United States, becomes irritated. Painters have arrived early in the morning from the contractor, but they aren't making much progress. It seems that the chemicals thrown off by the Xerox machine have accumulated in a brown scum on the ceiling which must be cleaned before they can proceed. The painters wipe futilely with their rags for an hour. Looking up at them, the bureau chief opines that they need to use a stiff brush. The painters ignore him and continue their wiping, finally throwing him these words: "Don't have a brush." "I do," replies the enterprising executive and returns after a moment with it. "Don't know how to use it," say the trade unionists. "I do," says the bureau chief, motioning them off the ladders. Very slowly, they climb down. He mounts, energetically, and in five minutes has cleared several square meters of the ceiling. The trade unionists are unimpressed, sullen. They take to the telephone. Hours later, after difficult negotiations between the bureau chief, the painting contractor, the workers, and their shop steward, the painters, finally convinced that no one is trying to take advantage of them, agree to use the brush.

So is life become group-defensive, politicized, divided, and blocked. Mixed into all this kind of thing is the passion of religion. For when ancient hierarchy broke down, creating the left-right axis and the matrix of modern European society, the new scheme was immediately filled with the harshness of religious warfare. In Catholic countries, the left, in general, aligned against the church. The church, in general, aligned itself with the right. In Protestant countries, the situation was more complex, but religious feeling also leaked into political, social, and economic groupings. Thus, parents and painters are not only fighting against the possibility of unreasonable economic exploitation by other groups, nor even the memories of unreasonable exploitation of yore, they are also fighting the past shadows and future possibilities of the Inquisition, the Index, and the priests who joined the Fascists, the Pétainists, and the Falangists. Its takes some historical imagination to understand the fierceness with which Europeans sometimes foolishly cling to their boxes and their often self-destructive habits. Old blood and divinity blind their eyes.

The passion, the absurdity, and the selfishness in these bitter habits of collective action, the reflex to stand with one group against another, are everywhere. The Italian government, though a member of the Common Market, wants to discourage imports from its partners, other national boxes. The government reduces the number of customs inspectors at the border and keeps their wages low. But then the inspectors' union strikes. In retaliation, inconvenienced truckers blockade major highways all over Europe. Box against box against box. In England, coal miners try a giant strike to bring down the government itself. In the same country, at one point, even the spies attempt to strike. In Paris, when the truckers block the roads, the populace, with ancient habit of those used to the war of groups, empties supermarket shelves of sugar and coffee: no one knows how bad things will get and how long the blockade will last. When, at last, the truckers get quicker service at the Italian customs, they restart the process by upping their demands and insisting on reduced prices for fuel. Though massive street violence is not as common as it used to be, street demonstrations are routine, another tradition of revolution and counterrevolution. Contention reigns within each nation and among them and thus revolutionary conditions persist but with less evident damage than in the past. To imagine the situation, no longer visualize the barricades of old but, as one European put it, "each one trying to get more of the blanket." Imagine many groups, with hands to pull and legs to kick, underneath one cover, each believing itself too much in the cold, and you have a useful picture of the underlying structure and dynamic at work in much of European society.

As we have observed, our own society is also organized into subgroups. But ours are not typically hard-sided, built-in, and baked-in by history. Even our political parties are loose alliances with hardly any ideology, practically disbanding between national elections. Far from politicizing individual kindergartens, we tend to have nonpartisan elections in whole municipalities. Such practices often puzzle and even infuriate Europeans, giving them more reason to call us unserious, naïve, and childish. It is hard for them to understand a more fluid social situation which derives from radically different historical circumstances: religious toleration, no religious wars, no tradition of fixed hierarchy, to name just a few. Even the Soviets can't make it out. As one Russian diplomat told me: "We can predict what the Western European nations will do ninety percent of the time. But you Americans are a mystery. Even with all our institutes which study you, we can't get better than chance, fifty percent." A German socialist, a professor of American history, a man who has taught and studied at Harvard, can't make it out either. He complains, bitterly: "You have many politicians—Hubert Humphrey, George McGovern, Walter Mondale—who have similar goals to ours: social democracy. But when they come through and I ask them why, unlike other Europeans, they have no formal ties to our party, they shrug. I tell them they are irresponsible!" I want to write for him a book about societies that are compartmentalized by history and those that are not, but I believe he would still not understand.

Europeans constantly miss certain fundamentals of our more fluid social situation. One I've encountered numerous times was well represented by the remarks of a Danish journalist: "I went to a religious meeting in America, some small sect, but it had thousands of members. A revival, I think they called it. The clapping, the singing, the ecstasy, it frightened me. I felt that an American Hitler could emerge from such a situation and take over such people!" Europeans have trouble understanding a decentralized and flexible people always on the move toward God, seldom contained for very long by any small sect or local congregation, sliding from belief to unbelief and back, and consequently often in need of revivals. When Europeans see an enthusiastic religious meeting here, they automatically infer its connection with a strong centralized state and vast groups of people organized into opposing blocs. If one of the blocs takes over the state, they know, watch out: Hitler.

How to explain our relatively decentralized politics, even in the Iron Age of our being a great power? How to explain our traditional separation of church and state or the separation of our many churches into an increasingly easy toleration? Enthusiasm in Europe has repeatedly turned into delirium and destruction on a colossal scale. Thus, one must be ever vigilant over there and be prepared to fight against the encroachments of other groups. To take an ideological example, at a dinner party a thoughtful American sociologist remarks that "Marxism's emphasis on social justice is very appealing to me but as an economic philosophy it is nonsense." An Anglo-Irish journalist doesn't address the complex personal observation but demands, with boxified fury, "Whose side are you on?" The American doesn't understand the question (hard-sided boxes of left-right is what he can't get) and the Irishman doesn't understand the implied social and historical context of the remark (fluidity, flexibility, social consensus).

But much more important for the European are the bonds which arise from his revolutionary past and present to limit his freedom as an individual and his possibilities as a social being. Though Europeans appear to be more intellectually individualistic than Americans, they often are not. In America, it is true that for many reasons, there is a well-known tendency for men to focus on practical affairs and in intellectual matters simply to embrace the reigning views of the majority in a conformist way. In Europe, however, the existence of strong social groups complete with tough ideologies forces a person to choose one. Then, he must defend it. Since others are attacking, he becomes skilled in dialectic, in inventing arguments, in mustering evidence—the eristic style of argument once more. The result is the appearance of intellectual vigor and independence, but truly individual intellects are as rare in Europe as in the United States. What one mostly gets are various conformities to the beliefs of boxes.

The lack of European individualism is most evident in action. This is particularly true in regard to livelihood. The European clings to his economic habits, and when the world economy changes, he refuses to move. His whole history and his belief that others are organized to prevent his moving easily makes mobility unthinkable for him. Whether farmer, steelworker, or a business executive, the European is quickly mobilized into being a sheep member of the group, which he needs for protection and to which he has sworn loyalty in order to advance his little interests.

Even when, as in the coal mines, the work is miserable and dangerous, the European clings to it and identifies himself with the box he has been born into or joined early in life. In an economic crisis, he wants the members of some other group to be flexible and to change, not his own. He attends not to statesman-like exhortations from elected officials to save the economies of England, France, or Germany, as the case may be, but if at any time his own group is under pressure, he listens for the sound of the phone, the call from the local party chief, the union leader, or the head of the trade association, summoning him to a meeting of his box, where he will plan to participate energetically in whatever act of reinforcement may seem necessary. It may be a peaceful mass march, the distribution of literature, acts of collective vandalism like telephone workers' cutting the wires, or even pitched battles with the government's police—all just to show that *this* box means business. From one point of view, it is a kind of revolutionary anarchy by group. From another point of view, it is again the opposite of individualism, a collective conformity rather than the taste for what truly defines individuality: action, adventure, personal exertion, triumph, pain, and even defeat.

Compare, briefly, the much greater individualism in action of the American who, if anything, suffers from too little basic social support for his economic welfare. But he has a lot of freedom to move—at least, many Americans who are not poor and members of despised minorities do. Already fifteen years ago, according to the Department of Labor, the average American changed careers (not just jobs) three times in his life. Even physicians, who express the most satisfaction with their jobs of all Americans, are starting to move: one meets doctors who say, "It's enough." They are off "to write," "to open a bookshop," "to go to law school." We change, in vocational and so many other ways, not only because we are restless and driven—which we are—but because we *can* change. We are not forced into collective compartments. In this way, Americans are much freer to chart and rechart a life course. Of course, the price of such existential freedom is anxiety, and God knows we have it. We pay also in a certain lack of civility. It is hard to be leisured, for example, amidst the ambition, fear, and even frenzy associated with the drive for individual achievement.

On the other hand, as we have seen, one encounters less and less civility in the contemporary European. The bookstore clerk and manager, the pharmacists and the train attendant, even the tobacconist, are doubtless irritated for many different reasons. But one is that boxification traps them in the vocational compartments where they have first landed. Paradoxically, they are able to express their irritation to anyone who crosses their path, because they are securely defended by their little box.

The complex, unyielding matrix in which they dwell also costs Europeans in their ability to be communal. It is true that many excesses of American individualism are corrected by such formal benefits which European boxes have won as long-lasting unemployment insurance, guaranteed medical and child care, and maternity leave. As social measures, however, all this is impersonal. What is it really like to live in a European city? Bad manners to strangers aside, does the social legislation won through revolution and group agitation translate into that subtle feeling of the supportive presence of "the others"?

These are difficult questions, but one person I talked with about community in Europe seemed to me to sum up many answers I was given. A Parisian, Vivianne is a woman of about thirty, trained in history in France and then in economics in America. She is a serious young professional and also a divorced single mother. She insists on talking in English, so she can practice what is her nearly perfect, colloquial, American speech. As I get to know her, I come to like her courage and her realism about things.

"My parents were French intellectuals. So, of course"—she laughs—"I was brought up as a Communist. I was told that when I went to America for five years, I would find people totally selfish and individualist, lacking any solidarity.

"But compared to Paris, where I've come back to since two years, Cleveland was social. Over there, mothers shared children and people were active in community organizations. An example: two days after having my baby in the university hospital, I went home, terrified of being alone. But all my neighbors were there.

People I'd never seen. And they kept coming back to hang up curtains, give advice, pass on some old baby clothes, two strollers, and a used playpen. When I needed milk and the shops were closed, I just went next door.

"But people here in Paris are much more privatistic. True, in Europe the family is supposed to take care of all these things. But the European family isn't what it was, you know. When my friends in Paris have children, they don't go to their families, they drive halfway across town to ask *my* advice: *I'm* the grandma, because I had a kid first.

"For me, people's relationship to children defines what 'community' means. My daughter, Diane, was born in the U.S. and arrived here only when she was five. Naturally, like any American kid, she rang all the bells in the building to find friends to play with. But the only people who opened up in this whole large apartment house—I think there are sixty units—were foreigners, Moroccan Jews. And even with them, after four years now, it's all still so complicated! The kids here go to music lessons, dance lessons, they have homework; everything is organized. There is no casual openness. I only met the mother of Diane's best school friend this year, today. It's *June!*

"But with the easy support I found in the States, I could be much more independent than I am here. Here I have to organize things very tightly. If I arrive home even five minutes late for when Diane gets back from school in the afternoon, I can't count on my neighbors being willing to take her in, let her wait, give her a glass of milk. True, there is state child care; but it is antiseptic and cold. There are not enough people to really take care and not enough places. Anybody I know who has even a little money looks for private care, and it's hard to find.

"Frankly, if I had to have a very young child here, I would not know how to do it. America, at the level of my own life, not the socialized economy and all kinds of 'benefits,' was more socialist than France, which I find more lonely and individually alienated. My parents say that I should become a member of the Communist party and that would help. I could take the kid somewhere then; but I can do that now. I would still have the real problem of community—the building."

A recital such as this suggests the intimate ways in which boxification destroys community. American rural neighborliness was imported to the cities because it was drastically needed. In Europe, organized groups were supposed to replace community but, instead, they have only supplied services. Just as boxification often prevents an active individualism, it kills the spontaneous and organic community sense.

Some effects of boxification on the European personality are subtler and harder to grasp. We have already alluded to the air of self-assured "rightness" with which the European advances his opinions. But this feeling of "rightness" can also extend to a person's desires and even to his very self. Part of the reason for this is that the European learns to feel himself to be not just a lone individual but a representative.

Only after years of residence do I gain insight into this transforming process by catching it at work on myself. One day, offended yet again by the bad manners of people I have been running into, and increasingly influenced by socializing with a number of acquaintances who identify themselves with the old hierarchy, I sit in my Florentine café and watch Italian young men with their brilliantined hair, their sloppy-chic, up-to-the-minute clothes, and I hear their rude, cheap remarks about girls who pass. "*Canaille,* the sweepings of the street," is what I find myself thinking—as if I had the right to use the terms of some counter-revolutionary *seigneur.* I am filled with contempt that changes to a general fury, not merely a personal but a collective feeling of how socially wrong are those ribald jokes, those sloppy provocative postures. In me there burns a superior rage that would easily give itself to extreme measures, to guillotines, garrotings, extermination camps. I feel myself transforming: I could kill for aristocratic good manners! *I* have become WE.

I catch myself with a shudder, then laugh. I recall a sculptor friend who had lived in Europe for many years—in England, France, and Italy—and then returned to New York. Several times, when he was put off by a supermarket clerk's lack of consideration or the brusque rudeness of a bus driver at rush hour, he would say astonishing things like: "I really shouldn't talk to people of your social class." I had attributed such un-American remarks to his artistic eccentricity. Now I see the influence of the European matrix.

Though they may not always state it, Europeans often feel and think so: "I shouldn't talk to people who are so stupid as not to be Communists, or Socialists, or who are stuffy aristocrats, or who are vulgar laborers," and so forth. A vague habit of social intolerance, fueled by remembered hierarchy and the fury of revolution both, allows each individual, no matter what his social position, to feel not only that he is right but also that what he thinks in fact represents the right, as embodied in the group. Being habitually identified with and conditioned by their group of affiliation, Europeans often imagine that they take on its size, power, and claim to infallibility. Each individual becomes the delegate plenipotentiary.

This mood, once I came to see it clearly, turned out to be not entirely unfamiliar. As a child on the Lower East Side of New York, I had known it in the Eastern European immigrants of my family and neighborhood. I remember outdoor fishmongers, their hands red from ice shards and covered with blood and scales, who could condemn others, even the whole world, from a position based on solid traditions of entitlement, of those who *belong* to something that is mighty, great, organized, and, therefore, dangerous. Naturally, such a state of being fuels the eristic quality of European argument. As an Italian professor puts it to me, only half-jokingly: "*We* don't argue to convince; we *know* we are right and that only a fool would not have seen our point long ago."

During my time in Europe, I have not only fallen into this mood—a disgrace for which I am partly grateful because it has shown me a concealed side of the European psyche—but I have even learned to cultivate it, as Europeans learn in their childhood. What one works at is developing that sense of self-importance derived from group affiliation, an attitude expressed by the question: "Don't you know who I *am?*"

One day, a friend calls from America. She says that she's coming to Florence and asks: "Would you mind calling the Castello ———— and arranging for me to visit their closed sculpture collection while I'm over there? You can say, if you need to, that I am a graduate of ———— University, which now owns it and that Professor Cadwallader recommends me." I hesitate but say yes. She quickly passes on to other matters.

When she has finished the call, I put down the phone with

mixed emotions. For I have learned that access to places here is not the easy thing it is back home. I'm sure the Castello is now run not for the benefit of the university, so far away, but for that of its local employees. In short, it is a boxified revolutionary social institution. But I resolve to try.

On Monday, I call. The directress, I am told, "is in the garden." I leave word for her to phone back.

No call.

On Tuesday, when I call again, she is apparently still in the garden. I leave elaborate messages, including Cadwallader's name, but she doesn't call back.

On Wednesday, it is the same.

With each day my irritation mounts.

Thursday, as sometimes happens with anger, its energy delivers the propulsive power for a creative takeoff. I begin to think out what Europeans instinctively know: "Probably there is an association of museum executives that allows them to behave like this, that protects them from having to work. In America, someone, at least, would have called back, or, if not, suggested how *I* should proceed. Here, they stonewall it." Then, increasingly annoyed at the injustice in this treatment, I begin to search in my mind for that psychic group support the European has learned to find from youth. "In the garden, indeed! Who finances the Castello, after all? It belongs to the university now. But who supports universities? These days all universities are partly supported with public funds. Taxes. That means *they* are denying me access to what is paid for with *my* money." Wild now, I am full of indignation: "Undemocratic! The Castello belongs to all of us Americans!"

To meet their box, I will put myself in boxes of my own. I calm myself. I call back once more. I have resolved to be full of Europeanness. "*Pronto.*" The secretary answers the phone in her usual laconic way. "Hello," I reply, in English this time. No longer do I try to be decent by speaking Italian—I admit to myself at last what I have dimly known for a long while: speaking their language makes me, in their eyes, nothing more than one of millions of anonymous nonpersons. Power is what they understand, and so I put myself into the box of America; the U.S.A. is powerful and even owns the Castello. Moreover, I put them in an embarrassing box of their own by forcing them to speak their bad English: Europeans believe that they should know English well these days. Next, because they violate several good American norms, including promptness and efficiency, I take a high tone, indeed. I swell inwardly, a regular viceroy, the representative of a great colonial power, a spokesman for the fairness of the New World. Naturally, as befits such collective power and right, I am polite. I menace but I do it quietly: "You see," I explain, "I have called before, recommended by Professor Cadwallader, but she has never seen *fit* to call back."

I let the unuttered warning linger in the air, counting on their European sensitivity to pick up the threat. I am not disappointed. The secretary, previously bored, abruptly changes tone herself and says excitedly to someone else near her: *"Dice che sia raccomandato dal Professore Cadwallader e sembra un po' arrabbiato."* "He says a certain Professor Cadwallader recommends him and he seems a bit angry." The directress, as if she smelled the subtle chemistry I have injected into the affair, abruptly seizes the phone: "Who is this?" she demands.

I remain calm at the counterchallenge in her tone and become, if possible, even more confident, more vice-regal. I make my introduction yet one more time but conclude with an air of absolute certainty: "I'm sure on Professor Cadwallader's recommendation you can squeeze my friend Professor Jones" (I decide to give her a title and thereby put her in a superior box too) "into your program of special visits." The directress clearly has no idea of who Professor Cadwallader is. But she fears from my manner that he—and I, for that matter—might command an influence on some subbox of the America-University-Castello complex. Suddenly she gushes into graciousness: "Of course, I'll try. We will do our best," she says, "but it is so difficult with these many, many visitors." Ever more sure of myself, full of that exquisite condescension natural to a leader, I sympathize. "I'm sure it is," say I. "The tour of Tuesday became full yesterday," she says. "Could Professor Jones come the following week?" "Impossible," I reply, dryly confident, "and I have been forced to call several times before, you know." *Dieu et mon droit* is the feeling at which I have arrived. I wait. Comes the capitulation: "I will put her down for four o'clock on Tuesday." The viceroy is satisfied, *l'État c'est Moi!* When I can work up this higher European mood, I *know* it is the only way to treat people.

No wonder Europeans are so often arrogant if they can, so easily, experience themselves as more than individuals, indeed, like gods. What a sweetness, what a strengthening vigor, what a utility it has. Of course, the magnification of the sense of self which boxification fosters also further enhances blockages to true self-expression in action. When one exalted self meets another, as happens constantly in these societies, the two forces often paralyze each other and the individual progress of both is stopped dead.

There is another even more pervasive and damaging way in which boxification affects the psyche of Europeans, further impeding freedom of movement. It infects European subjectivity itself, casting mysterious shadows inside the streaming inner awareness, the fantasy, and even the nighttime dreaming of individuals. Once again, my own view was a long time in coming, for hundreds of observations, reading, and innumerable conversations had not made it clear. Then, one night in Paris, that city which specializes in clear ideas, the pattern of the thing swiftly fell into place.

I was staying with French acquaintances, she a physician, he a lawyer. At the dinner table, each of us reviews his day for the others. When my turn comes, I complain about the phone service. "I know the phone people are working on improving the system, but still, when I look in the directory or call information, I only get the numbers I want maybe half the time." In a joking way, I exaggerate to make the point about what seems to my American understanding only simple inefficiency: "It's like Soviet Russia! And so foolish from a business standpoint—as if the telephone company doesn't want people to call each other."

"They don't," snaps Marianne. "At the least, they don't care one way or the other. I never call Information to try to get a number; it's generally useless; I stay within the circle of people I know." And then, her voice assuming an annoyed tone that seems to say she doesn't want to continue the explication of such events, she adds: "You miss the point, Stuart: this is *not* a democracy. Yes, they are trying to improve it, to break the practice of keeping all information in the hands of certain people, above all of keeping it centralized in Paris so they can maintain their power. But by now this is no longer a decision, it is a habit. It is built into the way things work, the social system itself. They really don't want it any other way; they don't want it to change."

As she concludes, I am aware she is telling me that as she knows her society, things are not open, free, and transparent. I am less sure what to make of her annoyance, some of which I feel is directed at me. I can't fathom it. These little realizations cross my awareness rapidly, however, for I am already reacting to what she has said, which seems so un-American. "Who is this *they?*" I wonder aloud, a touch of skepticism in my voice. "Sounds to me, Marianne, that you have an idea that somewhere a master class, some elite, is secretly directing everything."

"And probably not far wrong," Charles the lawyer flatly comments. Then, lawyerlike, he reviews the facts. "You told me that today you had a very hard time trying to call *Le Monde*. Even finding the number in the book was difficult, you said, because it was not at all prominently displayed. And you were surprised, because it is our most important, objective, and distinguished newspaper. At last, you found the number, but you kept getting a recording saying the number had been changed and to call Information. But when you called Information, they gave you the old number again. Finally, when you tracked down the current number through a friend, it was a little after five o'clock. You wanted to leave a message for a journalist but the phone operator at *Le Monde* told you: 'I'm sorry, *monsieur,* we don't take messages.' You were 'shocked,' you said. You compared America, where there is always someone to take a message at a major newspaper, anytime.

"But instead of being shocked," he concludes the review, "let us be analytical." He pauses. I note the characteristic French move into Reason and tell myself I enjoy it. With a slightly patronizing voice, even a little hard, he begins again. "Let us ask what the response you got at *Le Monde* means. Just that people don't want to be accommodating. Therefore, it must be in their interest to make the paper difficult of access. Maybe reporters and editors just don't want to make all-night stands but would rather go home. Perhaps it's just that simple. Or perhaps there is another aspect. Despite its relative objectivity, like all French papers *Le Monde* is more full of opinions than hard news. Well, one makes one's opinions at night, over dinner, reading, and so on:

thus, one can't be bothered to take phone calls from strangers. Or, one makes one's opinions constantly, even during the day, so who needs strangers to call?"

He rests, satisfied with himself for having penetrated a mystery. But there is still a heaviness in the air, some annoyance that radiates from him. It is subtle, but I feel it, a mystery in itself. Hoping either to illuminate or dispel it, I move on to other events of the day which have puzzled me.

I mention a mutual friend, Jean-Luc, with whom I have talked. The publisher of several important magazines, he has just written a book which has become a best seller. "You know what he told me," I say, "that even though he made his own publicity arrangements, and even though the French publisher had had plenty of time to make preparations, when he went to Switzerland yesterday to do an important TV show about his book, there wasn't a single copy in the whole country! American publishers at least would have organized themselves to back a sure thing like a best seller. Apparently, French publishers are even more inefficient than those in the States."

Charles jumps in to object: "You're seeing the system too rationally here, as if only the market and money and profit counted and people were trying to maximize those in a reasonable way. That may be true in the U.S. but not in France." I am bewildered by his violent move away from Reason and even more mystified, unsettled by this notion of a vague, institutionalized irrationality in the French publishing world and in French life in general. He takes up his thought: "I imagine what happened is that some people at the publisher didn't like the book, maybe the person in charge of foreign sales; or maybe someone is personally opposed to Jean-Luc; or believes that the house should publish some other kind of book; or doesn't like Jean-Luc because he's Jewish; or simply just didn't *feel* like promoting it. The person blocking it might not even have been a boss, it could have been an assistant.

"Marianne told you that life wasn't democratic and open here. You should also know that it doesn't operate according to reasonable rules of fair play. It operates according to the interests of individuals and groups."

I begin to feel oppressed by the heaviness of their assumptions about their lives: out there, there are others, who by design or whim are moving to block you; you know it, but you can't do much about it.

Charles expands the vision: "People use their power here, whenever they can. They use it to suppress information, for example, in constant censorship, one of the great habits in Italy, France, Germany, and even in England. And not just government censorship—everyone's censorship. And they use it to make propaganda, the reciprocal of censorship. And it's not only with information, but with everything that it is become a habit: a war devoted not only to promote our interests but also simply to *block* those of people we don't like, our enemies, or just 'the others.' Most Americans say the States isn't like this, except somewhat in politics. I wonder. In any case, most Americans don't have this constant will to revenge we do. Write it on your brain in capital letters—they are trying to block you, everyone is!"

Marianne gets up, as if she has had all she wants. Charles's tone has been rising. She looks bitterly at me. We say good night and I go off to bed. My thoughts toss around as I try to digest what has happened. Not only what has been said by way of social analysis, some of which is already quite familiar, but more the psychological meaning of that, its effects on subjectivity. I am particularly puzzled by the curiously dark tones that crept in over and over. These people, I reflect (and I have heard many other Europeans say things that lean clearly in the same direction), carry the burden of believing they live in a world in which others, everywhere, are out to frustrate them, especially groups of others.

Incredible. And yet, I know that if one reads newspapers in many European countries, there seems to be a consensus on this point. How else explain the continuous appearance in them of elaborate scandals, many the result of preceding scandals, in turn arising from others yet older—as if some group had begun plotting at the beginning of time and the years had only served to elaborate the original intrigue. In Italy, not to speak of other countries, the newspapers are nearly opaque to the foreigner, because to understand their stories you would have to know all that background, and how one affair implicates, progressively, the rich, the Catholic Church, the banks, the Masons, the Mafia, the labor unions, the landowners, and the main political parties as well as other powerful groups.

Indeed, the historical monuments of Europe themselves testify to such complex and perennial manipulations. Go to old castles and you will read, either in your guidebook or on marble plaques at the entrance, how these formidable fortresses, well provisioned and well defended, commanding seemingly impregnable heights and approaches, were taken, century after century, by foreign invaders. One asks oneself how it was possible. Research reveals it was done, at least half the time, not by sheer force of arms but by betrayal from within. Some individual, or more usually a group, secretly opened the postern, poisoned their own town's wells, made a deal with the enemy, betrayed, connived, and collaborated—in secret. European castles are architectural symbols of *conspiracy.*

Lying in bed and turning over these thoughts, I realize that the European naturally believes he lives in a world in which conspiracy is as ever-present as castles. This is an important reason why Europeans are always so suspicious and skeptical. It is also why, whenever something happens in life which frustrates them and which could possibly be attributed to the will of another acting in his own self-interest or simply against one's own, they make such an attribution. For them, life is like Newton's universe: every effect has a cause and even a deliberate one. Alert, Europeans are ever on guard to discover the secrets of the farthest reaches. They know that others are trying to muffle the reality they search and that the distant and partial signals they receive are not much with which to work. But still, like the most patient investigators, their radio antennae constantly turning, searching, they outwatch the night.

One understands now why Europeans were so baffled at our getting upset over a conspiracy like Watergate. For them, it was just business as usual. Moreover, they *know* that the Kennedys, Oswald, and King, for example, were not killed by lone adventurers, American-style. They *know* there was a group, probably many groups, behind the scenes.

As I come to these realizations in the Paris night, I better understand that other Europe which, I realize ever more clearly, I knew in childhood in New York. For those immigrants, products of the still more desperate background of Eastern Europe, life was even worse than any mere conspiracy.

Like so many American children, I was taught in school to have a patronizing contempt for my foreign-born parents. They didn't understand life. How could I know, at age ten, that what my father understood came from his experience of another very different society? Only many years afterward did I learn from him the circumstances of his emigration. At age eleven, he was elected head of his class's little protest group. The Jewish pupils in his school in Poland wanted to be treated the same as the other kids and not forced to sit in the back of the class. The word was passed about him; he was boxed-labeled as a Jew, a ringleader, and an anticzarist. The policeman of the village told my grandfather it would be best if the whole family got out of the country. The czar's bureaucracy had boxed the eleven-year-old for life.

I, on the other hand, had been taught that I was born in the land of the free, an open society where every individual had a chance. After my evening with Charles and Marianne, and all it brought into focus about the European habit of thinking about conspiracy, how full of comic misunderstanding seem the conversational struggles I used to have with my parents.

Item: Crest toothpaste. It was new on the market. At age seventeen, having been taught in my American school to appreciate new developments in hygiene, I was happy to bring the good tidings home to my European-born parents. Thus, one night, showing off a little but mainly trying to be helpful, I observed over dinner: "You ought to buy Crest toothpaste—it really prevents cavities; it has fluoride."

Between bites, my father only replied: "Nonsense."

I felt offended but persisted. "But, Dad, it's been endorsed by the American Dental Association."

"So what?" he asks, rhetorically, barely pausing in his eating. Then adds: "They got paid off."

I am puzzled at his dry harshness. And even more puzzled when my stepmother, her lips curling with anger, says: "You remember the quiz programs when the postman answered all those questions about opera—every one? 'The Sixty-four Thousand Dollar Question'?"

I nod.

"Your father knew it was fixed from the start. And, sure enough, it turned out later that they gave all the contestants who were so successful the answers. He knew. Listen to your father!"

"Of course," said he, wiping his mouth with his napkin. "How could a postman know all that?"

He concluded with a portentous general thought that closed the subject: "It's all a racket."

Tonight in Paris, years and years later, I finally put it together. Schooled in a boxified society, the European sees men enmeshed in a world typified not only by conspiracy but by a generalized *criminality*. It was that way in 1922, when my father came to America, and it is that way in Paris now. "It's all a racket."

And, at last, the reasons for one emotional consequence of this bitter vision come clear to me. Why have Marianne and Charles and my father and stepmother, most gentle people, become so irritated, even angry, in these conversations? Because it is annoying that others—naïve Americans—refuse to listen to what's good for them. Because children and other innocents must be told, and it is a nasty duty to have to disillusion people. Finally, and most infuriating, because one must again oneself face and publicly proclaim the harsh knowledge that social life is corrupt, that the cards are stacked, that what appears is not what is, and that others are engaged in evil combinations to get you.

Since that night in Paris, I have changed. When I was a child, I used to fight this European complex of cynicism, paranoia, and bitterness. Until recently, I used to fight it again in contemporary Europe. But at last I have come to an understanding of where the attitudes originate in history and how they are reinforced in the European present. As Charles says, corrupt conspiracy has become such a habit that there seems no way to change things anymore. An impulse toward positive action—reforming a school, attacking the Mafia, crating a new product—too often yields to the need to form a strong group of one's own in which all are united. One acts to define, perfect, and defend it as an instrument for the protection and betterment of all within. But the group thus formed excites the fears of others, who mount counterefforts at organization. Thus is the original cause lost to the System and each individual becomes a part of the problem rather than of the solution.

Just the assumption of criminal conspiracy alone, without regard to mobilization of one's own group, demands an enormous price. People who believe that everything is a racket, or that there is a willful decision not to make phones work well, are discouraged before they start anything. Think of the number of projects which must never be attempted. Consider, moreover, the European energy wasted in fantasy efforts to discern the hidden motives behind everything that happens. I used to be angry at Europeans for being so pessimistic and easily disheartened. Now I am equally inclined to take pity.

It is true that their complex attitudes serve those who have them in ways that are often far from worthy of pity: believing that everyone else is engaged in corrupt conspiracies justifies one's own selfish and concerted corruption. Tax evasion is the universal example. Thus, the poor argue that the rich are hiding their ill-gotten gains and escaping their tax obligations by sophisticated maneuvering and outright fraud. The rich, in turn, argue that the leftist parties and trade unions are conspiring to rob them of their legitimate wealth. All come to feel justified, according to the conspiracy theory, of doing everything possible not to pay taxes themselves. But such attitudes are not, in the end, very productive, or even satisfying. As one European puts it to me—he seemed to be speaking for the whole old continent— "Yeah, we're wised-up. We're smart, not innocent like Americans. But sometimes I think we're so smart we're stupid." More and more I am sorry for their sad, self-destructive knowledge.

PART FIVE
SPIRIT IN MATTER

Tho' much is taken, much abides.

—**Alfred, Lord Tennyson**

No one will ever succeed in defining happiness, but certainly one of its conditions is that a certain modest human scale not be overstepped. Happiness is also a host of small impressions which strike us, though we spare them no attention. . . . The streets of Paris have given me much happiness, as have the valleys and hills of the French provinces, where a slate roof in a cluster of green, a field, a footbridge, a grove, almost burst with the density of their unique particular existence, every kilometer abounding with things to see and touch. This is not the same as zooming down three hundred miles of California freeways situated amid menacing, monstrous vistas, the light lurid on the bare mountains.

—**Czeslaw Milosz**

Aristocratic ages will have a small group of men cultivating the arts who are themselves aristocrats. In literature, devoid for generations of material cares, they will write for each other and be interested in refined sensation, in taste, in conventions, in art for its own sake.

—**Alexis de Tocqueville**

At least the writer as such does have a role in Europe. It is not like in America where literature is produced by the teachers on the campuses for the students who themselves are future teachers.

—**Gore Vidal**

• When I return from my honeymoon with Jacqueline, two and a half weeks in Italy, beginning and ending with a brief visit in Brussels, I am astonished that the first question my mother-in-law poses after asking about our health and the weather on the trip is: "What did you eat?"

• A vulgar Danish-born skirt manufacturer who has prospered with her husband in America, has had all of two years of junior college, and drives a 450 SL Mercedes, which she claims is her preferred automobile "only because it's reliable," says: "Americans are uncultured."

• A Japanese-American woman, married to an elegant Vietnamese refugee and living in Germany, says: "I am glad to be away from Americans: they say whatever is on their minds; there is no grace."

• A French wine merchant on a plane tells me that "Americans are physically awkward; they don't know what to do with their bodies."

• An Austrian visitor to the United States uses, over and over again, the word "charming" to express her appreciation of what she sees, people she meets, places she goes. To an American, she seems foreign, even affected.

CHAPTER NINE

True Materialism

Some fifteen years ago, I was present at a small, excellent dinner party given by the Anglo-American popular philosopher Alan Watts. Alan was a marvelous combination of showman and modest person; he loved to play with life and ideas; and because of his personal history, he was extraordinarily cosmopolitan. Educated in England, he had worked and lived in America for thirty years and, in addition had spent much time in the Orient studying its cultures and religions. He liked to make epigrammatic, even paradoxical, statements, to enjoy their effect on others. He would laugh at his own witty remarks. That evening, I recall, he got off a pithy observation which baffled me for many years. What he said was logically correct, but it troubled my mind because it had no weight of meaning for me and so did not convince. "I can't understand," he said, "why people say that Americans are materialists. If this is a materialist country, then why don't Americans really care more about food? If this is a materialist country, why is there such a tendency to ruin the beautiful landscape?" I tried to shrug off the remarks as the cleverness of a clever man, the sensual advocacy of an avowed sensualist. Obviously, Americans *were* materialists, we all knew that. But still the observation bothered. I felt there must be something significant in it.

The American who really gets to know Europeans and who has eyes to see will slowly learn what true materialism is. What Alan Watts was talking about is before all else a love for matter founded on a belief in matter's substantial existence. Americans believe in ideas, in the ideal, in the future, in progress, in making money, and in achievements of all sorts. But, as many instances make clear, we do not truly believe in matter.

* * *

For humans, land must be the most fundamental of material things. Indeed, in older civilizations, land is not just land but a specific place which has ancestral meaning and nearly religious associations. But when Europeans came to America to settle, especially later on in the big migrations of the nineteenth century, land was infinitely available, it was cheap by comparison to Europe, it had no ancient meanings, and it was a splendid source of gain. Land bought and cleared, or simply bought and held, could be sold, not very much later, to succeeding settlers at a profit. A motto of the frontier moving westward in the nineteenth century was "settle and sell, settle and sell." Americans are still doing it. We treat land, from early times, as a commodity. In the United States, sacred land became a mere thing; its value was its price and the price fluctuated with the market. Land became the equivalent of so much spending power. Thereby, the most basic matter became reduced to the abstraction of a handful of greenbacks or, even more ethereally, of a few figures in your credit column at a bank, numbers on a page.

Europeans do not view land this way, nor did they in the past. Life was settled and land was scarce. Land once possessed was kept in the family. Passed down from generation to generation, whether at the level of the lord, landowning burgher, or peasant, it became a living presence in the family imagination. It was endlessly improved, down to the single rill and contour, fence post, conduit, and stone, in order to yield the most. It was caressed like a familiar lover or, better, like a mother. It acquired a deep familiarity and a holy awesomeness. The priest would come and bless it. Some years it was generous, others stingy; some years you would have to join it in a fight against flood or drought; you would have to struggle by its side.

When Europeans, or we ourselves, for that matter, say that Americans are rootless, this is part of what is meant. Roots can only belong in a particular piece of land. Pull them up once and all land tends to become mere soil, dirt, so much productivity, so many dollars, so much terrain to use. Today's Europeans—the urban majority now, not peasants or small farmers—still yearn for their land, lost or abandoned in the move to the cities. As soon as they can afford it, Europeans will buy themselves a little country place, becoming part-time amateur farmers. A Norwegian psychologist goes from Oslo to the family country place every year to plant her own potatoes for the winter. In Italy, at the other end of the continent, a retired man occupies himself with making wine each year from the little grape arbor behind his house in a small city. It is not a matter of trying to save money; money doesn't enter into it. Nor is it even a question of the quality of the product; the wine in the store is often better and not very expensive. Rather, the relationship to the earth, his own earth, is at the very essence of the act.

We have our share of people who love plants, who garden, who grow and eat their own produce. But with few exceptions, the magnitude of attachment to the land is of a different order. Strong attachment to land is, relatively speaking, un-American.

We are also unattached more generally. Few of us live as adults in the homes of our forebears, and a decreasing number live even in the same town as our parents. Community, in the old sense of a permanent human congregation on land sanctified by its historical existence, was transient even in the American West. A list of "extinct geographical locations," places settled and then abandoned between 1852 and 1912 in Kansas, comes to more than twenty-five hundred. Jamestown was a ghost town a century after its founding. In Europe, ghost towns existed too, but new towns were very often built upon them: one thinks of the many-layered cities of Troy, even the deserted villages of Goldsmith. In Italy, today, thousands of peasant hamlets, *borghi*, abandoned a mere fifteen years ago, have already been reoccupied by hectic urban people seeking country. Possessing such successiveness, place becomes substantial. Place is full of mystery; a history not fully knowable; it is haunted by ghostly presences; it is charged.

We are careful to keep our psychic distance from such fundamental matter as place. Given our habits of moving, it would be too painful to do otherwise. To stay in one place for us is to let grass grow under one's feet (as we say), a sensation the European hungers for but we detest. To stay in one place is to miss all sorts of potential opportunities, not only to make money, but to do good and also to expand oneself, to "grow," as we now say. Our way is to plant our roots in air and grow without any particular place. Even "community" to us is not a permanent place but rather a changeable agreement between free souls, an abstraction embodied not in location but in gestures, not in matter but in acts.

Though he, too, is now uprooted by the forces of modernism, democracy, and economic opportunity, the European still hankers after matter: his land. This is true even at the level of social policy. The expensive indulgence of Europeans toward their inefficient farmers—a mere 10 percent of the population—comes in large part from the broadly held materialistic feeling that the landscape, the particularity of its million little farms and orchards, the old life of attachment, must be preserved: it is good for everyone. Like a good meal, it satisfies.

After land comes its product, food. With some exceptions, Americans are not *very* interested in the things we eat or in eating itself. In this sense, Watts was right again in saying we are not materialists. Paradoxically, we are chronically overweight: when we eat, we tend to be swallowers rather than tasters; when we cease swallowing, we become dieting penitents. Many Americans who visit Europe are surprised to see relatively few Europeans who are really fat. On the other hand, European visitors to the United States are always surprised and even baffled by "the large number of enormously obese Americans," as one German physician puts it.

European food varies enormously in quality from country to country and some European countries (France, Belgium, Italy) make much more of food than others (England, Holland). But generally appreciating and even demanding very good food is not unusual in Europe. France, of course, is the classic case in point. As many American visitors who have made their way into Parisian homes know, living space is expensive and the mass of the population dwells in apartments that are not only crowded but often shabby and decrepit. However, an American diplomat living there remarked one day in a rainy, cold street: "Though most of them live in lousy little hovels and have lousy little lives, twice a day they know they are going to have a really good time. It helps." One can't imagine masses of Americans looking forward to food in this way.

Food to the European is more than defense or compensation. It is savored for its own sake. The American spirit, focused on production and the ideal, goals of personal advancement and world redemption, shrinks from caring so deeply about a corporeal mundanity. We recoil from it like Moses at the sight of the Israelites worshipping the golden calf. Despite the recent proliferation of American cookbooks, the multiplication of restaurants of every kind—French, Italian, Chinese, Japanese, German, and all the rest—much caring about food strikes us as affected and, indeed, in certain Americans it is often just that: a kind of artificial Europeanism, something one does to show that one is cultured, like going to the ballet or the museum. For the European, however, the enjoyment of food is, as they say, "simple."

An American from the Midwest who has lived in Italy for years remarks that one thing she particularly likes is that "over there, eating is eating." When I tell her that the tautology is not literally meaningful, she agrees to explain. "They take the *leisure* to do it. Even in Milan, that most modern of Italian cities, they still do not have breakfast meetings for business, and the lunch business meeting is still virtually unknown. Instead, they have their *attention* on the moment and they dedicate it to the food and the ceremony of eating.* At table, the food is discussed and food of other meals is remembered and compared with what one is eating now. Often, half the meal is taken up with talking about the food one is eating, the food one ate, the food one will eat, even how food is grown. It's no surprise that to Europeans, Americans seem ill at ease during meals. They say we eat on the hoof! That for us, even when the food is good, it is *primarily* functional. They say we don't really know what to talk about around food. That we are restless at table. Especially our business people, who like to keep the nonbusiness conversation light and wisecracking: nothing serious, real, or deep. In Europe, after the talk about food itself, conversation can become entertaining, even challenging, always in an atmosphere of *festa*, of ceremony."

This woman's husband, an Italo-American from Philadelphia, echoes her sentiments, particularly the point about how food is grown. "I get great pleasure from their concern with basics: all those detailed discussions about olive trees, harvesting fruit, growing tomatoes. They relish not only what they are eating but the whole process that led to the meal, they respect it. They talk about how vines are planted differently in different

---

*Americans began commonly using even breakfast for business more than a century ago.

provinces, tied one way in Puglia, another in Chianti, a third in Emilia. (Naturally, they always maintain that their province's way is the best.) They like to explain to visitors at home how the pasta you admire is so particularly good because the sauce, though simple, has an olive oil at its base that they got from the cousin who still lives in the country, four hundred miles away, where the oil is more flavored because the sun is stronger and the growing season longer. I love this concreteness!"

He is a professor, a small man, an intellectual who has lived in Italy for ten years. It is as if he has had to come back to the old continent to put his roots back into the material. He immerses himself in conversations about agriculture like one who has gotten too far from the earth. Like the mythic Antaeus, he gains back his strength, also a certain kind of peace, from his contact. He chooses to live far out of town in the country and raise his own chickens. Gradually, he adds geese, turkeys, rabbits, lettuce, tomatoes. The local *contadino* gives willing advice, happy to share these ancient, simple mysteries. The professor is squeamish, a city boy, about killing his animals for food, so the *contadino* does it, for the first two years. Afterward, he tells Alfredo it's time for him to do it himself. Alfredo learns to kill. He reaches into the cage and grabs the brown rabbit. Then in his left hand he holds it helpless by the long ears and with his right he takes a thick, round stick. He hits the back of the little head hard. The furry animal shudders its way to a mercifully quick death, transformed in seconds to a thing that stares blankly out of blue eyes in the sides of its head. Alfredo kills even though it still shocks him a little to do it. It is meaningful to him, part of some acceptance of things, of life and death. He peels off the skin and hangs the meat. Tomorrow he will eat it with a delicious but simple sauce. Once, to break the tense mood in the second after the slaughtering, I tell him that Alan Watts used to describe the world as "a mutual eating society." Alfredo laughs.

In Belgium, with its dreary climate and its endless history of foreign occupation, people pull into themselves and are quietly tough. Food and eating have what seems to American eyes an incredibly important place in the lives and imaginations of Belgians. Perhaps the motive is to escape from a harsh reality. But you would never know it. The thing itself is the apparent focus. The most elaborate meals are frequently mounted, especially at

Christmastime or other special occasions like birthdays or New Years. When foreigners are involved they quickly are enlisted in the European approach.

Every year, Jacqueline and I have Christmas dinner with her mother and another couple, she Belgian, he an American economist. All five of us are occupied in the long discussions of what will be eaten, where to get it, how to cook it, how to serve it, in what order. I learn to my astonishment that my mother-in-law believes any dinner party, especially one for a festive occasion, "takes three days. One day to shop. One day to cook. One day to clean up." There is talk about how, in the old days, one really ate seriously: five courses—soup, appetizer, and fish, then an interruption for *le trou normand* (the "hole" named after the Normans, a sort of halftime break when one rested at table and took a dry liqueur or a lightly flavored lemon sherbet), then onward to the roast and dessert.

We all laugh with sympathy at the old gourmandise, at the joyful, almost childlike excess of those old ceremonies. Our present-day special dinners in Belgium are pale affairs by comparison, but they often take six hours of carefully paced ingestion to complete. The other couple agrees to bring the appetizers: oysters carefully chosen at only the best fish market so that they are not too fat nor too lean, duck *pâté* with truffles covered with a glaze, *vol-au-vent*—delicate pastry cups filled with chicken bits and covered with a *béchamel* sauce. These are served in the salon with champagne. Merriment leads on to the lamb roast, which Jacqueline has prepared. The group praises its quality and someone recalls the old French saying that "a roast is the true test of a cook." With the roast come four vegetables carefully chosen and cooked, a salad with three types of lettuce torn by hand into tiny pieces, a vinaigrette prepared with much preliminary tasting. Two other kinds of wine are drunk with cheerful attention. My mother-in-law has prepared one of the desserts, a charlotte russe. Demitasse is accompanied by tiny fruits with an exquisite sugar glaze. During the meal, as each item is taken, one renders strict judgment. The city has been crisscrossed a dozen times to find the best of each thing. No merchant has been fully trusted, and now his performance is weighed and remarked and the dooms of praise or disgrace are sealed. Where an item fails to live up to its promise, threats of boycotting the store and attacking its reputation are made with a severity only controlled enough so not to spoil the festive atmosphere.

As an American, at first I found these carryings-on amusing, as all such exaggerations seem amusing. When actually eating a meal, of course, my amusement turns to delight at the exquisiteness of each production—with nearly all of which I have helped by cleaning, fetching, placing, or boiling water. But I try not to let it all get to me too much; I must save myself for greater things. My friend, the other American, is more assimilated into the European way than I. To me he seems a little contrived in his overly slow chewing and tasting; the food has become a project; enjoyment is a task to which he has given his considerable intelligence. I am suspicious of him. The others, the Europeans, unlike each of us, are easy amidst the elaboration, conscious of the excess but relishing it as one should any special feast. Though I enjoy myself, I don't entirely understand it. Even after six years, I am still a little uncomfortable. I find the thing foreign, un-American. And yet I am delighted a couple of years later when the five of us stage another New Year's Eve production of this order, and it is two o'clock, and we are thoroughly concentrated on the food, wine, and conversation, before anyone remarks that the New Year has come hours before, without our noticing it.

Call it living well. Three days later, my stomach is still upset, but I continue to think that overeating, when it is done with such care and, ultimately, simplicity of attitude, has its place in life.

Over many years of such adventures, in Belgium, France, Italy, and Germany, among other countries, I come gradually to agree with an American poet friend who had lived in Europe for ten years. When he came back to the United States he said: "There is nothing to eat in this country." He is wrong, and more wrong now than ever before, and, in any case, he exaggerates. But it is true that in some general way, the experience of food is not the same and its meaning is less—much less.

Our lack of true materialism is also reflected in our tradition of craft skills and our attitude toward product quality. A very popular contemporary novel, *Zen and the Art of Motorcycle Maintenance,* whatever its ultimate literary merit, has a long discussion of "quality" in its many senses. The central metaphor of the book, the care and carefulness with which one needs to treat things to maintain them in perfect order, has to do with a manufactured object—a BMW motorcycle. The author, however, has to refer dramatically not to our own culture but to a German object and an ancient Oriental tradition to make his point. I know a European car-racing champion who is married to an American and criticizes quality in American cars: "You are always ten years behind; your cars look good, great stylish behemoths once, now a little smaller; but when one opens the hood and looks underneath, they are primitive, no refinement."

Americans, especially after the start of industrialism, have been more interested in producing something expediently than in producing it exquisitely. The roots of this difference are historically complex. The European aristocracy monopolized nearly all manufactured products and set higher and higher standards for them. Craftspeople were compelled by this small group's ever-rising demands for quality increasingly to refine the things they made. European museums and palaces are full of such material elaboration—parquet floors, stone carvings, intricate woodwork in ceilings, glassware, ceramics, picture frames, all of a level of manufacture unthinkable in our country. Though quality has declined there, the demand for it still hangs in the air and conditions European attitudes toward products.

American democratic tradition worked the other way. A mass of potential consumers, with little wealth but a normal human attraction to the showy and the luxurious, created a market for goods manufactured quickly, cheaply, and in great numbers and, naturally, of a quality inferior to the aristocratically grounded crafts of Europe. For there, even the peasant, when he could afford to buy, had to order handmade things from craftspeople whose habits had been formed by aristocratic requirements for refined quality. In addition, the peasant buyers would naturally take their cue for what they would deem satisfactory from the work produced for the nobility.

Sheer scarcity of craft skills in our country also contributed to this difference. Skilled craftsmen did not migrate in any large number. In the early nineteenth century, the shortage of craftsmen and wide demand led to what Boorstin has called "a nearly craftless way of making things," the American factory system. The results were a new concept of prosperity and a desacralization of products. Timepieces, for example, had been the flower of the watchmaker's fine art. But once millions were made from standard parts, and once the brief joy in acquiring the novel object had passed, the watch became less interesting, less wonderful, less personal—like land—than in the older civilization. When products lost their uniqueness, they lost a lot of their human significance.

Still another element in our lack of interest in quality manufactures was the original and persistent American belief in progress and perfectibility. We believed not only that things simply *can* change, but that they could and would change for the better. Tocqueville recounts a charming anecdote in which he asks an ordinary American sailor in the 1820s why our ships were made so that they wouldn't last a long time: "He answered offhand that the art of navigation was making such quick progress that even the best of boats would be almost useless if it lasted more than a few years. . . . I recognized in these casual words of an uneducated man about a particular subject the general systematic conception by which a great people conducts all its affairs."

European craftsmen and, later, manufacturers looked with care at what they made, because they couldn't easily imagine the possibility of any great improvement in it. But in America, from the beginning of the industrial era, our eye was fixed not on the thing at hand but on the future, when this object would be replaced by yet another, new and better.

Despite the decline of their craftsmanship nowadays, Europeans are still influenced by the tradition. One sees this in the way old buildings there, built to last forever, are not struck down and replaced as often as here but are reused. The Florence police station is the old Medici palace, five hundred years of service. Europeans keep their cars eleven years, on the average; we keep ours only seven. Our cars would last as long, perhaps even longer than theirs; after all, our cars are simpler and they require less craftlike attention of expensive mechanics; but even now they themselves have less presence for us. Today, as before, our habit of planned obsolescence is an index of our rough-and-ready nonmaterialism.

CHAPTER TEN

More True Materialism

Though there are important exceptions, Europeans generally like and are more comfortable with their sensations than we
are. Even in the clean, repressed, and sanitary north of Europe,
there is a greater entering into the world of sensation—often in
very private moments. But in certain countries love of sensation
in all its human complexity is even more pronounced. A Spaniard
I meet on a plane flying back from New York tells me about his
visit. An enthusiastic young man, when asked to sum up what he
so much likes about the city, he says: "The smells of the different
neighborhoods; the variety of those smells—to me, that is the
greatness of New York!" Except for a few born sensualists, most
Americans must simply wonder at such a remark. How could one
love a city for its smells, especially when many that he enumerates
are disagreeable? One day, the BBC survey report notices that the
average Frenchman still bathes only once a week, but he com-
pensates by using a rich complex of perfumes, colognes, and
aftershaves, all mixed with ranker fragrances.

Smell, in fact, is the most evocative and intricate of human
sensations. One German woman intellectual, a writer, dark-
haired, soft-featured, but with strong blue eyes, tells me about
her lover. She lived in America for many years and she is trying
to explain to me how Americans and Europeans tend to differ
about sexuality. Her remarks are general at first. "Europeans are
perverse, Americans are hygienic and technical in their love-
making, they try to do it well and that's that: it's not complex."

Somewhat baffled, I ask: "What do you mean by 'perverse'
and 'complex' or 'hygienic' and 'technical'?"

A very long hesitation, a look into the distance, a meditative
pull on the cigarette, an interval of calculation, I imagine, about

how much she will reveal and in what way. Finally, she says: "My German boyfriend likes smells. He likes the smell of soap."

"Soap?"

"It goes back to the war or something. He and his mother were walking along a road and there was an air attack, a fighter. They jumped into a ditch. The whole experience is mixed up with his being with her, her carrying a bar of soap, which I suppose was precious during that period, the fear of the plane, his being next to her, next to her thigh, their hearts pounding. Who knows? Maybe he also saw her underwear. Being conscious of such an event, remembering it with awareness, letting it influence your sexuality—I don't know, it's European, somehow."

The young woman's sister, who is also with us, talks about an American friend, Daniel, from New York. He is not a lover of either sister, just a friend; a single man who visits them as often as he can. "When Daniel speaks about sex, it's always very explicit. There are facts—physical or psychological. I can't even get European men to talk that way when I try. For them, it would reduce the intricate to the simple; the mysterious and the tormenting—for sex is tormenting, isn't it?—to a project, a problem you can deal with nearly mechanically. Like people who talk about death easily—doctors. There's that sort of medical attitude toward sex among Americans. On the other hand, there's not enough leaving room for the subtleties and the contradictions. Americans try to cut them open; sexual experience becomes professionalized. All the parasitical feelings, the suckers that hang on to any such complex act, the memories, horrors, strong desires, disgusts, guilt—you try to cut them out."

This analysis, difficult for me to understand at first, eventually rings true, and is further illuminated by the analogy with food that the first sister brings up: "Americans are more and more interested in European food, but when they come here, especially the most enthusiastic, you have the feeling that they have denatured the actual experience. It is not so much a sensual experience they are having but an *abstract* thrill—of sitting down in a fancy restaurant with five wine glasses or something. The ideational context rather than the food is what seems to be eaten. But European food frequently has a disgusting aspect: violent French cheeses that smell like shit, eating brains, guts, and so on.

"For you, hygiene is such an important aspect of everything: sex, food, sport, even bodies. Like those absurd workouts popularized by certain movie stars: the body must be perfect, hard, tight, tough. It reminds me of those shiny American apples with their thin, tight skins and very little taste. No spare flesh; sport is good for you; food is good for you; learning how to eat like a supposed European will be good for you. There is a repression of sensation and an exaltation of self-improvement."

In fact, wherever people work hard in the modern, increasingly mental and rationalized way, there is a tendency to repress sensation. This is as true in Europe as it is in America. But Euros retain a lingering openness to sensation, derived from other times and another way of life. It is more than openness, however. When they criticize our habit of explicitness, about sex, for instance, our desire to *say* everything, Europeans often claim that in talking so much, we miss the multiple dimension of human material experience. They praise their own silent wrestling with the involved relationship between sensation and human desire, aspiration, and contradiction: it is a struggle that gives sensation the kind of dignity we would, generally, deny it.

From an American point of view, perhaps the most essential aspect of European materialism, even more important than land and food and underlying love for sensation, is their implicit belief that the body truly exists. We Americans, always mobile and upward bound, whether through class barriers or levels of spirituality or both, have little patience with the human body. We would, if we could, utterly deny its existence and importance. Since that, of course, is impossible, we attempt to dominate and shape it. We even work the most subtle attempts at mastery. Having learned from many European teachers—Freud, Reich, Selver, Rolf, and Feldenkrais, among others—some ways the body influences our whole lives, we have turned their findings upside down in order to put the body back in a subordinated place. Thus we have elaborated an entire subculture of body-based therapies that attempt to use will skillfully to reshape the body and bend it to our immaterial notions. We make the body into a tool. While most of the European body-awareness teachers were humble in the face of what Delmore Schwartz's poem calls "the withness of the body," we take their means and put them into an American agenda in which the fact of the body disappears beneath the discipline of the mind.

This tendency is so great that much illness is increasingly seen as our "fault," our mind over our body matter. A few years ago, one of America's most Europeanized intellectuals, Susan Sontag, afflicted with cancer, had to write an entire book to prove (1) that the illness was not her creation and (2) that in the face of exploding cells, there was little she could do about it with will and mind alone. The massive growth of interest in psychology in our country, carried so far that European observers like Jean-Louis Servan-Schreiber have remarked it is almost "the only intellectual discipline that is broadly known and taken seriously," is in its deepest motives yet another attempt of Puritan will to win out over material resistance. Increasingly, American doctors will attribute physical diseases about which they can do little to hypothetical "psychosomatic" origins, thereby encouraging the American patient to feel he is, in some arcane and fuzzy way, "responsible" for them. Most American patients shoulder the burden; it is in our tradition. Our view of will is such that we feel we should be able to pull ourselves up by our bootstraps, as the idiomatic American expression has it. If so, we should be able to do anything, even make our bodies well.

As a general rule, Europeans have no such heroic views of human psychological capacities. For one thing, they are much more conscious—in a casual and popular fashion—of genetics. They do not see the individual as completely free, as we tend to, and therefore responsible. They see him shaped and partly determined, even largely determined, by what has gone into his germ plasm. In marriage, for example, Americans have long been custodians of that idealism sociologists call the "romantic, companionate marriage," two souls joining in inspired love and friendship. Europeans tend to look upon marriage as having more material dimensions. They pay more explicit attention to wealth and class origins, fully aware how these social facts open some opportunities and close others. They also tend to be more conscious of marriage in its most physical aspect, as breeding, in the sense of the mating of two animals. We detest all such notions and procedures as we detest the body itself, and the possibility that it might limit our aspirations and progress toward the good and the prosperous. For us American idealists, to quote Delmore

Schwartz again, the body is "the heavy bear that goes with" us—a bestial alien without beauty or dignity.

Likewise, in discussing social subjects, Europeans will look for material origins to what seems to us an astonishing extent. This is one of the reasons for the success of Marxism there and its utter failure here. But Europeans will go much farther in this direction than dialectical materialism. A Portuguese surgeon, an internationally known pharmaceutical researcher, a man who also writes books about politics, who publishes poetry, a man obviously very well educated, hesitates not at all in invoking genetic explanations of phenomena where an American would apply only historical or sociological reasons.

One day in discussion he says: "The reason that violence in Europe became 'baked in,' as Milosz puts it, is genetic. Nowadays, one tends again to accept Lamarckian views: the imprint of experience and the surrounding world tends to be registered 'genetically,' and thus transmitted. The U.S. had only a brief four-year civil war, but Europe had hundreds of years of civil war. European violence, pessimism, hatred: it's in the genes now."

I am so astonished I can't reply, but later on I think how amazing it is that this scientific man, a serious intellectual, can so forget himself, even overlooking the paradox of his own argument: after all, did European violent tendencies disappear from their genes when Europeans moved to America? Perhaps he would argue that it just changed form in different historical and social circumstances. No matter. His very notion of how social events take place—in the depths of the body—is foreign to us.

This fundamental sense of the body's true existence often gives rise to European observations which a contemporary American will find "racist." For us, nurture is everything and nature nothing, and in our giving opportunities to masses of people of many races to become successful Americans in similar ways, we have gone a long way toward proving that race is vastly less important than many people used to think. We would go further and say that it is inconsequential. And perhaps that is so, for all practical purposes of social functioning. But Europeans are utterly at odds with such a view.

One day I casually ask an acquaintance who lives in Paris but comes from Romania: "I wonder why I am so moody. Not just today, but often." He answers, knowing my family came from

Russia and Poland: "Oh, that's just your Slavic atavism." Because Europeans are too little conscious of how their racist past has led to recurrent disasters, they make such observations innocently, seemingly unaware of the enormous potential dangers of allowing oneself even to think in such terms. We, nailed every day to the cross of our black-white agony, our long shame and our attempts to right the wrong, recoil now from such kinds of understanding. They strike us as "primitive," and we are right to be wary of the doors to depersonalization and worse which they can easily open.

And yet we would also do well to see in such observations that nurture is not everything but that nature counts also, that our bodies exist and they do not allow anything—always, everywhere, and under all circumstances—to be possible. One would think such a belief truistic but we tend, in fact, to act as if men were disincarnate heroes for whom no obstacle on the material plane can long endure.

Getting the proportions right in our minds, not just in general but also in the particular case, means accepting that fatality in the form of the body and in other guises exists, a concession that Americans resist making. But accepting it, at least some of the time, would lead us, again, back to deep parts of ourselves. We might even be led to pleasant experiences, like being able to enjoy a good meal without having our minds on the next big or trivial project. So often, doing those projects is motivated primarily by the hope to assure ourselves, once again, that we can conquer all.

We can't.

CHAPTER ELEVEN

Still More True Materialism

We will find similar European-American contrasts and parallel lessons if we look past the borders of our skins at European attitudes toward common objects. Anne, the wife of my British publisher, is an American who has lived in England for thirteen years. She says she is always "shocked," when she goes back home to visit the United States, "by the consumer society." "Do you mean the waste, the profligacy, the lack of European frugality?" I ask. "Yes, that's what I mean." Alick, her husband, says he had always considered Americans and Britons "cousins," the "same language and all that." But when he studied two years for a master's degree at the University of Chicago, and lived at International House, he "felt more comfortable with the fifty percent of the occupants who were foreigners, even though they were not native English speakers. It was the Americans' attitude toward things that I found so foreign to me." In similar terms, I have heard dozens of Europeans deplore American "conspicuous consumption" and "the waste." There are even many Europeans who find it impossible to enjoy those American adventure films in which many cars are destroyed in multiple crashes. They don't get the humor or the excitement. They frown and worry.

My wife, Jacqueline, only told me years later that an incident I remember only dimly upset her during her first months in America right after our marriage. We were in a café, a sleepy-afternoon kind of place in San Francisco, where we would go regularly to take the sun on the back deck and read books while sipping our coffee. During that period, I was making my way through a lot of popular fiction, procrastinating from addressing more serious matters. They were vacation-reading kinds of things, James Michener, for example. Turning the many pages, I would quiet the voice of Puritan conscience by telling myself how much history, geography, botany, zoology, and even geology I was learning, all the while strategically letting my unconscious rest itself in preparation for the important tasks to follow. That day, I was reading *Chesapeake*.

At a certain moment, J. put down her own book and asked: "Is what you are reading interesting?"

Both to give her something to amuse herself with and to allow myself to get back to the fictional self-hypnotism I was practicing, I smiled, bent the cheap paperback into two halves, and ripped the book apart. I handed her the first half, which I had already finished, cover and all, and plunged onward, stopping only for another quick smile at her. I recall that she hesitated, that she even took one deep breath, but said nothing and accepted the half-book. I paid no further attention.

Three years later, in a discussion of the differences between American and European attitudes toward things, the incident came up. We were at table with Françoise, the Belgian lawyer, and Peter, the American economist. "I remember my shock," Jacqueline says with a grin, "when Stuart did that. To destroy something just for a momentary convenience—and to destroy a book! I was horrified," she recalls. She smiles again to reassure me that the horror is past and that she isn't going to moralize about the matter. "In Europe, you just don't treat things, especially books, that way." She keeps smiling to indicate she knows it is only a cultural difference, that the book wasn't expensive, that the whole incident wasn't important. But the smile is, again, purposeful. For, like other Europeans, she is deeply shocked, even annoyed at such American carelessness with matter, though politeness and good sense usually keep her and others from making too much of it aloud.

For me, as for most Americans, objects have two main meanings: symbolic and functional. We accumulate matter, parade it around—whether clothes, cars, houses, or artworks—to symbolize that we can afford it, that we are successful. Functionally, we use things and use them up. We ride the thing like a steed whose flanks we have sweated and breath exhausted, to get from here to there. In both cases, the symbolic and functional meanings, the object in itself carries the quality of profound interchangeability. This is captured and taught in the recurrent phrase used with young children when they have broken or lost some-thing they value: "Don't cry. I'll buy you another one."

Not caring too much for a particular toy soldier or Teddy bear is part of the Americanization of children. Though there are many souls among us who genuinely love certain things, and though almost all of us have one or two things that are radiantly precious, basically, such clinging to matter is un-American. It would slow us up.

The evolution of Puritanism after Calvin allowed making money, acquiring, and consuming to be spiritually sanctioned as signs of a predestined salvation. But, even so, it is in the Spirit that our Puritan heart lies. This is a major reason why so few American families have ever managed to keep wealth for even three generations. Every year, one sees new names appearing on the list of the ten richest Americans. Because there is nothing so un-American as avarice, miserliness, or what seems "tightness," many fortunes have been entirely given away. As Carnegie, the great endower of library systems, peace foundations, and the like, said: "A kept dollar is like a stinking fish." Though born in Eu-rope himself, he adopted an American stance toward the material. In Europe, people hold onto fortunes and attempt to establish dynasties; in America, many rich people (and many more not so rich) deem it injurious to the manly individualism of their off-spring to save too much for them by way of inheritance. We are, we want to be, a generous and even prodigal people and we are glad when we are so.

So, I realize in remembering, when I ripped apart the book, aside from my functional motives, I was also making something of a deliberate cultural statement, one which I could have put into words like these:

"It is *only* a thing."

"It is cheap."

"It can always be recycled, whether it is ripped up or not."

"If you really like the book after having read it, we can buy another one, identical."

"Time is precious."

"This is leisure time, and it too is precious."

"Here, take this mere thing and use it. It is our being as humans—not brute matter—that we must respect."

How different Europeans are becomes clear around the table where the four of us are discussing the subject. Hearing about the ripped-up book, Françoise wonderingly shakes her head. She tells us: "When I need a piece of paper to write some notes, say a shopping list, I simply go to Peter's desk and take one from the wastebasket! I use the other side or, almost always, there are pieces of paper he has thrown away on which he has written almost nothing!" We all laugh, but I recall my mother-in-law saying once how amazed she was "the first time Stuart left me a note on a whole piece of typing paper to say that someone had called when I was out. Three small lines on that large piece of new paper! I always save paper one can write on—the back side of advertisements you get in the mail, official notices. I have a pile of them on my desk for such purposes."

Wondering, I ask Françoise and Jacqueline: "Is it the money? The fact that paper was more expensive until recently, or that there were wartime periods of scarcity?" I am searching for a functional explanation.

"I don't think so," the successful lawyer answers. "That's not the primary reason. Rather it is a tradition of respect for things in general and your own things in particular, one that makes life alive in a certain way. Peter throws away envelopes from the mail we get. It annoys me terribly. I save them; it makes a 'package.' There's the date the letter was mailed, for example; and if there's a photo or some enclosure, you can put it back in the envelope; the envelope is part of the letter; the whole is an ensemble. For me, things are not just inert and trivial. The envelope has the writing of the people who sent it, it is a record of a human gesture at a particular time. A typewritten address," she concedes, "I would care about less. But then there's the future: if I preserve the package, the envelope will conceal a mystery, the letter itself, which I won't remember but can, years later, rediscover. I can receive the letter again!" she announces, not without a certain bemused sense of triumph—the European analogue, if you like, of my triumph in ripping the book apart.

Jacqueline nods approvingly at what, to American ears, may sound like neurosis. We head, as D. H. Lawrence noted, for the Abstract; once again, the European takes more notice of the Concrete.

My wife, I have come to know since the *Chesapeake* incident, is as inclined this way as Françoise. At first sheepishly, then more boldly, Jacqueline describes her habits to the three of us. She has piles of stuff neatly collected in special corners of the house. In the attic, there are issues of *Time* from the fifties. She has her first car, an old MG Midget, on blocks in the back of the garage: she can't bear to part with it; she says she is saving it until its value as a cheap "classic" car rises, but I suspect there is much more at work. Her present car carries the same-number license plate as her father always had, B3049. To keep it, years after his death, the car is registered in her mother's name. When she explains this, on occasional demand at frontier crossings, even tough customs guards understand and are pleased. Françoise also understands as Jacqueline recounts these facts; the two European women smile.

Years ago, when I first came to live with her in Europe and passed much of the time in her Art Nouveau family home on Rue du Monastère in Brussels, I quickly had to get the idea. The house is full of old things, handed down from generation to generation—ancient furniture too large for even what most would consider a big house these days; paintings done by the father, the grandfather, paintings of the great-great-grandfather; artworks by other people, some, friends of the family; curios and knick-knacks, collected in this or preceding generations. I felt, and still feel, like a bull in a china shop. But even objects which have no obvious value as antiques nor any apparent sentimental value, what for me are mere things, for her and for other Europeans have aura; they are minor essences.

To me, again, this is idolatry. As an American, I am ultimately ascetic. By old habit, I tear myself from the grip of things to plunge on with the tasks of understanding, mastering, producing, and improving an environment (with luck we will make it the best ever seen!). Europeans are not nearly as much this way. Once, in the house on Rue du Monastère, I broke an ashtray (nothing precious, a souvenir of a trip from a hotel in southern France), and, like a guilty thing surprised, hid the pieces. I amazed myself, because I hardly understood what I did, and acting this way is not my usual style. Nor was it an example of that proverbial American straightforwardness—George Washington and his cherry tree—on which, like others, I generally pride myself. Could it have been that I had sensed the aura of the old house and, if you will pardon the mystical phraseology, the vibrations of the things in it?

To my greater astonishment, the dishonorable ruse did not work at all. Amid the many hundreds of objects, most of them in one way or another more valuable, they missed it, they missed the ashtray within a few hours of its disappearance! And this is not, let me assure you, because they are stingy or poor. When, later on, I broke a cup (a porcelain one, to be sure, but modern, not antique) and then a glass that had belonged to Jacqueline's godmother—one among a dozen and, like the cup, replaceable in the marketplace of such things—I was urged not to do dishes ever again.

I learned that these objects, for my new European family, were *not* replaceable; none of them. Once it had been acquired and used, no object could substitute for another. Certainly, one could find *apparent* duplicates, spend money, and get them. But that was not at all what was missed. Very important is the fact that these objects have felt our touch, received the look of our eyes, been held in our presence. They are therefore significant beyond their mere market value.

Earlier, I commented on the fact that European houses are often so carefully guarded—shutters, elaborate locks, and so forth. As I noted, the violent heritage of Europe accounts for much of that. Traditions of having had less are certainly at work here, too, along with a past in which more was very hard to come by and craftsmanship rendered certain objects especially valuable. But sheer *attachment* to whatever is in the house also counts. This attitude of caring for things communicates itself even to modern mass-produced items like envelopes and pieces of paper.

It is further amplified by the custom of inheritance. Things are often passed down from before and one naturally imagines oneself passing them on later. It is something one thinks about—the human genesis of an object in the family, and its next destiny with another member, to whom one will give it before death or will it after.

For all these reasons, there is a general belief in Europe that casual workers like housecleaners, roofers, plumbers, carpenters, and others, unless they are well known and therefore part of the family in its normally extended sense, are likely to be robbers. It's not just that outside people were often robbers. It's also the fact that *whatever* one has is covered with a mantle of preciousness.

Jacqueline and her family are perhaps a little more this way than many Europeans. Five generations of artist ancestors on both sides have contributed to a gentle but acute love of what can be seen, held, touched. And yet the comic result of the matter is only a slight exaggeration, if at all, of the normally European, and it is this: I no longer drive Jacqueline's car, nor do I wash or dry the dishes. At first, they thought I was clumsy (I never damaged the car but I precipitated the destruction of a door on an old *vitrine*). In fact, I *am* a little clumsy. But beyond that and overriding it, we all gradually realized, was the fact that I simply am American. I did not take sufficient care with objects. I did not care. And that made people nervous. And their nervousness made me nervous. In a word, Europeans love their things. I leave them alone.

When Europeans complain about the American lack of frugality, they miss the essential meanings of our getting and spending. They are horrified at the too-muchness, as it seems to them, of our lives: the three television sets, the phone for the adolescent children, the big steaks, the many jackets in the closets, the friends who have ten pairs of running shoes. What Europeans don't understand is that consumption and disposal are symbolic acts of self-assertion for us, exaggerated triumphs of the original Puritan will. Once again, as with our attitude toward food and the body, we celebrate the victory of spirit over matter.

In our wastefulness, we are being true to a partial interpretation of the Old Testament notion that God has given man dominion over the creation. Easy purchase and replacement of material things carry for us the charge of the transcendence of matter itself by free men. Grown-up Americans, early weaned away from the particular, have a profound contempt for individual objects which generalizes itself into a *contemptus mundi*. Consumption is a potlatch: a heroic, spiritually aristocratic soaring above the material as we throw it away or recycle it. An assertion that values like energy, mind, and will are more important than mere matter.

The easy use of money also has, therefore, a nearly spiritual dimension. This is only one reason that spending money in America makes you feel alive, but it is perhaps the most fundamental one. The pleasure is only apparently in the thing acquired. In fact, the deeper excitement is in the ability to acquire it, not just to use it or show one's personal success but to play with matter. Things are for play and so is money. Many Western societies have gamblers, but the United States has the most. Whole cities—Las Vegas and now Atlantic City—are devoted to it. And when we gamble, we bet the most. Some come to win but most are satisfied simply to play. This is a sort of childishness again, I suppose, but it is a free and gay childishness.

Naturally, the real pursuit of money is not so playful. Money is important everywhere, but in the United States it has peculiar meanings. A history of greater opportunity than Europeans have had makes financial success seem essential. The social strata of European life, the national boundaries with their linguistic gates, the nationalistic racism of Europeans, their general boxification, their prejudice against any but a social and intellectual elite coming to power, all these elements make the European less hopeful for himself, less optimistic about his chances for making it big. But Americans are supposed to have the opportunity Europeans have lacked. "Making it big" is spiritually enjoined as evidence that one has been saved. "Making it big" also carries the immediate spiritual rewards of showing that one's inner worth—will, grit, determination, purpose, intellect—has triumphed over matter. If one is supposed to make it, and if one is not making it, then one is *very* hurt, frustrated, and angry. If one *can* make it, one must. Europeans accept poverty—or rather what is now merely "relative deprivation," to use the sociologists' phrase—in ways Americans don't. We can get very violent if we are not progressing.

The spiral of spending is imperative, much of the reason why Americans have the lowest rate of saving in the world. Money, purchase, and consumption serve functional purposes: to save time, to keep you advancing, to support that blitzkrieg effort in work which makes one move forward, feel alive and triumphant. But even if you are successful, says an executive with a large salary, you're still exhausting yourself by working nights and weekends to get even further ahead. So you *must* have a comfortable car or two or three; you must have a full freezer, telephones in every room, TV sets in every room, and a psychiatrist to keep you functioning; when vacation times comes, you *must* be able to get away to rest. Not everybody in the world feels these needs in the same deep ways, and this allows Europeans, for instance, to be more leisured and take quite a different attitude toward money, saving, consumption, and things.

Our ultimate goal in gaining money, however, remains to gain more money and then, or all along, to play with it and the matter it symbolizes. Unlike the European, the American who cannot buy feels deflated, depressed, not quite alive. Financially successful Americans, those who can really throw money around (and all the things it can buy) are admired, envied: we other Americans *know* they are having a really good time. They seem to us to have transcended things while apparently immersing themselves in them. The things themselves lose importance as soon as they are bought. For these people, the Tantric doctrine seems true: Samsara, the whirligig of physical illusion, is Nirvana, blissful transcendence.

Europeans operate differently and have little understanding of such joys. Though many Europeanized American expatriates, when they come back to the United States after years of absence, are appalled by what now seems a foreign wastefulness, I am still American enough to enjoy it. My brother-in-law has been reasonably successful in the insurance business, and every year, when I pay my visit to the United States, I stop at his and my sister's house first. Arriving there fresh from careful, parsimonious, materialistic Europe as I do, I feel as if I can breathe at last: I have a TV to myself, an air-conditioned room to myself, there is always a spare car to be driven, I am taken to restaurants where portions of meat and vegetables are served so large that only hungry Hussars who had galloped all night could eat them; half that food is routinely, assertively, contemptuously, extravagantly, gloriously, heroically thrown away. At home, the freezer is full of reserves; cars are ridden hard, like so many pony express horses, to be traded for fresh ones as often as necessary. Though I occasionally experience *some* European disgust at such profligacy, I must confess that, as an American, more often I feel a great liberation from the European obsession with *things*. That obsessive clinging reminds me of a child with a filthy, smelly security blanket. It is beneath the notice of a proper man. It is dross, says my American self.

We Americans buy to destroy or even to give away. Our new habit of recycling proves we don't care about things. We love to give old stuff away to be transformed. We are the masters of matter. We like things big, really big; high, wide, and handsome. The European, on the contrary, seems to love his fences.

Which is the better attitude, ours or the European's? Is small the only beautiful? Yes, if there are limits. But are there limits? Somewhere, sometime, certainly. But have we reached them?

Who can tell? American consumption is part of the national faith that men and women, their dreams and their aspirations, are more important than earth. We don't have *time* to worry about things. We are moving on—why should we be restrained? Yet, in the European reverence for things there is something essentially human that seems instructive, something that has its own dignity, less large-scale and hurried. We could learn to rest with our things, instead of rushing to use them better or acquire more of them. As Americans, we *do* have another old and countervailing tradition of simplicity, but it was essentially ascetic. (Even Thoreau saw simplicity as a renunciation of possessions and love of the material world of nature as ultimately a means for transcendence.) There is something to be learned from European reverence, thoughtfulness, care. Surely the American rich, who have everything and want more, and the relatively deprived, who have less, can come to some sort of peace in finding again the earth and the things that are made from it.

CHAPTER TWELVE

The Aesthetic Attitude

An eminent professor, member of the stratospherically important Collège de France, is reviewing another, younger professor who is competing with thirty others for a good job in theoretical physics, one that will probably lead the winner to great heights of eminence in his own turn. The older man writes a note to the review committee describing his opinion of the younger man's research. To give weight to his praise, he invokes a frame of reference that would be repellent to a practical, businesslike American sensibility: "I find his work interesting. Even amusing."

The older man is speaking about a dozen learned articles full of mathematical equations, and in his summary of what is praiseworthy about them he evokes a set of values shared by his colleagues on the committee: we are not just here to be drudges, banging away at an evanescent truth like so many high-IQ idiots; we are also here to enjoy ourselves; and that enjoyment, proper to people like us, responsible as we are, includes our pleasure at the way a younger man has carried on his work with elegance, even a sort of mathematical wit and poise and imagination. We know that the final truth may escape us; by definition, it *will* escape us; but we, as sophisticated highly developed men, can give ourselves the time to enjoy the aesthetic quality of the effort.

In quite another field, an American psychotherapist who has worked for a long time in Europe, giving workshops training thousands of other therapists, offhandedly remarks: "Some of those people have poetic souls." It is not the sort of observation one would imagine anyone applying to a group of American therapists in training. The trainer gives an example: "I think of a Norwegian psychiatric nurse I worked with in a Gestalt therapy session. She had remarked: 'My people were farmers but we lived by the sea.' There was a deep melancholy on her face as she finished her statement and intuitively I felt it would be helpful for her to explore this abandoned part of her past. I told her to talk to the sea, as if it were present, a being. It was not the most crucial work we did together—nothing involving mother and father or the most urgent concerns of her life, but it was touching: 'How could I have left you? The seasons, the carefree days of childhood, the mountains? The mountains that kneel in the sea like gods!'"

What is at work in both these incidents is another way in which Europeans reconcile matter and spirit: the aesthetic attitude. I mean their tendency to take a nearly sensuous (aesthetic = sensation, as in the word *anaesthetic*), pleasure-filled, and even. at times passionately appreciative approach toward every aspect of existence: things, experiences, other people, ideas, whatever. It is an attitude eager to discover and create beauty in experience and in the world. It looks still to find and make art in life.

I have a younger friend in Brussels who makes his living as a journalist and who turns to me, as to several other older people, for general guidance in the pursuit of what is almost always a hazardous career. One evening, just come back from Paris where he has been prospecting new possibilities, he tells me that he is troubled. An editor of an American paper there told him: "Get together the names of some papers in the U.S., check out the name of the editor whose section you want to publish in, then write these guys. Tell 'em you're interested in writing about Europe. Tell them who you are, enclose two clips of published articles, and see if they'll bite. If they don't reply soon, call them."

My young friend, Charles, is that mixture of traditions which Nabokov calls "a salad of racial genes." His mother is Irish, his father is Czech, but he spent his youth in the United States; the parents lived with their son first in Geneva, then Paris; then they separated and Charles was principally raised in Brussels. Despite the American element in his background, it is the European in him which wins out as he describes his reaction (doubtfully) to the editor's advice: "It sounds very American as a way to proceed." There is a certain distaste in Charles's voice. As an American myself, the advice to be straightforward and eager seems perfectly natural. Accordingly, I have to search my knowledge of Europeans to imagine what Charles means to say. He means he's reluctant to make an approach that way. It seems too direct to him. It seems brassy. Ungraceful. Abrupt.

"Seems okay to me," say I, nevertheless. "Why not follow his advice?"

I push him because I know that his European reticence is irrelevant in this American context and that the advice he has been given is the most appropriate. He broods lightly, silently, knowing he couldn't possibly bring himself to beard strangers so directly. Even his denial of me is delicate, however. "Perhaps you're right," he says evasively, "but it isn't the way I'm used to doing things, you know."

What causes a European to react this way, even against his own interest? In a closed society—which Europe was and in some ways still is—it is good sense to be slow in one's approaches to others. Walking on eggs is a particularly good policy whenever important stakes—livelihood, marriage, major purchases or sales—are in the balance. In European journalism, everyone comes to know everyone else and first impressions can last for lifetimes. Therefore, nothing quick, nothing without deliberation, nothing brusque or direct will be acceptable. You must *know* the person you address, you must be introduced, you must reconnoiter him or her and the situation. Every European has understood this for centuries.

Moreover, the American goal orientation in action is foreign to a civilization where for so long, compared to the bustling American marketplace, there were few goals to seek. Consequently, a direct American approach—"Here-I-am, this-is-what-I-have-to-offer, if-you-don't-want-it-I-will-go-else-where"—is sublimely irrelevant.

But there is even more involved in Charles's way of being. Behind it stands again that tradition where aristocratic grace was cultivated as a virtue in itself. This tradition, assumed by all lower classes over centuries (especially the middle class to which journalists, for example, belong), still shapes some social behavior. There is, as we have seen, a part of the European soul that loves American directness, but finally it bothers them. It does not seem true to all of human nature. With people one knows or hopes to know, their human sensibilities, their natural love of grace and ease and gradualness must be understood and respected. Otherwise, at the least, one's own image as a sensitive person is at risk.

Reciprocally, we Americans, as long as we don't really have to *do* anything important with such persons, love European tentativeness, their slow dance of delicacy and ritual of careful approach. We find it lovely, redolent of the luxury—so hard for us to come by—of not doing, not striving, not being efficient or effective. Unfortunately, too often, we come to reject the validity of the more delicate approach when we learn that it isn't usually symbolic of any deep ethical concern for others but rather is a result of ingrained good manners. When we see that these manners are not generally based on goodness, on Hebrew and Christian values of being a good person and treating others well, we reject the silver we are given and wave away social delicacy with a fever of republican directness.

When that happens, still more misunderstanding arises. The European feels even more roughly handled than before and accuses us of a "lack of fineness," of "caring only for money." We, in turn, feel misinterpreted and maligned, on top of feeling that we've been tricked and disillusioned!

Fortunately, we can correct or prevent this cycle of increasing misunderstanding if we learn to see European social delicacy as the expression of an aesthetic attitude which reminds us that nonutilitarian values are important to our own humanity.

The European aesthetic attitude also extends to the body. I am not saying that all or even most Europeans are devotees of grace in the way they hold themselves or move, nor even that they are universally conscious of what they put on their bodies. Indeed, Americans are often now as well or better dressed than Europeans. But there is a subtle difference that bears examining.

One day years ago, flying back to the United States on a crowded jumbo jet, I get talking with a bearded Frenchman from Brittany. He is a part-time farmer, he tells me, a descendant of generations of farmers, but he makes most of his living as an industrial designer. Thus, he is at once a man of the land and a sophisticated consultant to international business. In our conversation, he makes one statement that lingers in my memory: "Americans—they are physically awkward. Even when they aren't moving, they are restless, and it looks like they are uncomfortable. They don't know what to do with their bodies; they don't know where to put their legs; they put a knee up against a table when they are sitting in a business meeting, they even put their feet and legs up on tables, shoes and all; they cross one leg over the other instead of keeping them together. When they walk, it is frequently a heavy, unattractive style of moving, bouncing up and down or side to side, rough, as if they either didn't know better or didn't want to know better."

Since I heard this and other comments like it, I have taken pains to look, and it is true that we move with a sort of jerkiness, that sitting, standing, and walking, we move more crudely than many Europeans, who from childhood are taught to control their restlessness. Going to visit a friend in Connecticut, I take a train on the New Haven Railroad from New York. I sit near the front of the car. It is summertime, and the last passengers getting on find themselves without seats. Two of them, young women about twenty years old, create a solution. On the right is an area reserved for baggage that will not fit above the passengers' seats. Along with their own bags, the two simply sit down there on the carpeted floor. They do not know each other but, obviously being college students on their way to Boston, wearing the international uniform of their status—blouse, jeans, backpack—they quickly get into easy conversation. I can only hear snatches of it as they talk about where they go to school and who they know in common, but I observe them from time to time, trying with a writer's curiosity to hear more of what they are saying and to guess, in advance, what kinds of people they are and with what concerns.

One is a loud red-haired New Yorker. She is nervous, even agitated; she smokes a lot; she tries to please and be liked; she is defensive and needy. Her gestures are abrupt and somewhat exaggerated. She is intentionally sloppy in dress and movements, large and open. Her hair, constantly falling down and needing to be put back in its place, is part of a well-established style of deliberate nonchalance, a studied naturalness. I overhear that she is an art student.

The other young woman mostly listens, with a kind of pleasant-faced attention. I observe, after a while, that they are equally good-looking but that the little dark-haired one at first seems much prettier. Her gestures are small, delicate, fine, even though they are lively. As she listens, there is a look in her eyes that seems to come from farther back, as if she is not all there but in back of herself, watching and controlling her attention and the way she looks, controlling how forthcoming she will be. She seems more soignée, more meditative. Her own hair is casually done, but it does not fall down or cause her problems. The redhead exudes, despite her obvious vulnerability and lack of ease, a more brawny assertiveness, as if she came from a wilder, rougher environment. Finally, by paying close attention and concentrating, I hear enough of the few words the dark-haired girl is able to utter to learn that she is Greek. Though there are many exceptions to the pattern, in bearing, movement, and style of personal presence, each woman typifies her civilization.

An internationally known Italian professor of psychotherapy tells me that when his American female colleagues come to see him in Europe, whatever their other concerns, they often say they feel "inferior" to European women: "'*They* know how to dress, how to do their hair, how to use makeup—I don't know how they know, but they do.'"

It is all a small matter but revealing of how we differ from Europeans. In America, personal style and refinement are looked upon with suspicion as betokening a placing of manner over substance, truth, and, above all, results. In America, it is considered "feminine," in the derogatory sense, to be too conscious of appearances, even for women. We are still afraid of what seems excessive "artfulness." In the older and more settled European civilization, finesse in appearance, posture, and movement assumes greater importance and legitimacy, a legacy of the aristocratic tradition. True, Europeans may have other motives to their style—manipulation, defensiveness, keeping up appearances, watching and waiting to make sure their movements are safe or opportune—but some of their grace is derived from sheer pleasure of refinement.

When I first met Jacqueline, I found myself impressed as we walked around San Francisco that she would remark upon this or that vista with the word *charming*. Though I have since learned that this is an ordinary expression in French people's mouths, I still find it meaningful. It calls attention to an inner world where matter and spirit meet. We have already noticed how the European more readily accepts and relishes the existence of material things. We can now look at how the material and the spiritual are constantly being subtly intermingled rather than, as is our tendency, subordinated one to another or even kept apart.

The words that strike one in Europe as expressions of the aesthetic attitude are two-directional. I hear *charming,* used over and over; I also hear *poetic;* and, in Italy, though they are mostly gone, one still hears the words *bello* and *bella* as terms of high praise for every satisfying aspect of life. Such words do more than describe material aspects of a scene, a painting, or a child's smile, as they do more than express a positive reaction to an external event. They also serve to affirm the existence of an inner human world which is sensitive to beauty. When I, as European, say I am "charmed" by something, for example, it calls up in me a whole inner realm where magic takes place. Though this realm does nothing to advance me, the nation, or God, it is important. Using such words is a daily validating of the aesthetic attitude and moves one, in turn, to search for something to please the inner realm.

Here is another way in which European materialism rises toward spirit, another place where the European spirit embraces matter. From a different perspective, we can say that the everyday presence of the aesthetic attitude in European diction reminds us that object and subject are seeking each other. The object that is not just out there but also "charms," or that is "poetic," is no longer a mere alien thing. It is recognized as calling up in one a subjective correspondent to itself, an inner fixed desire for the lovely; a part of oneself that is animated and energized by the external. Thus, on a hundred small daily occasions, the European heals or even ignores splits that for us remain very real.

I asked an English acquaintance's eighty-year-old aunt, shortly before she became ill and then died rather suddenly, what she thought was the biggest change in society since she had been a girl. She hardly took time to think before saying: "There was more poetry in life then." Over the years, I have pondered what she meant, and as an American I have been amazed that her culture allowed her to take one of her final stands on such flimsy, nonutilitarian grounds.

On another occasion, I talk with a Belgian social worker about America and she thinks back on her trip to the United States, years ago, and talks intensely but casually of "the poetry of the Southwest." The same woman, no artist, not even someone particularly interested in art, impresses me when, as the discussion shifts to the landscapes of Tuscany, she describes them as *"prenant"*—the hills "take you," she says. Or when talking about the light of San Francisco she says it is *"éclatant, l'air est très pur, une combinaison qui donne beaucoup d'énergie"*—"bursting, and the air is very pure, a combination that gives one a great deal of energy." It is the precision of her awareness and her ability to express it that strikes me. The material world is not foreign to the inner but integrated with it and humanized; just as the human being himself is humanized by his communion with the delights of the outer world. Everyday use of words like *charming, poetic,* and *bello* expresses a part of the human spirit and counterbalances the technicalization and bureaucratization of modern life which are our daily denatured bread.

Even Europeans like Jacqueline, who are strong admirers of Americans and our culture, will use the common words of the aesthetic attitude to criticize our shortcomings. One day, in talking about the difference between Europe and the United States, she says that we Americans lack "imagination." When I ask her what she means, she cites an example as ordinary as fashion: "In general, even now, Americans must still look to Europe for the fantasy that can create interesting clothes." She expands the concept, invoking again that pregnant word "poetry."

"Poesis—making. There is not much 'making' of the imaginatively new, as a habit, in the United States. Almost everything that is beautiful and made comes from somewhere else—Europe or China or Japan. This stems from a lack of imagination. It derives from history, or rather the lack of history having to do with such things. You can't do it because it is not taught; it isn't around; it isn't in the air. There is a lack of polish, really—work done in polishing a world, even landscape. Landscapes in America may be beautiful but they are either empty or crude. And you feel the lack if you are a European, everywhere: in fashion, hairstyles, houses, dishes, and so forth. Where, even, are the geraniums in every window that you have in Bavaria? Or the numberless gardens of England? Naturally, there are millions of

exceptions, but my point stands. I'm a very ordinary person, but I used to amuse myself in restaurants imagining people in different costumes. I gave the fat man a peruke, for instance. I can do that because I grew up with a certain tradition which encourages and supplies the inner materials and methods for such fantasies. Here, in America, only the exceptional individual would be moved in such a direction."

In another conversation, this time with a German consultant on international development, I come to see that when Europeans use words like *imagination* they have yet another level of meaning. We are talking about movies and he criticizes Woody Allen, whose latest film has just won a prize at the Venice Film Festival. "I find Woody Allen boring," he says. "It's his complete lack of imagination. All of his films are the same." He goes on to say that despite the elaborately envisioned machines of the early films, or the complex images of later works like *Zelig,* Allen remains always "in images," on the surface, and not in the realm of the "imagination." He says: "There is no creative penetration to something that excites and touches the soul."

Whether one agrees with him or not about Allen's films, the man has focused on something important. When Europeans use the term *imagination* or others like it, they are pointing in the direction of the mysterious and compelling depth of the human being. To them, an "imaginative" moment succeeds in doing more than putting individuals in contact with their own private worlds. At these deep levels, we enter the realm of archetypes and our private worlds intersect. Thus, aesthetic moments conveyed by common words relieve us, momentarily and partially, of the experience of our aloneness. We share what we need, what we desire, and what we are afraid of. By talking about the "poetic," in nature or in art, the "*bello,*" the "charming," the "imaginative," and even the "amusing," the European establishes his solidarity, however subtle and evanescent, with those who hear him. The European reaches out across social space to say to others: "There, don't you see it too? Isn't it something that stirs you too?" He calls up, an acceptance of our subtler feelings and deep wishes. He affirms the individual and collective right to these human faculties and to their exploration and expression.

True, the "poetic," as the English aunt said, is much diminished. What Tocqueville wrote long ago of our own country applies more and more to all democracies and industrial societies: "The hope to better one's lot, competition, and the lure of success anticipated all goad men to activity in their chosen careers and forbid them to stray one moment from the track." Nevertheless, daily straying still takes place in Europe and the special common words help make it possible.

It is hard for an American to grasp, much less sum up, the essentials of the aesthetic attitude. Not long ago, however, I met in Düsseldorf a typically frenetic American businessman who had lived in Europe for a long time. He did a good job of compressing some of the elements into expression. "I think all peoples have the same essential values—the Ten Commandments. Maybe there's a little difference in emphasis here and there. But I believe that, compared to us, when the European adds up his life, he adds up a lot more pleasure. In Europe, an interchange with a person, for example, can be marvelous in itself, *without it being a means to an end*. The vacation, to take another instance, is an end in itself, an achievement in itself. The American, on the contrary, looks on it as a distraction, or a period of necessary preparation to working hard again. Americans are on a treadmill and Europeans are not on a treadmill. I heard that a famous sociologist has summed up American culture in two words—'instrumental pragmatism.' That sounds right to me. I guess for Europe I would characterize their attitude as 'sensual existentialism.'"

CHAPTER THIRTEEN

"Tell Them You're a Writer"

The aesthetic attitude is given specific expression in the high status accorded by Europeans to art and artists. Though we are changing and Europeans are too, ours is a civilization that does not accord art or intellect an important place in its set of values. Tocqueville wrote: "In America everyone finds opportunities unknown anywhere else for making or increasing his fortune. *A breathless cupidity perpetually distracts the mind of man from the pleasures of the imagination and the labors of the intellect* [my italics] and urges it on to nothing but the pursuit of wealth." Unhappily, these hard words still catch and explain some part of a fundamental difference between us and the people who remain in older civilizations. There is an emphasis in our culture on action, especially commerce, which tends to diminish the efforts of artists and intellectuals and to rob them of social prestige in ways not at all European.

I have lived in Europe several times over three decades, first as a graduate student in literature for nearly two years and then as a research director, editor, and working psychologist for briefer periods. It was only a few years ago, however, that, in deep midlife dissatisfaction with the path my work was taking, having married Jacqueline seven months before, I had the courage to cut out for Europe with little other agenda than the hope that a new direction would emerge. It was a move into a kind of limbo: I was leaving home, language, community, and job—the numerous definers of role and identity—for I didn't know what. Indeed, the only socially explicable definer that I had was a contract to write a personal sort of book on friendship, a subject that was giving me an immense amount of trouble and that threatened to be unyielding and to defeat me at last.

As Jacqueline and I were about to land at the airport in Brussels, I asked with sudden anxiety, used as I was as an American to defining myself by my occupation: "Will people ask me what I do?"

"Yes," she said, "Europeans do that now."

"What can I say?" I asked her, fearing the social disapproval of the busy, the engaged, the more-or-less well placed and employed.

"Tell them you're a writer."

The suggestion only plunged my thoughts into further turmoil. Like most Americans, I believed that saying one was a writer meant, first, that one made one's entire living as a writer—something I had never done. Further, to say that one was a writer could also mean that one was deeply called to a vocation and that one was a very good writer, even a great writer—again, aspirations I did not entertain. Finally, to say that one was a writer without being, at the very least, famous, seemed pretentious.

I shared some of these hesitations with her. "Oh, no," she said "*a writer is just a writer.* Just say it—you are writing a book, aren't you?"

"Well, I am trying, but it isn't going forward very much."

"You *have* written books, haven't you?"

"Yes, but always as part of some other professional activity, or some personal quest; I never thought of myself as someone who was primarily a writer."

"Just say you are a writer," she said firmly. Then she added, reassuringly: "I think it will be all right." Finished with discussing what seemed to her an obvious matter, she looked out the window at the rainy fields approaching us from below.

A couple of months later, I had made some halting progress on my book. Then, in the middle of a gray November afternoon, my mother-in-law, a woman of great sensitivity, especially to music, which she taught and performed when she was younger, yet neither an intellectual nor a professional artist, told me with great excitement that she was about to watch on television the admittance of Marguerite Yourcenar to the French Academy, the first woman to enter among the "Immortals" of French letters.

I could not quite fathom my mother-in-law's unusual

breathlessness nor the different but similarly intense seriousness which Jacqueline showed at the news and with which she sat herself down before the large color screen. Not having read Yourcenar's work, I allowed myself to be drawn into their afternoon's activity without any real curiosity or concern. At least I could kill some time and keep my mind off my own difficult writing project. Faced as I was by lack of inspiration and doubts about the financial viability of the enterprise anyway, I turned with grudging and guilty gratitude to the tube.

Coverage began with an announcement that the program was being broadcast in "Eurovision," the special network that crosses national and linguistic boundaries to unite the continent around important events: major bicycle races, the coronation of a pope, the signing of an international treaty. That attention usually reserved for the panoplies of popular sport or international religion and politics was going to be turned onto the honoring of a writer, albeit a very gifted and celebrated one, was my first astonishment.

I expected, quite naturally for an American used to our own cultural television, something like "Meet the Press": a closet affair with a few people, gray and underbudgeted. On the other hand, it could easily have been something dominated by grand spectacle: a princess's wedding with crowds, horses, and marching bands.

It was neither—or perhaps a very cunning combination of both. The camera stared long and monotonously at the severe, neoclassical interior of the building which, the announcer said, housed the Academy. As we waited for what I supposed would be the action to begin, he explained in a hushed and reverential voice that the Academy had been founded by Louis XIII and the empty amphitheater of seats, which resembled a kind of parliament house, was reserved only for the members, each one elected by his intellectual or artistic peers. The election usually came late in life and never more than forty belonged. You could only get elected if some other member died. There were distinguished historians, novelists, philosophers, men of letters, poets, and so forth in the Academy. But Marguerite Yourcenar, we were told a number of times, would be the first woman.

All very interesting, thought I, but let's get on with it. No one else, however, neither Jacqueline nor my mother-in-law nor the people working the television production, seemed in a hurry. The crisp pace of American life in general and expensive network television coverage in particular were both absent. The announcer filled the time we passed watching the empty seats and high columns by telling more and more about the history of the Academy, more about Yourcenar, more about the events that would happen later—the sort of thing they do for the queen's birthday or an installation of a pope. But instead of showing us massed pageantry and vast St. Peter's Square, we were left staring for fully half an hour at this empty, elegant interior.

Action, at last. In filed the Academicians, mostly old, often nearly decrepit, and after election honored to their last breath. The announcer now raced to detail their identities and achievements. My French was not then up to every phrase and most of their names were unknown to me, but the announcer lavished learned attention on each one, as if the TV public would know them. Though I believed she knew no more than I who the various Academicians were and what they had been honored for, my mother-in-law watched with quietly smiling satisfaction. The Academicians came in each wearing a kind of early-nineteenth-century military uniform—gold braid and stiff cloth, stripes down the sides of their trousers—and each wearing a cape and a short, elaborately decorated sword.

I think it was the swords that finally got to me.

In America, a writer could aspire to a kind of minor wealth, but little more social prestige than money and some celebrity might bring. Mario Puzo made a few million dollars here and there, not as great as a major businessman, certainly less than a major movie actor. And how many made it even that far? As Puzo himself says, narrating a Hollywood party scene in his popular novel *The Godfather,* the much more celebrated actors and actresses, the much richer producers and directors, accepted the invited writer as a minor entity, an accessory figure, a highly paid flunky, even though everything they did was based on his work and words.

In America, an *intellectual* writer such as Norman Mailer or Susan Sontag could aspire to, at best, an intermittent and secondary celebrity. Take the latter, the one who has written much less for a broad public. Despite an occasional appearance in *People* magazine, her picture on the cover of *Vanity Fair,* who in the mainstream of our society has even heard of her? And what American institution could honor her in such a way as to command national, not to speak of international, attention? Aside from her membership in the American Academy and Institute of Arts and Letters, an institution not noted for displaying its pomp and circumstance on network television, at most she could look for an honorary degree or two from some college or university—honors conferred, to our eyes, by mere schoolmasters. Even Norman Mailer, when he was covering Muhammad Ali for a book called *The Fight,* was introduced by the boxer as a writer who had gotten very large advances, though no sums as great as a really successful and celebrated American like The Boxer himself. The makers of the year's best television advertisements get more public honor than most of America's important writers.

But look at this, I thought: Swords! And capes! And uniforms designed in Napoleon's time. And a building constructed in the seventeenth century. And, hey, wait, get this—look who's coming in to sit before the amphitheater of Academicians' seats: the then president of the whole goddamned country, Valéry Giscard d'Estaing his arrogant self. He's coming to do honor to this old woman writer who has lived for years in North America and has flown in for the affair. But he—and this is something—doesn't merit a sword, or a cape, or a uniform. Only pinstripes for him. And he has to sit down *below* the semicircular tiers of "Immortals," with his sensibly but elegantly dressed spouse, and just watch. He is not even asked what he thinks of this event, its feminist aspect or any other aspect. Representative of the nation and the state, he is merely invited. The artist doesn't get a patronizing invitation to dinner at the White House; instead, the White House comes to honor the artist. Reverently, as always, the announcer explains that since the time of Louis XIII, the head of state is commanded to be the "Protector of the Academy."

As the hours, for so they do, march slowly forward, it begins to sink in that things might really be different over here. That the TV cameras following for over two hours, first the procession of these thirty-nine creaky men, then an interminable speech of acceptance by Yourcenar in praise of the recently deceased geologist-writer she is replacing, then yet another speech—a bit more sprightly—by the literary editor of *Le Monde,* the aristocratic Jean d'Ormesson, all amount to a suffering of the intellectual and artistic life, with its many slow and boring moments, of a kind we would not dream of allowing in the United States of America. We will be bored by politicians, by the law, by business, even by sports, but not by such people as these.

I am not saying, of course, that all modern Europeans have a feeling for such events. But enough of them do to warrant taking the French president away from matters of nuclear submarines and reactors, inflation and unemployment and foreign affairs, to appear at an event like this and not get a chance to speak. And enough of them do to warrant hours of important TV time all over the continent being devoted to an old woman getting her precious chair.

In the face of such an incident, one begins to realize that calling oneself a writer, as Jacqueline had urged me to do, has a whole different meaning from what it might have in the United States. First, no apology is necessary—writers are all right. The snobbish Belgian lawyers, doctors, and businessmen I had been meeting are of no higher standing in the eyes of society, even if they make more money. Nor is it important that one is not a famous writer. All writers are worthy of honor. As Jacqueline later puts it to me in a careless aside: "Anybody who works hard can be a doctor, lawyer, or businessman and, sometimes, make a lot of money. But not anyone can be a writer."

An accumulation of events like this makes one aware that a special, un-American atmosphere surrounds art and intellect in Europe. Gradually, I begin to get the idea. My old reading as humanities student and professor, so far behind me after years of executive jobs, begins to come back to me and assume, if not yet a new meaning, a new reality, one socially developed and validated. I recall the solemn tradition praising the poet, the man of imaginative letters and speech. From Homer and Aristotle down through Sidney and Shelley and Coleridge, they had written of the poet or writer as connected by a natural magnetism to God, as more philosophic than the historian of mere facts, of serving to preserve community and emotional well-being and health, of being an unacknowledged legislator of mankind, and so forth. In the end, *anyone* who was seriously engaged in trying to penetrate the human questions that writers work at, and then to reveal them to others—well, he was at least as good, if not as rich, as a millionaire. He had made the serious attempt to reach up and seize a grace from art, to face the beautiful, terrible, and ridiculous, or, more modestly, to give us back an image of our mind.

Such notions would seem, in contemporary Europe as in America, merely the theories of long-dead literary philosophers. Except one finds them appearing repeatedly in the texture of European life. It is different living in a place where the president of France after Giscard, stocky, short, Socialist François Mitterrand, primarily thinks of himself neither as politician nor statesman but as *écrivain,* writer. He convincingly asserts that though his several books of reminiscences and sketches are modest achievements, it is the writerly identity which means the most to him. It makes a further impression on one that people don't think this an affectation but accept it as a reasonable way to behave.

Furthermore, art is not only valued as something remote to be rewarded in academies. People act as if they know its importance and how it is produced—they are insiders. This comes out in many subtle ways, as for instance the indulgence given to "artists." I listen to two women, Angelica and Rosina, talk about Rosina's husband, a man who is both a real-estate salesman and a part-time sculptor. They are in hot debate. Angelica insists: "I know your husband is difficult, but you must understand that he is an artist!" Afterward, Rosina, who works as a teller in a bank, is amazed. She tells me: "Can you imagine? Angelica's trying to say I don't understand about artists! I know that Carlo is more than a real-estate salesman. I know that I have to be indulgent with his moods. Everyone would understand that!"

In America, Carlo would be seen, with what seems to us obvious logic, as a real-estate salesman who makes statues in his spare time. In Italy, and in much of the rest of Europe, he would be seen as essentially a creator who sells real estate to put bread on the table. More important, the resentment of the wife and the heavy-handed advice of the friend bespeak a mutual familiarity with a common conception of the creative enterprise. Creators are liable to be difficult husbands because they are different kinds of people: EVERYBODY KNOWS THAT! Creators, therefore, are to be indulged, they are engaged in singularly unsettling work, exploring an inner realm where pain and confusion can occur. From that inner realm come treasures. Therefore, the artist must be respected. EVERYBODY KNOWS THAT! Art and artists, then, are both special and ordinary. They are different from the usual, but it is a well-known difference. This assumed familiarity gives every cultural activity a legitimacy as absolute as eating, building, doing laundry. Art has its place and dignity.

Living in that atmosphere, one can be brought up short by contrast with American assumptions. One day in Brussels, I listen to a Voice of America broadcast about the birthday of Edgar Allan Poe. He is described as a great poet and short-story writer, not appreciated in his time. Because I have gradually become acculturated in matters having to do with art and artists, I continue listening with nearly European ears. An American professor of literary history comes on the air to say: "Poe is remembered most for his tales of the macabre, but he turned to that material because of what we would call today 'market research.' He was one of the first to try to find out what people wanted and to give it to them in order to make a living and be commercially successful. Because poetry didn't sell then, any more than it does now, he turned to short stories in the macabre mood and achieved a certain celebrity; nothing like the reputation for high art he won, later on, in France, for his neglected poems."

I find myself listening and imagining the European shudder, the superior smile, at this American version of Poe's working habits and artistic-commercial strategy. The European listener knows Poe as the great Poet, for so he has been held to be since his canonization by the alienated, artistocratic translations of Charles Baudelaire. It's not that the European couldn't appreciate Poe's troubles in making a living; rather, he would be disturbed by the casualness of the description of him as an artist turned marketeer.

The European would be astonished that the American professor takes the thing so matter-of-factly: they ought to express a certain horror at the artist's abject dependence on the open market. Though literature is commercialized in Europe too, the European pretends that it isn't, protests that it should not be, and finds many ways to maintain an aristocratic attitude toward the artist—a man who works for those who have the leisure, the security, and the tradition to cultivate the best taste and to reward talent. Memories of a society in which lord and church dignitaries took care of such functions are deep. The helpless exposure of an

American artist to market forces, and the consequent sense that there are no other powers deep within our national character to bring the artist to honor, seem disgusting, rude, rough—a real cornball way of running a society.

Living in Europe further dissolves my native attitudes. At times, my doubts about the validity and importance of art, mind, culture, and "artists" disappear entirely and I find myself one with the Old World attitude that accords an absolute validity and prestige to these enterprises.

I am not alone. Perennially, American intellectuals and artists have sought Europe for this reason. There they find the legitimacy of their interests and passionate commitments affirmed. Though for many reasons, the grand days of American expatriatism are over, Europe is still full of American intellectuals and artists, sometimes novices, sometimes accomplished, seeking for a time the atmosphere that they hope will make their concerns seem normal and important. They still find that nourishment from a whole society which in America can only be found in small groups, specialist corners of a multispecialist nation.

One writer I know, who has lived in Europe for several years, let me see some pages of his journal. They revealed the intimate experiences of this contrast between Europe and America:

> It has been long in coming but I have finally conquered some doubts. These last days I let myself be filled, like any European intellectual, by the knowledge that in *this* society, people have always supported the kinds of things I am doing. It has made me stronger, and also better able to work, and more seriously.
>
> I am going off to America for a visit tomorrow and I feel good. The dignity Europe accords to art is with me. My last book, I learned a few days ago, will be published over here, in France and Holland. Small editions, but that is not what matters. Now, I belong to the great cultural enterprise of Europe where things of the mind are held in true esteem.

The next day he flew to America, and that night he wrote this in his journal:

> Though I clutch these soaring thoughts and feelings to me, they are difficult to hold. When I land in America

today, moments after the cheerful Customs inspector tells me: "Welcome back!," the flush of glad homecoming passes. I face at New York City's Kennedy airport a crying, hyperactive world: bustling porters, frantic taxi dispatchers with walkie-talkies, immense limousines, arrogant and secretive with dark windows and Star Wars antennas on their trunk lids, rushing businessmen scrambling for a place on the airport bus, and defeated broom pushers moving cigarette butts around old linoleum floors. It is all the commercial epitome of the monstrous in our great country. Here, I realize, I am nothing. My artistic triumphs, though small, are honored there but here in America, who the hell cares? Especially in New York. Small time stuff. Chicken feed. I am not making it.

And it's not just me. Who's *really* making it here? One person in a million? There's suddenly no legitimate social existence for me again. The women on the television sets I watch, extraordinary creatures I see everywhere—in the newspapers, in the magazines—are all incredibly better looking, better built, better dressed and better humored, than any women I know, ever have known, or could know. I feel unsteady. Insecure. I don't earn enough. I'm no longer young enough.

"What the hell's wrong with me?" That's what I think, suddenly plunged from the heights of aristocratic superiority. I came here feeling great and now I have fleeting images of senectitude, futility. Within twenty-four hours of arriving on my home soil, I find myself wondering if life is really worth it!

Maybe, I think, I'm just tired. Maybe it's jet lag. But I have, nonetheless, these fleeting images of ending it all. I find myself eating too much, even though the food has no taste. Food and I, both nothing. America reduces all to nothing to make us anxious so we will work faster. Production is all, quality of no importance, I think. Artists, intellectuals, and writers are reduced to less than nothing. All in a few hours. I must get hold of myself. . . .

The day after my arrival I go to interview a new literary agent. Living far away in Europe and needing to make *some* money with my writing, I am willing to make a realistic bow and get a person to represent me in the marketplace. I am no landed gent, after all. I get off the bus at Upper Fifth Avenue. Pretty posh. Uniformed doorman, a concierge, an elevator operator. I'm a little intimidated. Whisked I am to the thirtieth floor. An obviously gay fellow in his twenties opens the door. His boss, the agent, a woman nearly sixty, heavy, fat, powerfully planted on thick legs, stands looking out over the East River and talking on the phone about an advance for a book: "We won't take less than half a mil," says she. When the call is over and she has heard my plans for the next book, she leans forward and lights into me: "Four years! To write a book! John, here, wrote three books in the last two and has a full-time job! And you are thinking of submitting to publishers a long uncorrected first draft? You must be crazy. This is a business, now, writing. Are you a masochist? You've got to take the time out from writing and work up a selling proposal. You've got to give those editors a dream. That's it, 'Sell a dream,'" she half-muses, pleased with her phrase even though she has clearly used it hundreds of times. "Why, if Leo Tolstoy walked in with *War and Peace* now they wouldn't read it! Editors get fired, get promoted, and get bonuses. They don't have time to *read*!"

I listen, cowed, trying to tell myself to be reasonable and prudent and take in what she offers, advice based on hard experience, no doubt. I try to be American and practical. But it doesn't work. Anymore.

I hate what she is saying. I hate that line, so often uttered to American writers, as if we were children needing to be told it over and over, "Writing is a business." If it is, it is not the usual kind of business. And if it has become one in which *War and Peace* couldn't get a reading, then it's time to fight. I leave the woman and her productive assistant. I am not going to take their way.

In fact, this writer has been true to his word. At enormous personal sacrifice, he has continued to follow his interests and talents rather than aim his productions primarily at the marketplace. To do so, he has had to keep himself in exile in Europe, where, he says, "they have the right attitude and it helps me have the right attitude."

It is true, of course, that there is another side to the affair. Perhaps European artists and intellectuals take themselves *too* seriously, and America, if it reduces them far too much, does remind them of the importance of humility. Milosz, reflecting on his own deflation in the United States, puts it well:

> Here one must come to terms with one's own pride. In his optimistic moments, every writer considers himself a genius, and if he lives in his own small country, whose language differs from its neighbors', there will be no lack of support for his favorite self-image. . . . [But here] even if one has some renown, he is, in his everyday dealings with people, anonymous, and so is, again, one among many, but in another, larger sense. Whatever satisfies our vanity becomes a very effective *divertissement,* of the kind to which men resort, according to Pascal, to veil the futility of our endeavors and our fear of death. At least one *divertissement,* the most important one, recognition, is rarely attainable in America, where we are all particles of a lonely crowd. . . . America pushes to the wall and compels a kind of stoic virtue; to do your best and at the same time to preserve a certain detachment that derives from an awareness of the ignorance, childishness, and incompleteness of all people, oneself included.

Nevertheless, the perennial critiques of American Philistinism still have their point. We are *all* wounded by America and its too exclusively commercial civilization: especially in that part of us represented by art and thought. It is the old Puritan wound: the violence done to the whole man when beauty was persecuted during Cromwell's days. We are mostly Roundheads in the United States, but while in Europe the Roundheads ride from time to time, the ghosts of Cavaliers are still in their saddles, protecting the prestige of art and mind.

CHAPTER FOURTEEN

Culture

Now some qualifications are needed. Over the last forty years, Americans have been moving in a European direction at what seems a rapid rate. Sex has received frank attention; food is much more important and a great deal of attention is given to various ways of preparing it; California wines have been known to beat the French at their own game. Pleasure is no longer a dirty word and, indeed, we pursue it with energy, even, paradoxically, with seriousness.

Moreover, our universities are packed with students and professors. If tens of millions of college graduates do not emerge cultured, many are highly educated and have had at least a minimal exposure to the worlds of beauty and thought. I have no doubt that nowadays the average American has read more Plato in translation than the average European.

As an experienced but somewhat self-satisfied American cultural attaché in Greece put it to me: "Europe's fascination with itself is due to the fact that it has a history, but *we* [meaning Americans] have the contemporary culture. We have the leisure and the resources, even though most culture is only privately supported and not, as here, publicly funded. We probably have more museums, libraries, and symphony orchestras than all of Europe combined!"

It's his business to know and I, for one, believe him. The ability of our flexible society to take on new agendas and pursue them in massively energetic ways is impressive. Though we are only beginners in our move toward matter, the body, food, sex, art, culture, and learning, our achievements are already formidable. The Europeanization of America may already be as great as the Americanization of Europe. We have bit the luscious apple and there is certainly no turning back.

On the other hand, we tend to give Europeans too much credit and to sell ourselves short. We see ourselves still as the unlettered nation we were. We imagine that Europeans are vastly superior repositories of learning, taste, and cultivation. In southern Germany one evening, I was introduced to another American at a dinner party given by a retired couple living in a mountain village. His accent, his simplicity of manners, his tall frame, his lanky posture, his tweed jacket off some department store rack, even his cordovan dress shoes, all were typically middle-class American. A clean, neat, intelligent, college graduate about thirty years old. What was unusual was that he had lived in the village for three years now, and that he was a self-employed maker of harpsichords—antique reproductions for which he searched out old wood in attics and found old painters who could put the finishing touches on them. All the rest, he told me, he did himself.

I engaged him about his European experience and wanted to know why he had come to work here and why he stayed. He told me about how he had dropped out of law school, to his parents' alarm, and then sent away for a do-it-yourself harpsichord kit. He spent over a year making it, made another, continued to teach himself, completed a formal apprenticeship, and finally emigrated to Germany to find a quieter life and other more important differences: "In America, when I tell people I'm making a harpsichord, they are liable to think it is some kind of harp! More often, some kind of dulcimer. But here, even the peasants know what it is. There is a certain depth of culture. A respect for classical music. Here, I'm honored for my interest in it. Besides, in the States, a high craftsman [he used the adjective without embarrassment] is a person of relatively low status, but here they still appreciate fine work."

Some of this I could understand—respect for craft, for instance—but the rest puzzled me mightily. What America did he inhabit, I wondered, where harpsichords were so unknown? While strictly blue-collar America, if you can still find it, might continue in ignorance of harpsichords, I suppose, the vast middle classes with their minimum smattering of college education couldn't be so dim. Not more than German peasants!

Later on in our conversation, I threw it up to him, all our new cultivation back home. A reasonable man, he was not in-

clined to deny facts; nor was he anti-American. He began thinking about the matter and lapsed into silence. Then, after our
hostess had removed all the dishes and placed them in the dish-
washer, he fessed up.

"Yes, you know, the harpsichord revival in modern times—
well, it's American. The first books compiling old works about
harpsichord-building in seventeenth- and eighteenth-century
Europe—it was a couple of guys who had gone to Harvard who
put them out. And the first manufacturing of harpsichords in
modern times—that was also American. And this guy I'm im-
porting from London to help me with the construction of a major project—making ten different kinds of eighteenth-century
harpsichords for the Händel celebration coming up—he's an
American, too."

I was pleased, because I get annoyed when we undervalue
our own achievements and overvalue what Europeans are doing. "So it would appear," I said, to drive home the point, "that
America is just a very foundry of high culture at the moment,
wouldn't it?"

"I can't deny it." He smiled, pleased to make a new discovery; a typical, open-minded, self-correcting American.

One must also observe that Europeans have lost a great deal
of their own high culture. I have already alluded to the disappearance of Italian peasants who could quote Dante and Manzoni, and sing whole operas. Similarly, one finds that the old
studies of our Western cultural tradition which formed the basis
of European secondary education are fading away. Even Greek
and Latin are being withdrawn. In the very German village our
harpsichord-maker inhabits, he himself admitted that younger
people are more interested in television and bubble gum than
harpsichords and, like many between ten and forty years old in
Europe, had avidly embraced technical and mass culture. Though
13 percent of French adults read no fewer than five serious books
a month, the other 87 percent hardly read any books at all, ever,
once they have finished school.

Nor was Europe ever free of social considerations in its attitude toward culture. When the great Renaissance merchant Lu-
cas Rome insisted that his son learn Latin, it was intended as a
step away from ordinary business. Learning Latin was then and
for many centuries later a means of social promotion from com-

merce toward the clergy or to functions connected with it. In the late eighteenth century, when the pattern of training for the European administrative elite was institutionalized, "culture" became not only a question of having the right stuff but also of seeming to be the right sort by virtue of having done the proper literary studies. Elegance became partly a trapping.

Most often in the European middle classes, a concern with culture was and still is a mixture of economic, social, and intrinsic motives, so closely joined that no one can really tell them apart anymore. Mind work has long been the key to success in a more or less democratic society. As opportunity for social mobility slowly developed over the centuries, those who would rise trained their minds with culture because that was a way of preparing to fill those increasingly intellectual roles needed in a complex society. Culture also became a way of distinguishing oneself from those who worked with their hands, the laboring classes.

So European doctors and lawyers, increasingly heavily taxed and, therefore, not earning *that* much more money, make much, instead, of their "fine tastes" and "sophistication." When this happens, and it happens often, European "culture," like some recent American interest in "good food," confuses the unessential with the essential and to the extent the confusion takes place, an interest in culture becomes little more than a social manipulation, an attempt to make oneself seem and feel more important than others, to lean on the prestige accorded to culture which derives from a time when only aristocrats could afford to have it.

But giving full credit to ourselves for recent American "Europeanization" and recognizing that Europeans often mix economic and social concerns with those of culture, it remains true that they have a greater interest in and respect for the aesthetic and intellectual than we generally do. This being so, however, only drives us on to deeper questions: If Europeans are more engrossed in "culture," how does this engagement affect them as people? Does it mean that they are truly civilized? More decent? More caring about other human values and other human beings?

One evening, shortly after my marriage to Jacqueline and our move back to Europe, we went to a dinner party in Brussels given by some distant acquaintances of Jacqueline's family. From the beginning, refinement, cultivation, and the aesthetic attitude were all in the air. Our host, a retired lawyer, was certainly more elegant than his American counterpart. His blue blazer was *very* well cut, his hair perfectly trimmed, trained, and disciplined into an attitude that the French express by their word *distingué*. His wife, nearly seventy but still pretty, was all smiles, well made up, and shimmering in the feminine way of European women when they are turning on the charm: hints of bright teeth in red lips, sparkling eyes, arch little looks, radiant poise.

The house itself was impeccable, tastefully filled with relics of trips, aesthetic trophies of sculptures, paintings, and Oriental rugs. The other people—the hostess's sister, the sister's son-in-law and two daughters, and the hostess's son—are all similarly shining with that attractively modulated glitter of European social presence.

To detail the gradual discovery of less pleasant realities underneath these cultivated appearances would take, and perhaps deserves, a novel. Instead, let me concentrate on only a few moments. The son-in-law said he was a "food consultant," someone who had helped plan the assault of American hamburger chains on Brussels nearly ten years before. Despite his careful clothes and perfect shoes, he is, I see, a rough-looking man, the picture of bourgeois crassness: belly punching out his good cotton shirt and silk tie, a face flushed as if to reveal either incipient alcoholism or a choleric bad temper. But, in answer to a question from his mother-in-law, the man discloses that, fat moneygrubber or not, his *real* interests lie elsewhere: he spends nearly every weekend in the south of Belgium, *excavating Roman ruins!*

What a difference from the stereotyped American business consultant I had been comparing him to. Here is his true passion—the history of his little country, the patient reconstruction of the past, a fragment of a mosaic here, the lintel of a Roman storehouse there. "The Romans," he explains to me, "occupied the lowlands of southern Belgium and minor ruins are to be found in many places. That's where the word *Wallon*—meaning today the French-speaking Belgians—comes from, Latin *vallum*, valley."

I am suddenly enchanted. New as I am to this sort of scene, I thrill to such unexpected culture in an ordinary citizen. I say to myself, as does any eager American visitor: "God, I'm in Europe! One certainly doesn't run into this at home!"

But as the evening progresses, I find myself becoming more

critical. These people bore each other, just as in middle-class formal dinners back home, but here there is more culture around. However, even when the conversation approaches some interesting subject, like Roman archaeology, it does not truly enter it. Most of what is said is empty, the same avoidance of the personal and the real. It begins to seem that what Europeans have over us is nothing more than a higher level of chitchat.

As time wears on, however, other depths appear, the more troubling because set off by the snowy heights of cultivation. At one point, the red-nosed hamburger expert-cum-archaeologist says, pointing to his wife across the little card table at which four of us sit to pick at the *langoustine* and the carefully marinated tomato salad: "Bah, women are inferior, of course. They are stupid in what they talk about. All they care for is clothes, children, and trying to control their men. But we Europeans, we are clever, we don't let them. You Americans are dominated by your wives."

Aside from my astonishment, I am impressed, if anything, by the economy, the compression with which he manages to insult me, his wife, and mine, all at once. And he does it in a tone that pretends nothing is really being said that might offend—just an intellectual observation about sex and national differences.

To my right, at another card table covered with white linen, I notice that similar assaults and struggles are in progress. The sister turns her chair slightly in order to cross her legs in my direction. When she has my attention, she moves on quickly in search of other mini-triumphs, turning her head to her brother-in-law and giving him a tiny flirtatious smile. And pausing only to lift the silver tines of her fork with their precious cargo of shellfish to her lips, she tells her sister that she is not sure *her* dress is quite the thing.

Over and over again, I have found that beneath the polished appearances of culture, if you hold them long enough in your view, you will hear among Europeans the grunt and clash of weapon on shield, the bang of egotistical mace on heavy buckler, the harsh splintering of a lance and the puffing into temporary retreats: all the back and forth of the armored conflict of social selves endlessly contending for place and mastery. But unlike the battles of the highway, the street demonstration, and the anonymous urban contact with strangers, these rough encounters are muted. Likewise, there is no American "haw-haw" or slap on the back, no loud voices. It is a subterranean noise that one can hear in European dining and living rooms, a noise that the visitor must learn to attend to with an inner ear, a sound that rumbles like a ghostly subway far beneath the structures of cultivation.

Much too often, European "culture," however elaborated, must be considered superficial. This is especially annoying when, as is frequently the case, the same "culture" is used to criticize Americans for their own purported lack of "humanity." A Swedish physician, a university professor specializing in cancer research, a woman who attends international conferences on several continents and who meets Americans both at home and abroad, says to me: "I find that there is nothing to your medical scientists. They are shallow. They lack humanity. Let us say that they are 'technicians.'" Not yet forty, very pretty, dark and tall, she adds to her patronizing remarks: "They are interested only in 'making money.'" She scornfully wiggles the middle fingers of both her hands to indicate she is quoting an incessant American refrain. Though her English is near perfect, she pronounces the wiggled phrase as if it were a peculiar foreign idea, something untranslatable in her own language. "This obsession with getting ahead," she continues, "is a cloud that obscures all other human concerns."

But this time I am not taken in. I know the woman who is speaking and I have seen her at the hospital tell a patient who has timidly questioned her recommended treatment: "Stop! It is *I* who command here! No questions or get out." This is also a woman extremely conscious of her status, one who fights like any ambitious professional on our side of the waters to get ahead, to be better known, to get every ounce of respect due her. And who also wants to impress with her femininity, her beauty, and the fancy clothes her banker husband can buy her. I look at her silk suit cut in the latest French fashion, a single diamond, two carats heavy, dangling between her breasts, and I wonder: "What's so different from her and the moneygrubbing, driven, anxious people she critizes in America?" Ingrid is a focused careerist. She gloats at her permanent appointment, long-sought and finally achieved, at an international cancer research institute in Switzerland. On Swedish television, she cuts off a visiting English col-

league on a panel show, tough, confident, and bruising her way
forward in the public eye: "I disagree! The diagnosis was faulty.
The patient never had that rare cancer to begin with." The implication lingers on the screen that *she* would have known better.

And what does her "culture," for this is what she criticizes
Americans for lacking, amount to? Badly remembered fragments
of high school Latin, a little art history, recollections of quick
visits to foreign monuments. I know that on her vacations with
her husband—she has refused to have children lest it interfere
with her career—she reads only just enough serious books of
current interest to give her something to say during those
required-to-be-informed-and-cultured European social conversations. Once that task is over, she gives herself to junk fiction,
usually, it must be admitted, stuff written on the American model
or, ironic though it is, knowing her attitudes, to actual translations from American popular novels.

So often, "culture" comes to seem merely a proverbial ve-
neer on either business as usual or even tougher business. And
yet it is not simply that Europeans are hypocritical in their pre-
tentiousness. Sometimes they are merely being conventional.
They enact and then describe stereotyped attitudes: Europeans
must be cultured and Americans should be criticized for not
being so.

Worst of all, however, is the European who, when I complain about the frequent fracture between what I would call "culture" on the one hand—that is to say, not only high culture but
all those sophisticated, wordly, elegant, mannered, refined attitudes and postures—and such values as "goodness," "modesty,"
"sweetness," or "decency," replies: "But, Stuart, no one has ever
said that culture or cultivation made people *better,* in the sense of
'good.'" It is an acquaintance, a person I am fond of, an English
historian, no less, who says so. She says it, I think, because she is
naturally argumentative, European style, and because she is for-
getful, human style. I am so stunned that I cannot think what to
reply, but when I go home afterward, I remember what should
be said.

It is false that no one ever claimed culture or cultivation
makes people better. Indeed, that was the whole idea of culture.

The Renaissance interest in learning, the study of Greeks and Romans, was begun because Europeans thought that those precursors knew best how to live and be virtuous. By studying the ancients, one sought a path to high humanity—vision, wisdom, goodness. Hence we still study the "humanities" in American colleges, however well or badly, because that culture is supposed to have a humanizing and civilizing function.

But why should it surprise me, I think, as I begin to wrestle through these issues, that a historian could forget the original function of all that studying, of studying history itself? The so-called American "academy" too often shows the same contradiction between knowledge and culture on the one hand and meanness of spirit, empty specialization, backbiting, and ego-boosting on the other. It's just that I have previously believed this contradiction between culture and decency to be a uniquely American artifact: the low social status accorded to American intellectuals caused the institutionalization of cheap bitterness alongside great learning. Now, however, I see that even in societies like Europe's where "culture" is honored, in practice it is often used for defensive and aggressive purposes.

Perhaps, on the scale it presently exists, this culture-mongering is something new, a decline from the central inspirations of Renaissance times. But if so, what a falling off there has been. Far worse is the appalling fact that before the Second World War, one country stood out in Europe for its cultivation of the arts, philosophy, history, the classics, theology, and science. Never before in the history of man had so many people learned so much nor been so busy with culture. Opera companies were everywhere, symphonies and chorales flourished in every village, high schools were legendary for their seriousness, and a mass of citizens—not the majority, but a large number—became celebrated for how much they knew and how much they loved the beautiful. The country, of course, was what would become Nazi Germany.

Is there a necessary conflict, then, between cultivation and true civilization?

It is possible that the answer is "Yes."

I talk to many people. In a Midwestern town, I visit again

an aged college mentor. Long retired from teaching, he has still the air of an old-fashioned gentleman. Naturally elegant, he can use a walking stick this close to the cornfields without seeming in any way affected. He is a distinguished literary scholar and a dedicated Christian and he puts the matter in historical perspective: "Europeans have partly lost the roots of their culture and their civilization has suffered for it. To me, the most lasting of civilizations is the Jewish. *Jordan amenta:* toning down the Greek element in Christianity and fortifying the Hebraic side is my way of answering your questions and doubts about where 'culture' fits.

"The Hebraic people, who cannot be called a cultured people, had ten commandments, which can be reduced to two: 'Love God' and 'Love thy neighbor.' And there was an eleventh commandment: 'You shall have no *secular* culture.' Poetry for God, yes. But no secular architecture or jewelry, pottery or sculpture, music or paintings. 'You will have no fame for those things. You will, however, love God, even though you are mean to Him.'

"The New Testament has, in its first three Gospels, no philosophy. There is not a word about culture. In John, there is the first of some new philosophy and in Paul you have the first new man—he was a Roman citizen and could think in Greek. But he had no culture. He, and others, *can be great without culture.*

"To me, if you're not 'Jewish,' your civilization is likely to have no real foundation and your culture be devoted to emptiness. When the Italians became Jews by becoming Christians—in the Middle Ages and through the Renaissance—they built and painted and sculpted great things."

I reflect on the profundity of his observations. Though I am literally a Jew by birth, I am, in my heart, secularized. But as an American, a philosophic descendent of "Hebraic" Puritans, I know where my first loyalties lie, and if I cannot place them in God, I place them in moral rather than aesthetic values.

As if he reads my mind, he says: "America is perhaps the most Jewish of developed countries nowadays. This is evident in many everyday ways. The American religious tradition, for example, makes for a simple civility that is rare elsewhere. It leads, sometimes, to a failure of polished 'manners,' of 'politeness.' But it is still touching and true. I had a haircut the other day and the barber called me 'Andy.' My name is Andrew, I'm eighty-three,

I'm a retired professor, and so on. He's thirty, new in town, from Texas. He says, 'Thanks, Andy.' It's not very cultured, is it? *But he has that kind of sweetness,* a sort of Christian love, which is perhaps more valuable than if I were in the old Italy and people were to call me *professore.*"

I go away and ponder some more. If I *have* to choose, I will always take the plain American Hebraism over polished European ways, an honest heart over any amount of refinement. But my hope is that we will not have to choose. That, on the one hand, we will avoid the corruption of "culture" without a constant anchor in true decency; and, on the other hand, we will avoid the lack of roundness which a merely Hebraic way of being, however grand and essential, leaves us with.

No one can imagine the eventual results of the Europeanization of America. When the Romans imported Greek civilization, they got more than Pindar and Homer—they also received all of decadent Hellenistic thought.

Maybe we too will go the way of all hardy peoples, losing our simplicity, vigor, and sense of right in the process of sophistication and maturation. One day, however, Jacqueline, who ponders these questions with me as I search, makes an important distinction: "Perhaps this is the first time in history that one people, the American, flees its roots and then, when it becomes itself, its own nation, goes back to find them again."

Though not all Americans have their origins in Europe, our collective cultural roots are there. Historically, we fled Europe and its ways in order to be free, to prosper, and to pursue high social and religious ideals. It would be too much to say that we have been representing the Good and Europe the Beautiful. No, we have been too often wicked and there are tens of millions of idealistic men and women all over Europe. Nevertheless, in a general way, within the Western mind as a whole, America has always stood for the ultimate hope of a better world, particularly in the ethical meaning of the term. Perhaps now that we are, as a country, more advanced in age, we can combine European beauty, grace, and cultivation with our more Puritan values. Perhaps a higher synthesis is possible.

Jacqueline herself impressed me, shortly after her first visit to California, when she opened up this vision. We were walking one day through the small valleys and over the hills of San Francisco. I was enchanted with her profound inner cultivation. Not only her exquisite manners, but also the refinement of her "gentle heart," as the troubadours might have put it, her delicate attention when listening to others speak their mind, her fine aesthetic sensibility in human relations. It was with considerable astonishment that I heard this sensitive but strong creature exclaim: "But this is the most civilized country in the entire Western world!"

What on earth could she mean? Only gradually, after many months, even years, in Europe, did I see that she was speaking of an emerging attempt taking place in many ways all over the United States: to combine aesthetic values with true civilization. In contemporary Europe, which she, like many Europeans, often criticized, "manners, for instance, are too frequently mere show—something one has been taught. But in the United States, often," she said, "there is an open decency and simple everyday caring, a desire to please, that is hard to find to the same extent anywhere else in the world." Another value she loved was "the lack of pretense," the less-armored American who feels himself in little danger and wears much less heavy a social mask.

Later on, sadly, she came to learn that we had our many faults. But those first impressions of a combination of grace and decency in the usages of everyday life remain. In fact, that combination is on our national agenda and represents an emerging synthesis of European values with American, the Puritan with the Cavalier.

Our problems in working toward such a synthesis in the United States are many and large. Nevertheless, one can learn to take much of use from the present Old World. Even its empty cultural snobbery is not entirely vacuous. Insistence on "culture," though frequently little more than lip service, may also recall us to a high ideal which can inform our striving ways. With imagination, we can let European snobbery remind us of where it comes from, an aristocratic time when men and women paid careful attention to values like grace, finesse, quality, elegance, honor, contemplation. Or, since even that age was less pure than it should have been, we can take present cultural snobbery and follow it farther back, not in mere time, but to the higher roots in the collective spirit of man, where all the ideals ever exist to inform and chasten us.

I am suggesting a new strategy to the American visitor. Not only to take what one can from what is presently available—a solid European materialism that still lingers, for instance—but to use even the hypocritical shows of excellences, like bread crumbs dropped to form a path which, if we follow, can lead us out of the woods and home, back to something beautiful and important. Even the bludgeoning eristic habits of European argument, so typical of their shows of "culture" these days, can be used. They can be seen through and can remind us of a time when men—at least men of a certain type—could be truly independent of the striving and anxiety that too often lead us to easy conformity and false agreements. We don't ourselves have to become defended and opinionated asses. Rather we can follow the eristic style to its origins in the search for truth and the willingness to take an independent stand.

In short, contemporary European Philistinism, so often disguised as "culture," can serve to remind us, if we forbear, of true culture. We can follow the waters upstream to the source. Older Europeans called this anagogic thinking, positive theology, the seeing of the divine behind the earthly disguise.

PART SIX

DEPTH

All educated Americans, first or last, go to Europe.
—Ralph Waldo Emerson

The lamps are going out all over Europe. We shall not see them lit again in our lifetime.
—Edward, Viscount Grey of Fallodon

Like many searchers before and since, Somerset Maugham's American, Larry, off to Paris in *The Razor's Edge,* seeks "answers to the big questions." For their part, some of today's Europeans still lay an implicit claim to "depth" when they criticize Americans for "superficiality." But I believe that most Americans have instinctively known for at least fifteen years that Europe has lost much of its depth. This is the fundamental reason why a continent which was so fascinating to us in the past, even up to the early sixties, is no longer of intense interest. Many people I talk to remark this decreased curiosity. A French actress who is also a part-time businesswoman tells me that "when Americans come nowadays, the only thing they feel inferior about is restaurant food. They brag that everything else that is modern is better back home, everything from the theater to manufactured goods." An American publisher who began specializing in translating serious European books four decades ago says: "I still like to go back there, we keep our apartment in Paris, but whether it's in philosophy, history, theater, or fiction, I can't find much to publish anymore." A Madrid professor who has run a Spanish-language program for American college students for twenty years says: "Yes, Europe in general, Spain certainly, has lost much of the charisma it used to have for Americans before the seventies." The professor continues: "It is hard to imagine an American saying what Maugham's Larry did, nowadays; even his thinking it; don't you agree?" I do.

Indeed, the American usually comes to Europe now no longer to sit at the feet of the mother civilization but merely to take in its artifacts. Ideally, tourism means no more than hitting the high spots and in the process becoming enriched by culture. Viewed schematically, it looks like this:

FINISH

• COMING HOME, AFTER
THREE WEEKS, SOAR-
ING.

• REPEAT FIVE TIMES IN FIVE
CITIES.

• DAY 4: THAT BEAUTIFUL SQUARE.

• DAY 3: THAT THREE-STAR MEAL.

• DAY 2: THAT CHARMING CAFÉ BY THE FOUN-
TAIN.

• DAY 1: THAT WONDERFUL MUSEUM.

ARRIVAL. FIGHT JET LAG AND GET OUT THERE.

START

We don't go to Europe for Europe anymore, we go for certain preselected experiences we've read or heard about. How different from the past when, as Emerson said, we *had* to go to
Europe. Then, we needed to study what an older, more traditional society had to give. We have already seen how many of
those traditions have been broken, but as recently as the postwar
period, certainly as late as 1958, when I first came to Europe,
one could feel oneself squarely in the tradition of American seekers. I was in the path of every intellectual or aspirant intellectual,
every artist or aspirant artist, every American revolted at the shallow drive and intellectual conformity from which our country
periodically suffers, and from which it suffered greatly in the late
forties and fifties.

But, particularly in that postwar period, there was more to
Europe for us than ancient traditions and escape from American
defects. When ruined cities had not yet been entirely rebuilt and
many Europeans still suffered the poverty and dislocations of that
enormous civil conflict, we felt there were special lessons which
people who had lived through periods of great tragedy could
impart. We came with a certain humility. We came to breathe the
air of recent Resistance, to know something of the Opposition
that had been honored by dreadful brass and marble plaques
placed high in every city and village square: "In honor of three
corporals of carabinieri, machine-gunned by the Nazi tyranny,
the City of Fiesole places this monument." . . ."In honor of Major
Benoît, killed while attempting to dive-bomb his airplane into

the Brussels headquarters of the Gestapo." . . ."In memory of two hundred French villagers, slaughtered in reprisal for the killing by partisans of a Nazi sergeant."

These were deep mysteries for us: heroism unimaginable against odds unimaginable.

We came to see the ruins of bombing, to touch horror that even our worst slums and our own most detestable violations couldn't suggest. We came to see or be near the camps, made into memorial museums, where millions—no fewer—suffered and died. We came to learn what the depths of the human soul were that could bring seemingly ordinary men and women to resist such crimes. We came to hear stories about collaboration. To smell the shame of conformity to great force and to rub timidly against the mysteries of human weakness in its most disgusting forms, and to know ourselves thereby. For all weakness partakes, like all strength and honor, of the same human depth, and we needed to know about it.

The depth of Europe therefore was not only in its ruins but in its suffering. The formulations of European existentialism, that culture of abuse, absurdity, resistance, and revolt already explored by such earlier philosophers as Heidegger and Kierkegaard, became known to many of us through the works of Camus, Sartre, Marcel, Buber, and Bonhoeffer, among others. For all this we came with eagerness, because we sensed that they, the Europeans, knew more about what was what, deep down.

That confrontation by Euros with the immediacies of horror and heroism, and all the human profundities that lie between, is long past. Some wounds have healed; still more have been put out of sight. The social welfare system works to take the hard edges off life, and in considerable measure succeeds. Yet Europe has so much lost its depth and dignity that where once one spoke of "Resistance," now an entire continent, richer in a material way than ever before, refuses itself even the dignity of fully supporting its own defense. The universal deep truth that comes through suffering has been in large measure replaced by a hundred habitual maneuvers to avoid sufferings. The mass of the current generation are much too self-protected to understand tragedy and to accept and live the old wisdom, older indeed than the Second World War. Instead of a knowledge of the deep things, everywhere one encounters in Europe the sentiment that one is "de-

serving." There is a general, quiet, elbowing-its-way kind of ar-
rogance.

A contentious people to begin with, Europeans have forgotten both the depths of suffering and of forgiveness. If, in the
main, we are not much better, we are no longer much worse.
Indeed, Europeans are rapidly losing their own traditional depth
without, for the most part, acquiring that redemptive transcen-
dental aspiration and sweetness that mark the better sides of the
American character.

Frequently, we Americans are blamed for the decline in Europeans' depth. The argument can take many forms, but generally they claim that Marshall Plan aid was given not from generosity but to insure the political and economic stability that would
allow American companies in. "They brought in hard-sell advertising techniques and junk food and images of a consumer society
and then seduced Europeans into buying the American shallow
way of life."

Let us concede that some of this analysis touches on truth.
But are Europeans as hollow as this analysis makes them out to
be? Was T. S. Eliot right, when he wrote in the middle of the first
war, so long ago, that Europeans were already empty knights,
"hollow men, headpiece filled with straw"? Is *that* why they ca-
pitulated so easily to Campbell's Soup? Monsanto Chemicals?
Carnation Milk? I have heard the United States and its corpora-
tions blamed over and over again for the trivialization of Europe.
But what, I ask myself, has happened to the brave existentialist
doctrine of the late forties and fifties of *responsibility for oneself*?
It's not something you hear much about in Europe anymore.

Though many of the essentials of the past are gone, there
are depths that remain. An American who would be something
more than only a thrill-seeking tourist can still discover certain
profundities, if he looks carefully.

First, while the typical European personality has become
rather shallow compared to that of the past, there are exceptions.
I think of the Europeans I have met who are deeply concerned
about their society, who are engaged in patient work to make it

more just, more beautiful, and who daily, year after year, shrug off the organized selfishness of their countrymen, preferring to seek other aspirations. A British senior economist who patiently works for unity within the much despised European Community comes to mind; an Italian political chief who battles for true democracy in a country which has little tradition in that direction; a French editor who, before he sends his journalists into the field, every day examines himself and his motives with a scrupulousness that is in the great tradition of self-reflection from Socrates to Montaigne to Camus.

And then there are those Europeans who seem true remnants of the past. I think here of the smaller and smaller number of blue-collar workers, peasants, and aristocrats. Sometimes, among such people—our *facchino* is an example—one meets with a simple grace, a sweetness of manners that is heartfelt, truly touching, and full of the deep decencies which arise from old codes and solidarities, both secular and religious. Such qualities are easier to find in those relatively isolated places like rural Norway, with strong traditions of family life still largely intact, or rural Greece with its traditional village hospitality, or parts of Portugal and Ireland.

More generally, one can find, if not the deepest profundities, certain real depths in the collective attitudes of people who have met life's difficulties and chances over many more hundreds of years than we have. The Belgians, for example, have been justly lampooned as the most bourgeois and therefore snobbish nation in the world. But if one looks beneath that annoyingly tight social presentation, one finds a private merriment (with people they completely trust, viz., naturally, family) and a sheer capacity for endurance that are admirable in the extreme. Push a Belgian hard and the easy pusillanimity that comes from forever toeing invisible marks of respectability turns to stony firmness. It is a quality that has helped them survive a hundred invasions and one upon which even Julius Caesar remarked. There are such admirable traits in all the great peoples of Europe: Italian flexibility, British stoicism, German courage to rebuild and to keep building in the shadow of nuclear missiles just across the border.

Even under the more shallow habits, manners, and ways of thinking that one runs into every day, one can find deeper meanings. By using an imaginative strategy, we can find the sources of culture in the hypocritical shows of it. Likewise, the snobbism of so many Europeans is, from an imaginative point of view, the distorted, stepped-down, aristocratic trait of *transcendence*. The Europeans, and their number now is legion, who pretend to worth, even greater worth than others, are striving for a sense of self that belonged by birth and right to those old aristocrats who had *fierté* and to the peasants who rightly imitated them. By such exercises, we can see the traditional value imprisoned within what will otherwise seem only its betrayal.

But useful as the imagination is to finding some European depth, its satisfactions lack tangibility. Fortunately, there are a few very important aspects of the European which still offer us, more or less immediately, some human profundity hard to get at home.

To start with the most simple and apparent, despite the guarded European presentation of self, there are still many moments when truth is permitted to shine through. I think of something so ordinary as the appearance of a newscaster, a beautiful woman whose charming manner is colored by intelligent wit. She presents the nightly news from Paris on a national network. I watch this newscast often, not only when I am in France but also when I travel to other countries where it is received—Italy, Belgium, Switzerland, Holland, and Luxembourg. At first sight, she seems only a French version of the American anchorperson—sheer good looks and pleasantness. But there is a singular difference. Despite her interesting and varied wardrobe, her carefully done hair, nails, and makeup, and her real beauty, one sometimes gets to see her on the air when she doesn't look her best: for example, when the skin is a little pulpy and the eyes tired. Small matters, but typical of a vein you can still find in Europe, where there exists no universal expectation that one can and should always be perfect, even in appearance. Mme. Ockrent is a true media star, but her occasional performances when she looks less than machine-tooled provide one among thousands of tiny corrections to the American exhortation: "You should always be successful!" While this is a precious half-truth, one that keeps us properly striving, it is not a sufficient wisdom.

At a deeper level, the reality of life's chances, its sadness, even its tragedy, are still rather easily available in Europe. I think of a simple photograph of Jacqueline and her mother at the Tuscan hotel where I first met my wife. She and her parents had known it as guests for over forty years. It is a lovely place that was once a convent and before that a villa belonging to the great Medici in their most splendid days. Its gardens are full of fragrant flowers nearly all the year round. Not long ago, Jacqueline's mother, widowed, aged, still handsome, had come for a visit to Florence and we had all gone to this beloved place. The kind owner, a friend now, offered to take a picture of us. When the photograph was developed and printed, there I was with an American smile all over my face. Jacqueline and her mother, perhaps conscious of the older woman's advancing age and declining health, perhaps filled with memories, do not smile. Full of dignity, they have a certain sober elegance in their expressions. As I look at the picture, weeks after it is taken, I also think I detect a hint of brooding on all that is contingent—for instance, the evanescent flowers that surround us in the snapshot. I think that one of the real reasons some Americans like New York City (and others detest it) is that in that uniquely Europeanized American town, in the streets and on the subways, you can see the same looks of sadness, of a kind of tragic knowledge, right on the faces of people. Here is the visible side of human depth which is not aspiration, dynamism, and hope for triumph, but the contrary. To look at many people in Europe is still to see the tears of things that we too often try to exclude from our improving, go-getting, American awareness.

We all know what this tragic depth is about. It is, of course, what Jung—considering it in its most general aspect—called the "shadow."

For Americans, the shadow is that darkness cast by our strenuous light, a blackness we cannot outrun even though we try. Europeans are happy that we have had, in recent years, a lot of trouble outrunning our shadow. Though in general they would rather that we had not failed in Vietnam, they also believe that it was probably good for the collective American character that we did. A Swede who has worked for many years in an office of the United States Information Agency tells me: "I think your country is growing. It has grown up a lot. I think the Vietnam 'blow,' let's call it, created an uncertainty, a sense that the United States did not know everything they needed to know. So Americans became a little more ready to listen. There is a new widespread interest in other peoples. When I used to travel in America in the fifties and sixties, ordinary people (I do not speak of artists or intellectuals) were rough with foreigners. Now, however, many people are less sure and they are more ready to listen. During the Vietnam period, they even asked what I thought. It could never have happened before. America was everything then and there was no self-consciousness." Europeans like this man point out that American films invariably used to have a happy, even triumphant ending. Now our film endings are sometimes problematic, even dark, often ambiguous.

Oftentimes European awareness of the unhappy side of life is expressed with bitterness. An Italian count who prefers to live isolated in the country with his horses, rather than watch the decay of manners and grace in the city, responds to a bewildered American who is struck by the rough treatment she gets in the shops by saying: "*Gente di merda.*" "Shitty people." And he goes on to say with abrupt acidity that, in general, "people *are* shit." This is not a dried-up, embittered old man but a young, handsome, rich, and courteous aristocrat. Such a misanthropic indictment, surprisingly frequent in the European, goes beyond the pessimism and cynicism we have talked about earlier. It is part of the tragic knowledge—the least attractive part. A furious, deep-down hatred of others and even of life itself springs from the personal and collective memory of repeated violations: the rapes not only of women, of fortunes or of small pittances difficultly acquired, but also of all self-respect, of hope, even of life itself. It is the total violation so memorably captured in Bergman's *Virgin Spring*. Such bitterness is not always in evidence, naturally, but it speaks, when one sees it, of the very darkest side of existence—one which we may not like but which we must acknowledge as part of the human experience. One wishes that Europeans, especially these days, would go beyond Old World venomousness, misanthropy, and fury to some of their still-deeper traditional values that are more helpful responses to life's darkness: faith, courage, adventurousness, and dignity. Nevertheless, I respect and stand in awe of their knowledge of the dark.

*   *   *

At its best, European knowledge of the tragic side of life can be manifested in a wise acceptance. A Belgian psychotherapist, a good friend who was born, right after the war, of parents who had somehow survived Auschwitz, tells me a story that is deeply impressive. She herself has struggled to escape from the shadow of that background which, as she put it one day, "chilled my mother's heart, the milk she gave me, and my infant self. When both your parents lived and saw too much, it is often hard, in my depths, to find the desire to live—it becomes a problem.

"Let me tell you a case of one of my clients that is even worse than mine."

As she takes a deeper breath than usual before beginning, I observe that I brace myself. I know that my reaction to what I am about to hear will be like the reaction one had to seeing the Vietnam war broadcast on the television news night after night: horror so complete and so beyond most of our experience that it is difficult to pay attention, difficult to take in, impossible to know how to help.

She begins with her client's background. "Before the war broke out, my client's father had been married to another woman than his mother. When the father moved to France, he left the first wife and two children in Hungary. Later, she and both kids were killed by the Nazis."

Working to keep my attention focused by posing circumstantial questions, I ask: "When?" as if we were talking about just another ordinary matter, one that responds to the gathering of precise detail.

"We don't know when, or how, since you ask. Until after the war, the father didn't know if his children and first wife were dead or not. From then on, he spent his whole life being full of guilt for leaving them. He had to live with the fact that he had left for no compelling reason; just because he wanted to: he felt like it."

She pauses and I struggle to let this recital make some impression on me suitable to my friend's own feelings, ones which she doesn't express in the moment but which I sense she has. Not only is her client someone with whose history and problems she has lived intimately for a long time, his story is one with which she compares her own: "worse than mine," she had said.

"On the mother's side, the whole family were killed. Except

for three aunts and a cousin, who are all now permanently held in mental hospitals in Switzerland. They each went crazy during the postwar years."

"How many others were there?"

"Oh, I don't know, probably the usual big family of that period—a couple of hundred—sisters, brothers, aunts, uncles, cousins. I'm foggy myself about the details."

I realize that my friend doesn't want to dwell too much on the specifics, because each of those hundreds of murders would be a separate blow to everyday composure.

"The man has only a sister.

"Four years ago, I took him into therapy. He's my 'brother'—his story is mine. Of course, I get supervised the most in regard to him.

"During the war, his parents often had to leave him with peasants hiding in caves. *Every time* he would cry, they'd put a warm potato in his mouth so they would be safe.

"After the war, when my client grew up, the first thing he did was marry a German woman, have three kids, and leave all of them.

"We have agreed that he was avenging his father."

I have to stop her a minute until I grasp the mad logic. She waits for me, then resumes.

"He has had a recurrent, important dream. In it, he discovers a murdered baby in a prison, full of blood. Of course, it is the murder, if you like, of him as a child.

"Then the dream switches. He's waiting for an elevator. When the door opens, there's a monster in the car. In the face of it, he goes mad.

"What my supervisor said, a man of twenty-five years' experience, was that what was killed in the dream was the man's very self. That is, his ability to have an individual life, to become an independent person.

"Confronted with a social monster, as we all are in fact, there was, because of this man's collective history, nothing to support him."

I don't follow and tell her so, though the heaviness of her words, like a huge hand, has pushed me down and made me feel weak.

"His negative personal reality, his terrible imaginings because of it, and social history, all together, were too much for him.

"So the man lives in his body but *he* dies."

It is a disturbing statement from a psychotherapist, but she continues, not with professional detachment but with a kind of hard-won acceptance of the inevitable: "Frankly, I don't think he can make it. In our work together, we opened up and went to face the experience of the pain, death, and violence in the world. But the confrontation nearly caused him to kill himself. So we backed off. And I got him out of that place of death.

"But it may be impossible and too dangerous for him to really pass through and liberate himself from the experience of his past, which cripples him."

It is a sober moment as I contemplate not only the man's fate but, by implication, my friend's. To what extent is she, lively as I know her usually to be, permanently damaged, even killed, by her parents' background?

She resumes. "There have been some positive results of the therapy, however. He used to fail at everything—be unfaithful to his wives, beat his abandoned children, throw away money when he got some. Now he knows that those patterns came from getting too close to the pain, withdrawing from success because of the inner sadness, killing himself again, not having a self—however you want to put it. So, instead of thinking of himself as unreliable, he sees and understands what is against him and acts with deliberation. He has become reliable, not an avoider; he has finished his training and become a therapist himself.

"But he's still dead deep inside. I'm not sure we will make it through to his living a truly individual life. His life. The best may be a reduction of suffering and of his self-destructive and antisocial behavior. His core is still bound by the death of his inner self, which was caused by the many deaths—too many—around him."

She stops. I ask myself, again: "What does one say?" And I do not know. I don't have the qualifications to know. Perhaps I can, with effort, understand a little. To hear. Not to forget. To know, if only abstractly, that depths of suffering exist beyond those I can imagine. I also admire my friend's own battle to overcome impossible childhood conditionings, although I can only vaguely surmise what those were and the excruciating struggles she has had to make against them. I admire her client who, though imperfectly and in perpetual doubt, still lives. "As a therapist," she tells me, "working to help others, he's not really sure if he's bringing people with whom he works to life or to death, but he pushes forward on a kind of stoic or, perhaps, desperate faith." I can only wonder at her ability and his, to extents beyond my ken, to accept the tragic, the irreparable, the hideous, in their own lives and in life generally.

One doesn't hear such stories every day in Europe—far from it. But there are many around, and when one does hear, one can forgive other Europeans for not talking—not just about those stories, but about anything too deep, too close, too hurtful. One can forgive some of the put-on and pretense. Though one wishes all Europeans were capable, like my friend and her client, of facing the deep levels of personal and social horror they inherit, one can understand why, as they sometimes say, they are "tired." Despite all the high-powered cars they drive too fast on their modern freeways, it is a tired old world they have inherited.

And yet life, with its demand for more than comprehension and forgiveness on our part and for more than repression and avoidance on the part of the Europeans, somehow goes on. Human ties, for one thing, must still be made, and Europeans still make them with a positive spirit that goes almost as deep as the bitter negativity their history has left them.

In many respects, to be sure, they go about forming relationships much as we do—with increasing faithlessness and superficiality. The mobilities of modern life—physical, geographical, vocational, psychological, political, and even spiritual—create a society that changes no matter how much Europeans try to box it in, and this change tends to dissolve relationships. Not too long ago, Europeans used to laugh at the problems that fragile relationships brought us, considering them "bizarrely American": divorce, problem children, drug addiction. Yet these torments have found their place in European life as well.

If one considers friendship, for instance, one finds there is not much difference in the contemporary European and American patterns. The vast majority of European adult men, for example, like their American counterparts, have not a single, deep, current friendship. The word *current* is important here. Many European men have occasional fond memories of friendship, but it is extremely rare to find one who has a friend of importance in his present life—I mean one whom he sees or talks to, or even inwardly cherishes, as frequently as once a week. Nevertheless, Europeans still put a high *formal* value on relationship, and this tends to make a difference, to add, at least, another dimension, to give it significant status, and, therefore, a certain weight.

Rollo May, the American psychologist who has lived both in Greece and Germany for extended periods, told me about an experience he had when he moved from New York City to the West Coast. "When I arrived I went to a party and this famous psychiatrist was there who had written many books. We had never met before, but we knew each other by reputation. We chatted. I expected nothing, but as we were saying good-bye he felt moved to tell me, 'I'm very sorry, but I hope you won't think since you've just moved out here that we can be friends. It's nothing personal, but I have all the people I can afford in my life.' He was simply telling me that he was very busy and so he didn't have time for me, a newcomer. It was an extraordinary statement even for an American. But I can't possibly *imagine* a European saying such a thing out loud."

May is perfectly correct. A European might think it—indeed, he would be more inclined to do so than the enthusiastic, open, and warmer-habited American. But he would never say it. The European is still more enclosed in a fixed social milieu and so he still believes that relationships must be acknowledged as important. They are not to be subordinated to lesser values like practical convenience and crammed schedules.

There is also an *obligation* felt in such relationships, a correct way to behave to others. An American executive was leading a group discussion of product preparation at his company's German subsidiary. He noticed that though he made some general points about product quality which he considered important, the European executives didn't take any notes. After a time, the American inquired, with some heat: "Why don't you write these things down—don't you want to give the man a good product?" They replied; "Of course we'll do that. That's what he would expect, after all. We don't have to write it down."

The Europeans were already sensitive to the obligations of

their relationship to the customer. As the executive said to me, in trying to analyze the interchange: "Europeans assume a lot. They assume that the customer, someone known to them whom they expect to continue doing business with, is due a certain sort of service. In business in the U.S., on the contrary, all assumptions are made explicit, written down, and sent to lawyers. Here in Europe, it's different—you don't live in a world where everything changes every minute. People feel more *bound* to do certain things."

Thus, the sense of obligation exists because of the expectation that relationships will have *continuity*. This expectation—often unconscious—shapes behavior not only in business but also in personal life. Europeans persevere in a relationship, and this tenacity generates its own kind of depth, because long relationships simply acquire profundity in some mysterious way—even if people are not any warmer, more loving, or even any more hating than in briefer ones. Like the accumulation of rings in a tree, sheer duration leads to greater substance.

A corollary to this expectation of persistence is that the past of a relationship is still honored. In the U.S., the past is at best a source of nostalgic good memories, but ultimately it does not count, for we look to the present and, above all, the future. In Europe, though the past is disappearing as a value, it still matters and, if not in the tightest way any more, it often still binds relationships. My best Italian friend of youth, dead, fifteen years ago, at age thirty in an automobile accident that tragically cut off a promising life as politician and man of letters, is not forgotten. I think of him often, of course. But the man's uncle, Donato, who raised him when the boy's mother and father died young, remembers our friendship in more active ways. For years, when I came to Florence for visits, he insisted on taking me to more expensive restaurants than he could afford to drink to the memory. And when I wanted to live in Florence but couldn't find an apartment because of Italy's rigorously rent-controlled real-estate situation (no landlord will rent his property long-term because of it), Donato found me a no-rent apartment belonging to two of his younger friends. They had bought it as an investment against inflation and wanted it occupied but didn't want to rent it at the low prices fixed by the law. The dead Franco, Donato, his uncle, the new couple, Anna and Daniele Zavani, I, and even my new wife, Jacqueline, are thus become a league of individuals—loyal, bound by the past, friends in fact because many years before two of us had been close and the friend of my friend is my friend, even if my friend dies.

Tenacity is admirable, but whether European relationships still have some more intrinsic and deep juiciness is another question. Nowadays, even in Italy, no one can be imagined writing those operas in which human sentiment and attachment are so very important that jealousy can beget passionate murder and betrayal can lead to suicide. Twenty-five years ago, when I first came to Italy, such stories were the newspapers' daily meat; now they are rare, and people mock the passionate events as quaint curiosities perpetrated by the ignorant. Relationships are much more casual than they used to be. A middle-aged Italian professor says: "I came back from eight years teaching in Manhattan to my hometown, Florence, because I missed my friends. But now that I am back, we hardly see each other anymore. It's strange. No one seems to have the time. Things have changed." Sound familiar?

Nevertheless, the collective memory of a special kind of contact haunts the continent and, at least occasionally, it produces a depth we lack. A conversation I had with French psychologist Hugo Pottier, who had returned to Lille after working many years in the U.S., was particularly illuminating. "The French are much less friendly than Americans and are even standoffish," he acknowledged. "Americans have a level of emotion I love: words, movement, action! But intimacy is something else. I think we have it and that Americans do not. It took me a while to get back to it, having been away so long."

I express my doubts, because I don't see a lot of intimacy in Europe, even in most of the families I know well and with whom I have lived.

"Maybe. Or perhaps you miss it. It is not easy to catch. In Europe, for one thing, intimacy is not expressed in words that much. Here, there's more modesty than in the States." I know that when he says "modesty" he is translating French *pudeur*. But a more accurate translation would also have to embrace several other English-language ideas: reticence, reserve, bashfulness, a sense of shame. "There's an extreme modesty in France," he says. "Some of it comes from a different rhythm. Take the movies: a French director will spend fifteen minutes simply building an atmosphere. But in an American film, Westerns are typical, if two people aren't killed in the first five minutes, the audience is bored.

"Let me give you a concrete example of that different European rhythm allowing intimacy. It comes out of my professional work. With some American psychologist colleagues, I lead a professional training program every year for French psychotherapists here in Lille. These are therapists who have never been exposed to contemporary American group techniques and theory. Usually, these French therapists have never even been in any group where strangers gather together and speak frankly for days.

"In the States, when Americans come for this same sort of training, they are respectful to start and let us be the leaders. But here, Europeans begin with mental aggressiveness. My American colleagues thought it was, to use their jargon, a 'kill-the-leader-thing,' that primitive rebellion against authority which groups can spontaneously go through, though in the States it is one that takes place *after* the group is happily off and running. When I had only been back in France a short while, I myself thought that's what the French therapists were doing. I missed the easy American openness and agreeableness.

"But gradually I came to see that the European assault on the leaders had certain functions. They were testing us. They wanted us to show them the most of our intellectual quality before they would follow. And, in addition, they were making clear their own positions, as far as they knew them, in potential opposition to whatever our teaching might be. It is a form of *pudeur*. Over and over in the group I found that this contentiousness was not merely a psychological defense but a technique for getting us to *be*, to show ourselves in some deep way.

"What can happen afterward is a subtle new level of being together. Something that goes beyond the typical American reaction when, after a few days of a training session, the participants *say* things like: 'Gee, this is great!,' and 'I never felt so open and so easy with new people as I do in this group!,' and 'I love you all!'

"I, myself, love that enthusiasm about group lovingness. But what can happen here is deeper, I think. I'll never forget the first time that kind of group affection was expressed in Lille. It wasn't with words. More like a tone. Or, in this instance, a sound. Suddenly, this guy produced a saxophone. He started to play. Someone else started singing. Others clapped. It lasted, tops, fifteen minutes. *A soft, deep, beautiful, tender sound.* No big expression. No words. No doing. None of these very American impulses were allowed to cut off the experience of depth in intimacy. And not everybody had to participate. People could stay individuals.

"We were all struck by the thing—especially my American colleagues. It's not that French people or Europeans generally don't know how to talk about things that are usually hidden—sex, shit, and what not. We did that before Americans, though you now do it more easily. But the deep tenderness, the *tendresse, that* we do not talk about. It would be a violation. We express it more subtly and, perhaps when we feel it, we feel it more profoundly.

"People in the U.S., I think, put words on this intimacy too quickly, make movement too quickly.

"Let me give you an image. You put little bits of silver paper in a ball of water and shake it up. Everything glitters. Americans would be inclined to exclaim: 'Wow!' or 'Wonderful!' They won't wait until the glitter drops into a sediment. They see the pretty movement but not the deeper thing which doesn't glitter anymore. It's not something I say or do, you see, but something I am. If I get excited by it before I *am* it, it goes away."

When he pauses for a moment, I have time to think of how expressive, to use the sociologists' term, we Americans have become in recent decades—intimate self-revelation has become a style. The insinuating radio voice, the drug experiences of the sixties and after, the spread of psychology with its emphasis on telling all, self-help groups, a hundred trends have contributed toward our habits of self-disclosure through words. Even the self-revelatory tendencies of modern literature have played their part. In reaction, certain Americans, who want to revolt against this easy openness, often exaggerate European *pudeur,* adopting the eristic style without ever allowing the special sweetness about which Hugo speaks to be felt, much less for it to emerge in expressions, like saxophone crooning, however indirect.

As I look now at Hugo, I see him reconsidering. I imagine

him remembering the warm, friendly, American training he had, which, as he had often told me, got him out of his "cold and excessive French intellectuality." And then I imagine him contemplating his more recent French experience these last years.

Then, with European skepticism and American openness combined, he interrupts the train of his own argument, asking: "But how true is this? Maybe it's just a *myth*. In the Jungian sense. Something which as a European I am in love with inside of me. Certainly, some of it is mythical. But so what? I'm talking about a myth that is collectively important. In America I missed this depth of *tendresse*. Maybe it's your Puritan background and you are really too vulnerable on that level. I have a few American friends who will exchange true tenderness with me but they tend, when they are not around, to withdraw it. We talk on the transoceanic phone but it doesn't come through. French people, however, will hold it for ten years, and once that level has been reached, you can get it right away at the renewal of contact.

"It comes from the heart, but it is not merely personal or interpersonal; it is also transpersonal, human but abstract. Some people call it sharing the *poésie* of things. We have it in our literature, our movies, our past, our cultural identity. Yes, it is a fading quality, but it is something we desire. And," he concludes, as if in his struggle to clarify such an evanescent quality he has reached a place of rest, "it is also a myth. But *nous l'adorons*. We adore it. It gives me an image of Love."

I look out the large windows in the upper room where we have talked. Early-morning clouds have yielded to a watery sun, pleasant after yesterday's snow flurries. Like Hugo, I am partly doubtful of these generalizations. Intimacy in Europe is so hard to find these days and reticence in itself is no measure of intimacy, especially verbal reticence. The great love poems of yore that make up most of European lyric poetry were not reticent. Who writes them now? Is it possible that contemporary European reticence is more a retreat from intimacy and depth than a cause of it? And yet is it not obviously true that Americans, with all our eager sweet agreeableness, are perhaps often too quick to talk about and act on deeper feelings?

Pondering these doubts and what Hugo has said I came at last to acknowledge that something of the old European depth in relationship still survives, here and there. I meet it, I realize, very occasionally, myself. A kind of black American soul without the black. Many Italians still have a little of it. When I call Donato, the sixty-year-old uncle of my dead friend, which is infrequently enough to surprise him, his reaction, not uncommon among Italians, is first a soft "OOOOOooooo" sort of sound. As if my remembered image, all that I am to him and that he likes, is allowed to penetrate his very being, to come back to him. He *never* says, with American haste; "Gee, it's good to hear from you!" It is the real contact of which Hugo speaks. It has beauty and it is worthy of honor.

But worthy as they are, all the aspects of depth that we have touched upon don't amount to all we need and once expected to find. One wants more. How inspiring it would be, for instance, to encounter the magical powers of the old Italian ways to transform evil. Once there was a worldly wisdom which sprang from being conquered a hundred times and learning to triumph over the conquerers. During the Second World War, for instance, the Waffen SS made Rome's best hotel their headquarters. They were fierce, booted, belted, starched, and heel-clicking. But within a few weeks, the Italian staff had domesticated the monsters. Witnesses remember visiting the headquarters and seeing SS colonels padding around the grand marble lobbies, at ease, in their bedroom slippers.

One night in the Paris Métro, I wait with my Belgian friend, Roland Dupont, for the train to come. He is a Belgian theoretical physicist with a strong humanistic education—a lover of history, literature, and wit. He is a good example of that small group of Europeans who have traveled the world and put together the two cultures of America and Europe and the other two cultures of science and the humanities—not in a theoretical but in a personal way.

Across the tracks, a drunken bum, what the French call a *clochard,* sits on a bench. We watch, and listen, for the drunk speaks to the gathering number of people waiting for the late-night trains on both platforms.

The *clochard* grumbles insults at the crowds. Then he looks

into his little box and draws out things to eat. He holds them up
to exhibit and grandly proclaims: *"C'est* le *pâté de chevreuil!"* And
then, *"C'est du Bour*sin!" He says. "It is *the* pâté of venison!" And
then, "It is Bour*sin* cheese," soft with garlic flavoring. "Like a
duke," observes my friend Roland. "He is there like a duke. A
disappointed duke, perhaps, but a duke just the same."

After munching a few bites, the *clochard* launches into a long
harangue, some of which I hear, some of which is masked by the
coming of a train across the tracks. He continues nevertheless but
is interrupted again by the train on our side. We get on. The
coach has many empty seats and Roland and I are able to sit next
to each other and speak. "What strikes me," says Roland, "is not
merely the man's pride, his sense of self-worth [*orgueil*] but his
elocution! He is like a *maître d'hôtel,* did you notice? He made
his words ring: *'C'est du BourSIN!'* I couldn't say it the way he
did. There was also the aesthetic side—he was cultivated. So he
was *minable,* a low person of no importance, *un clochard,* but he
became, suddenly, not a *clochard.* It all served as introduction to
his declamation. He called the public as 'witnesses.' He declared
himself 'a voice who speaks for all': *Je suis une voix qui parle pour
les autres.'* He said that he had known war: *'J'ai connu la guerre.'*
That he had been a soldier. And then, you remember, he slowly
pointed at the whole crowd of us on the opposite side of the
tracks, one by one, his long finger outstretched, and he declared:
'C'est ça la France: regardez la décadence!' 'Look at France, over
there,' he said, 'look at the decadence!'"

My friend, the physicist-humanist, recalls with a certain tenderness a film he had seen recently in which there was a conversation, harangues of a philosophical sort, between bums in Paris.
He says: "The bums are now the people who are free. We are
slaves. They mock us. They discuss important questions like so
many philosophers and *grands seigneurs."* The door of our car
opens and a couple of tired late-night people get off and a couple
of other tired late-night people get on. My friend says sadly, after
the doors clack shut and the train moves on toward the next
station: "Europe is leaving itself to the bums."

Europe! *Homo Europus!* Europeans! Come back to yourselves! Come back to us! Impress us again with your depth in-

stead of blaming your ills on American TV serials and commercials!

We need you to stop complaining about your "decadence" and "helplessness" and how "history has passed you by" and how you are "a small continent" and how you are "overshadowed by the superpowers"—and all the other excuses from 350 million people with the greatest collective wealth and the most dynamic history in the world. I believe, many of us believe, that you can still help us all find our way. But if you continue with your boxes, your shallow defendedness, with your increasingly empty parade of "culture," with anti-American scorn or mindless pro-American imitation, you will be of no use to us or to yourselves.

To vary the plea of Solidarity, "Let Europe be Europe!"

You might reply, of course: "But why isn't the U.S. what it was—more visionary, more idealistic, less constipated and dumb and foolish in its foreign policies, less exploitive? Where is the old genius and nobility in today's America?"

And your accusations would be right. But that doesn't change the point. It only adds to it and leads me to end with this final double hope, which though difficult points us toward the restoration of separate values and their better synthesis: *Let America return to itself!* and *Let Europe be Europe!*

Other Books from John Muir Publications

Adventure Vacations: From Trekking in New Guinea to Swimming in Siberia, Richard Bangs (65-76-9) 256 pp. $15.95

Asia Through the Back Door, 3rd ed., Rick Steves and John Gottberg (65-48-3) 326 pp. $15.95

Being a Father: Family, Work, and Self, *Mothering* Magazine (65-69-6) 176 pp. $12.95

Buddhist America: Centers, Retreats, Practices, Don Morreale (28-94-X) 400 pp. $12.95

Bus Touring: Charter Vacations, U.S.A., Stuart Warren with Douglas Bloch (28-95-8) 168 pp. $9.95

California Public Gardens: A Visitor's Guide, Eric Sigg (65-56-4) 304 pp. $15.95 (Available 3/91)

Catholic America: Self-Renewal Centers and Retreats, Patricia Christian-Meyer (65-20-3) 325 pp. $13.95

Complete Guide to Bed & Breakfasts, Inns & Guesthouses, Pamela Lanier (65-43-2) 520 pp. $15.95

Costa Rica: A Natural Destination, Ree Strange Sheck (65-51-3) 280 pp. $15.95

Elderhostels: The Students' Choice, Mildred Hyman (65-28-9) 224 pp. $12.95

Environmental Vacations: Volunteer Projects to Save the Planet, Stephanie Ocko (65-78-5) 240 pp. $14.95 (Available 10/90)

Europe 101: History & Art for the Traveler, 4th ed., Rick Steves and Gene Openshaw (65-79-3) 372 pp. $15.95

Europe Through the Back Door, 9th ed., Rick Steves (65-42-4) 432 pp. $16.95

Floating Vacations: River, Lake, and Ocean Adventures, Michael White (65-32-7) 256 pp. $17.95

Gypsying After 40: A Guide to Adventure and Self-Discovery, Bob Harris (28-71-0) 264 pp. $12.95

The Heart of Jerusalem, Arlynn Nellhaus (28-79-6) 336 pp. $12.95

Indian America: A Traveler's Companion, Eagle/Walking Turtle (65-29-7) 424 pp. $16.95

The Indian Way: Learning to Communicate with Mother Earth, Gary McLain (Young Readers, 8 yrs. +) (65-73-4) 114 pp. $9.95

The Kids' Environment Book: What's Awry and Why, Anne Pedersen (10 yrs. +) (65-74-2) 192 pp. $12.95 (Available 1/91)

Mona Winks: Self-Guided Tours of Europe's Top Museums, Rick Steves and Gene Openshaw (28-85-0) 456 pp. $14.95

The On and Off the Road Cookbook, Carl Franz (28-27-3) 272 pp. $8.50

Paintbrushes and Pistols: How the Taos Artists Sold the West, Schwarz and Taggett (65-65-3) 280 pp. $17.95

The People's Guide to Mexico, Carl Franz (65-60-2) 608 pp. $17.95

The People's Guide to RV Camping in Mexico, Carl Franz with Steve Rogers (28-91-5) 320 pp. $13.95

Preconception: A Woman's Guide to Preparing for Pregnancy and Parenthood, Brenda E. Aikey-Keller (65-44-0) 232 pp. $14.95

Rads, Ergs, and Cheeseburgers: The Kids' Guide to Energy and the Environment, Bill Yanda (8 yrs. +) (65-75-0) 96 pp. $12.95 (Available 2/91)

Ranch Vacations: The Complete Guide to Guest and Resort, Fly-Fishing, and Cross-Country Skiing Ranches, Eugene Kilgore (65-30-0) 392 pp. $18.95

Schooling at Home: Parents, Kids, and Learning, *Mothering* Magazine (65-52-1) 264 pp. $14.95

The Shopper's Guide to Art and Crafts in the Hawaiian Islands, Arnold Schuchter (65-61-0) 256 pp. $12.95 (Available 11/90)

The Shopper's Guide to Mexico, Steve Rogers and Tina Rosa (28-90-7) 224 pp. $9.95

Ski Tech's Guide to Equipment, Skiwear, and Accessories, edited by Bill Tanler (65-45-9) 144 pp. $11.95

Ski Tech's Guide to Maintenance and Repair, edited by Bill Tanler (65-46-7) 144 pp. $11.95

Teens: A Fresh Look, Mothering Magazine (65-54-8) 240 pp. $14.95

A Traveler's Guide to Asian Culture, Kevin Chambers (65-14-9) 224 pp. $13.95

Traveler's Guide to Healing Centers and Retreats in North America, Martine Rudee and Jonathan Blease (65-15-7) 240 pp. $11.95

Understanding Europeans, Stuart Miller (65-77-7) 272 pp. $14.95

Undiscovered Islands of the Caribbean, Burl Willes (65-55-6) 232 pp. $14.95

Undiscovered Islands of the Mediterranean, Linda Lancione Moyer and Burl Willes (65-53-X) 232 pp. $14.95

A Viewer's Guide to Art: A Glossary of Gods, People, and Creatures, Shaw and Warren (65-66-1) 152 pp. $9.95 (Available 3/91)

22 Days Series

These pocket-size itineraries (4½" x 8") are a refreshing departure from ordinary guidebooks. Each offers 22 flexible daily itineraries that can be used to get the most out of vacations of any length. Included are not only "must see" attractions but also little-known villages and hidden "jewels" as well as valuable general information.

22 Days Around the World, Roger Rapoport and Burl Willes (65-31-9) 200 pp. $9.95

22 Days Around the Great Lakes, Arnold Schuchter (65-62-9) 176 pp. $9.95 (Available 1/91)

22 Days in Alaska, Pamela Lanier (28-68-0) 128 pp. $7.95

22 Days in the American Southwest, 2nd ed., Richard Harris (28-88-5) 176 pp. $9.95

22 Days in Asia, Roger Rapoport and Burl Willes (65-17-3) 136 pp. $7.95

22 Days in Australia, 3rd ed., John Gottberg (65-40-8) 148 pp. $7.95

22 Days in California, 2nd ed., Roger Rapoport (65-64-5) 176 pp. $9.95

22 Days in China, Gaylon Duke and Zenia Victor (28-72-9) 144 pp. $7.95

22 Days in Europe, 5th ed., Rick Steves (65-63-7) 192 pp. $9.95

22 Days in Florida, Richard Harris (65-27-0) 136 pp. $7.95

22 Days in France, Rick Steves (65-07-6) 154 pp. $7.95

22 Days in Germany, Austria & Switzerland, 3rd ed., Rick Steves (65-39-4) 136 pp. $7.95

22 Days in Great Britain, 3rd ed., Rick Steves (65-38-6) 144 pp. $7.95

22 Days in Hawaii, 2nd ed., Arnold Schuchter (65-50-5) 144 pp. $7.95

22 Days in India, Anurag Mathur (28-87-7) 136 pp. $7.95

22 Days in Japan, David Old (28-73-7) 136 pp. $7.95

22 Days in Mexico, 2nd ed., Steve Rogers and Tina Rosa (65-41-6) 128 pp. $7.95

22 Days in New England, Anne Wright (28-96-6) 128 pp. $7.95

22 Days in New Zealand, Arnold Schuchter (28-86-9) 136 pp. $7.95

22 Days in Norway, Denmark & Sweden, Rick Steves (28-83-4) 136 pp. $7.95

22 Days in the Pacific Northwest, Richard Harris (28-97-4) 136 pp. $7.95

22 Days in the Rockies, Roger Rapoport (65-68-8) 176 pp. $9.95

22 Days in Spain & Portugal, 3rd ed., Rick Steves (65-06-8) 136 pp. $7.95

22 Days in Texas, Richard Harris (65-47-5) 176 pp. $9.95 (Available 11/90)

22 Days in Thailand, Derk Richardson (65-57-2) 176 pp. $9.95

22 Days in the West Indies, Cyndy & Sam Morreale (28-74-5) 136 pp. $7.95

"Kidding Around" Travel Guides for Children

Written for kids eight years of age and older. Generously illustrated in two colors with imaginative characters and images. An adventure to read and a treasure to keep.

Kidding Around Atlanta, Anne Pedersen (65-35-1) 64 pp. $9.95

Kidding Around Boston, Helen Byers (65-36-X) 64 pp. $9.95

Kidding Around Chicago, Lauren Davis (65-70-X) 64 pp. $9.95

Kidding Around the Hawaiian Islands, Sarah Lovett (65-37-8) 64 pp. $9.95

Kidding Around London, Sarah Lovett (65-24-6) 64 pp. $9.95

Kidding Around Los Angeles, Judy Cash (65-34-3) 64 pp. $9.95

Kidding Around the National Parks of the Southwest, Sarah Lovett 108 pp. $12.95

Kidding Around New York City, Sarah Lovett (65-33-5) 64 pp. $9.95

Kidding Around Philadelphia, Rebecca Clay (65-71-8) 64 pp. $9.95

Kidding Around San Francisco, Rosemary Zibart (65-23-8) 64 pp. $9.95

Kidding Around Washington, D.C., Anne Pedersen (65-25-4) 64 pp. $9.95

Automotive Repair Manuals

How to Keep Your VW Alive (65-80-7) 440 pp. $19.95

How to Keep Your Subaru Alive (65-11-4) 480 pp. $19.95

How to Keep Your Toyota Pickup Alive (28-81-3) 392 pp. $19.95

How to Keep Your Datsun/ Nissan Alive (28-65-6) 544 pp. $19.95

Other Automotive Books

The Greaseless Guide to Car Care Confidence: Take the Terror Out of Talking to Your Mechanic, Mary Jackson (65-19-X) 224 pp. $14.95

Off-Road Emergency Repair & Survival, James Ristow (65-26-2) 160 pp. $9.95

Ordering Information

If you cannot find our books in your local bookstore, you can order directly from us. Please check the "Available" date above. If you send us money for a book not yet available, we will hold your money until we can ship you the book. Your books will be sent to you via UPS (for U.S. destinations). UPS will not deliver to a P.O. Box; please give us a street address. Include $2.75 for the first item ordered and $.50 for each additional item to cover shipping and handling costs. For airmail within the U.S., enclose $4.00. All foreign orders will be shipped surface rate; please enclose $3.00 for the first item and $1.00 for each additional item. Please inquire about foreign airmail rates.

Method of Payment

Your order may be paid by check, money order, or credit card. We cannot be responsible for cash sent through the mail. All payments must be made in U.S. dollars drawn on a U.S. bank. Canadian postal money orders in U.S. dollars are acceptable. For VISA, MasterCard, or American Express orders, include your card number, expiration date, and your signature, or call (800) 888-7504. Books ordered on American Express cards can be shipped only to the billing address of the cardholder. Sorry, no C.O.D.'s. Residents of sunny New Mexico, add 5.625% tax to the total.

Address all orders and inquiries to:
John Muir Publications
P.O. Box 613
Santa Fe, NM 87504
(505) 982-4078
(800) 888-7504